A Political History of the Two Irelands

Also by Brian M. Walker

DANCING TO HISTORY'S TUNE: HISTORY, MYTH AND POLITICS IN IRELAND

DEGREES OF EXCELLENCE: THE STORY OF QUEEN'S, BELFAST, 1845–1995 (co-authored with Alf McCreary)

PARLIAMENTARY ELECTION RESULTS IN IRELAND, 1801–1922 (edited)

PARLIAMENTARY ELECTION RESULTS IN IRELAND, 1918–92 (edited)

PAST AND PRESENT: HISTORY, IDENTITY AND POLITICS IN IRELAND

PROVINCE, CITY AND PEOPLE: BELFAST AND ITS REGION (co-edited with R.H. Buchanan)

SENTRY HILL: AN ULSTER FARM AND FAMILY

THE OXFORD HISTORY OF THE IRISH BOOK (Co-general editor with Robert Welch)

ULSTER: AN ILLUSTRATED HISTORY (co-edited with Ciaran Brady and Mary O'Dowd)

ULSTER POLITICS: THE FORMATIVE YEARS, 1868–86

A Political History of the Two Irelands

From Partition to Peace

Brian M. Walker
School of Politics, International Studies and Philosophy,
Queen's University Belfast, UK

First published 2012 by
PALGRAVE MACMILLAN

Palgrave Macmillan in the UK is an imprint of Macmillan Publishers Limited,
registered in England, company number 785998, of Houndmills, Basingstoke,
Hampshire RG21 6XS.

Palgrave Macmillan in the US is a division of St Martin's Press LLC,
175 Fifth Avenue, New York, NY 10010.

Palgrave Macmillan is the global academic imprint of the above companies
and has companies and representatives throughout the world.

Palgrave® and Macmillan® are registered trademarks in the United States,
the United Kingdom, Europe and other countries.

ISBN 978–0–230–30166–5   hardback
ISBN 978–0–230–36147–8   paperback

This book is printed on paper suitable for recycling and made from fully
managed and sustained forest sources. Logging, pulping and manufacturing
processes are expected to conform to the environmental regulations of the
country of origin.

A catalogue record for this book is available from the British Library.

A catalog record for this book is available from the Library of Congress.

03
12

Printed and bound in Great Britain by
CPI Antony Rowe, Chippenham and Eastbourne

For Ronnie Buchanan

Contents

Acknowledgements   viii

Abbreviations   ix

Introduction   x

Part I

1   Action and reaction: majority identities, 1921–60   3

2   Parallel universes: minority identities, 1921–60   44

3   Remembering and forgetting: commemorations and
    identity, 1921–60   86

Part II

4   Conflict and conciliation: identities and change,
    1960–2011   107

5   Remembering and reclaiming: commemorations and
    identity, 1960–2011   155

6   The past and the present: history, identity and the
    peace process   178

Conclusion   203

Notes   206

Select Bibliography   237

Index   242

Acknowledgements

The phrase in my title, the 'Two Irelands', refers to Northern Ireland and the Irish Free State, later the Republic of Ireland, or north and south, or unionist and nationalist. I must acknowledge that David Fitzpatrick recently used this phrase in the title of his book, *The Two Irelands, 1912–1939*. I want also to acknowledge the assistance which I have received from many institutions and individuals in the writing of this book. I am especially indebted to the staff in the library of Queen's University Belfast, the newspaper library at Belfast Central Library, the Linen Hall Library, Belfast, and the National Library of Ireland, Dublin.

I have greatly appreciated the support of my colleagues in the School of Politics, International Studies and Philosophy at Queen's, especially John Barry, Keith Breen, Yvonne Galligan, John Garry, Adrian Guelke, Ruth Dilly, Lee McGowan, Margaret O'Callaghan and Graham Walker. I am very grateful to Paul Bew, George Boyce, Tom Garvin, Cathal McCall, Bill Vaughan, and Christopher Woods, who read part or all of my manuscript. Of course, they are not responsible for my final draft. Others who gave valuable help or advice at various stages include Don Akenson, Arthur Aughey, Eugenio Biagini, Norma Dawson, Marianne Elliott, Richard English, David Fitzpatrick, Gordon Gillespie, Will Hazleton, Jack Johnston, Jane Leonard, Patrick Maume and Tim Smith. I wish to thank Amber Stone-Galilee and Liz Blackmore at Palgrave Macmillan for their encouragement and helpful suggestions.

This book reflects my research and teaching interests over recent years on the subject of identity in Ireland. I acknowledge gratefully the response of my students which has helped me to work out ideas on this issue. Another version of the chapter on commemorations, 1921–60, appeared in my book, *Past and Present: History, Identity and Politics in Ireland*. Some of the material in the chapter on history and identity was used in an article 'Ancient Enmities and Modern Conflict; History and Politics in Northern Ireland' in *Nationalism and Ethnic Politics*.

Two final notes of thanks are appropriate. I am very grateful to my wife Evelyn and children Katherine and David for their patience and support during the time spent on the research and writing of this book. I wish to dedicate the book to Ronnie Buchanan, former director of the Institute of Irish Studies, by way of thanks for all his wise advice and encouragement.

Abbreviations

DUP	Democratic Unionist Party
GAA	Gaelic Athletic Association
IRA	Irish Republican Army
MP	Member of Parliament
NILP	Northern Ireland Labour Party
NIWC	Northern Ireland Women's Coalition
PUP	Progressive Unionist Party
RIC	Royal Irish Constabulary
RUC	Royal Ulster Constabulary
SDLP	Social Democratic and Labour Party
TD	Teachta Dála (dáil deputy)
UDA	Ulster Defence Association
UDP	Ulster Democratic Party
UUP	Ulster Unionist Party
UVF	Ulster Volunteer Force

Introduction

Not very long ago, violence in Northern Ireland attracted world-wide attention. In a 30-year period, from 1968 to 1998, over 3000 people were killed in a conflict which many outside observers found difficult to understand. Recently, we have witnessed significant change in Northern Ireland, with an almost complete end to violence and the creation of a system of government that has broad community support. A former unionist leader, Ian Paisley, has described new political developments in Northern Ireland as a 'modern miracle'.[1] In 2009, the Irish President, Mary McAleese, talked of greatly improved relationships within Northern Ireland, between both parts of Ireland and between Ireland and Britain. She remarked: 'all three sets of relationships had been twisted by the forces of history'.[2] In 2011 we saw not only the power-sharing executive in the north complete its four-year term of office, but also the first visit of a British monarch to the south since 1921. There are still tensions between the main parties in the situation but it is clear that matters have improved dramatically. This book seeks to explain the origins and nature of the conflict, and also to reveal how it was possible, eventually, to establish relative peace and significant accommodation.

The main argument presented here is that at the centre of the conflict has been a struggle over identity, arising from key divisions, particularly over nationality but also over religion. Six chapters examine developments over the period from 1921 to the present. This study is concerned with the political history of the two Irelands, namely Northern Ireland and the Irish Free State (later the Republic of Ireland), north and south, or unionist and nationalist. It is not possible to understand what happened in the north of Ireland without understanding what occurred in the south, and vice versa. Each state was greatly influenced by the other. As well, developments in the two parts of Ireland were similar in many ways, and by looking at both parts together we get a better sense of the factors that influenced the political process. In particular, this book explores how ideas of identity have served to impact markedly on politics in Northern Ireland and the Republic of Ireland, as well as between north and south and between all sections and Britain. It is argued here that prescriptive, exclusive and confrontational ideas of identity grew in the two parts of Ireland in the decades after 1921. This development helped to lead to the outbreak of violence in 1968 and to inhibit meaningful accommodation of the different sides for decades. In recent years, however, more inclusive and pluralist concepts of identity have evolved, which have allowed for a substantial degree of conciliation.

Our starting date of 1921 marks the partition of Ireland which led to the establishment of two polities, namely Northern Ireland and the Irish Free State, later the Republic of Ireland. An earlier date might have been chosen, although it would be a matter of debate which date would be more appropriate. This historical period, from 1921 to the present, has been picked because the aim is to examine the key developments that occurred during this time and had such an important effect. Without doubt, the situation in 1921 had significant roots in the past, but this period had its own special dynamics which greatly influenced how these new states would develop and how political identities within them would change. The end part of this period witnessed important acts of accommodation and conciliation. In 1998 the Belfast Agreement, known also as the Good Friday Agreement, established new relations between the two communities in Northern Ireland, between north and south and between Britain and Ireland. The year 2007 saw not only the establishment of a Sinn Féin/Democratic Unionist Party led power-sharing executive in Northern Ireland, but also the official meeting between the Northern Ireland First Minister Dr Ian Paisley and the Irish Taoiseach Bertie Ahern at the River Boyne, the scene of the famous seventeenth-century battle. Four years later the northern executive completed its first term of office. In May 2011, Queen Elizabeth carried out an official visit to the south. These new arrangements and events reflect the impact of changed identities on how people deal today with their political world and their political opponents.

The term 'identity' is used here in a broad sense, to mean how individuals, and particularly communities of individuals, understand and express themselves. In this study my main interest is political identity. Such political identity, however, goes beyond purely political matters to involve significant other dimensions, especially religion and religious division. Over the last hundred years or so in Ireland there have been two major communities, unionist and nationalist, with their particular national identities. This central dispute over nationality, for a united independent Ireland or union with Great Britain, has involved important ideas of Irish or British identity. During this period there has been great change in the form and expression of Irish and British identities. At the same time, we should be aware that there was sometimes overlap between identities, as seen in unionists who continued to regard themselves as Irish and nationalists who still valued the British connection. Such ideas of identity have been central for individuals and communities, as they affect not only how people view themselves but how they see their opponents. At the same time people are greatly influenced by the character and expression of their opponents' identity. The discourse around differing and often opposing identities is at the core of politics in Ireland.

Special structural or historical arguments have often been invoked to explain the conflict in twentieth-century Ireland, with its opposing nationalist and unionist sides and an influential religious division. It is stressed here, however, that the situation is best seen in a contemporary European context. The nineteenth and early twentieth century witnessed the emergence of nationalism as a key factor in the politics of many European countries. The years 1918–22, saw the establishment of new states not only in Ireland but in Central and Eastern Europe as well. Many of the new states, such as Poland, also contained majorities in favour of these new arrangements and minorities opposed to them. Conflict over nationality has remained a central issue in the politics of many European countries. We have seen this very clearly, not just in the early twentieth century but also in its last decades, especially in many countries of Central and Eastern Europe, including Czechoslovakia, and to less extent in some countries of Western Europe, as in Spain.

For much of the late nineteenth and twentieth centuries, religion survived too as a matter of political importance in many parts of Europe, such as Holland in the west and the former Yugoslavia in the east. Therefore, we should not be surprised to see that religion has continued as a significant dividing factor in both parts of Ireland over the last hundred years. Curiously, much of recent analysis of twentieth-century Irish history, in particular concerning the conflict in Northern Ireland, has failed to recognise the European context and has regarded developments here as abnormal or inexplicable. Setting these issues of nationality and religion in a broad twentieth-century European setting allows a much better understanding of politics in Ireland than viewing them from a simplistic Anglo-American framework, which has led to a failure to understand the importance of such matters in modern times, not just in Ireland.

This book has two sections. The first examines what happened in the years from 1921 to the early 1960s. In the opening chapter, majority identities in both new polities are examined. There is good evidence that, after initial difficulties and violence, leaders, north and south, made some effort to establish broad and tolerant societies. In succeeding decades, however, owing to both internal and external factors, important changes occurred among the main sections which led to prescriptive, exclusive and confrontational identities. The second chapter looks at the fortunes over this period of the unionist/Protestant minority in the south and the nationalist/Catholic minority in the north. In the first decade there was hope that both groups would play full parts in their new societies, but such hope did not prevail and both experienced marginalisation. Social and economic bias affected their position, but much more important was their exclusion from the dominant identity of the state to which they belonged. The third chapter looks at important commemorations and anniversaries in both states. It explores how people's appreciation of their identity and history, as expressed in how they marked these events, changed markedly, even in the short period examined here.

The second part deals with the decades from the 1960s to the present. Chapter 4 covers events from the 1960s and the outbreak of violent conflict. It deals with all the main groups in both the north and the south. It is argued that exclusive and antagonistic identities were a major factor in the failure to achieve some degree of accommodation in the early period which led to decades of violence and political paralysis. We then see the emergence of changed identities and perspectives, which meant that many could now more easily take steps towards peace and new institutions of government with broad support. Chapter 5 looks at how commemorations were marked in this period. At the beginning, such events were frequently occasions for confrontation and the exposition of exclusive senses of identity, but by the end they often served to promote more inclusive and pluralist ideas. A final chapter explores how views of history have influenced identities. It is argued that 'perceptions' of the past have been very important in Ireland, north and south. At the beginning of this period such 'perceptions' often had a detrimental effect on efforts to find peace. Over the last four decades, however, there have been important changes in how people have viewed their history, and this has aided attempts at reaching a settlement.

This book examines the fraught dynamics of identity politics both within and between the two Irelands from 1921 to the present. What it means to be Irish or British, or to be nationalist or unionist, has changed markedly over the last 90 years. For many today, identities have been reshaped and reinterpreted to become more pluralist and prepared to accommodate differences. In contrast to Northern Ireland Prime Minister, Lord Craigavon, who in April 1934 praised a 'Protestant parliament and a Protestant state', unionist leader, David Trimble, in 1998 pledged to provide a 'pluralist parliament for a pluralist people'.[3] In similar contrast, the Irish President, Eamon de Valera, in 1962 stated that 'if in the north there are people who spiritually want to be English rather than Irish, they can go and we will see that they get adequate, right compensation for their property'; his successor, Mary Robinson in 1995 declared that, to her, Irishness as a concept seemed to be 'at its strongest when it reaches out to everyone on this island and shows itself capable of honouring and listening to those whose sense of identity, and whose cultural values, may be more British than Irish'.[4] Of course, there are still matters of dispute and controversy and not everyone has accepted the changes, but these issues are now argued within a generally agreed framework and in relative peace. Without recent dramatic changes to identity among so many people and communities, today's structures and institutions could never have got off the ground nor survived. Only with the strengthening and development of such pluralist identities can peace and stability be assured in the future.

Part I

1
Action and reaction: majority identities, 1921–60

The early 1920s saw the creation of two new polities in Ireland, north and south. Under the Government of Ireland Act of 1920, six north-eastern counties became Northern Ireland, with its own government and parliament for local matters while remaining under the British government and parliament for other matters. As a result of the Anglo-Irish Treaty of 1921, the other 26 counties were formed into the Irish Free State, which also had its own government and parliament, but acquired dominion status. Over the next three decades a number of legal or constitutional changes occurred to the status of the two states. Eventually in 1949 an Irish republic was declared: in the same year the British parliament guaranteed the right of Northern Ireland to remain within the UK. During this whole period, from 1920 to the early 1960s, other crucial changes occurred in the mainstream political identity in each state. Also, major developments occurred in important religious and cultural dimensions of these identities. Such evolution of identity had significant consequences, not only on relations between communities in each society but also between north and south. At the same time, these developments affected the ultimate long-term stability and viability of both states. This chapter examines how and why these changes occurred in majority identities.

For a time in the 1920s there is evidence that some leading politicians, in the two parts of Ireland, sought to encourage a broad and inclusive character for their respective political communities. In a message to his Orange supporters in Northern Ireland and abroad on 12 July 1923, Sir James Craig, the Northern Ireland prime minister, stated: 'It is our earnest desire to live in peace and amity with the Free State, and to encourage in every way a better understanding between all classes and creeds'.[1] In his St Patrick Day's speech of 17 March 1926, W.T. Cosgrave, the southern head of government, declared that the destinies of the country, north and south, were now in the hands of Irishmen and urged brotherly toleration and co-operation.[2] Speeches of politicians in the 1930s, however, often contained evidence of a very different approach which reflected the emergence of exclusive and prescriptive ideas of identity. In 1934 Craig spoke proudly of a 'Protestant parliament and a Protestant state' – even though about one-third of the population of Northern Ireland was Catholic.[3] In 1935, the new southern leader, Eamon de Valera, declared enthusiastically that Ireland remained 'a Catholic nation' – although Protestants were nearly one quarter of the population of Ireland.[4]

Interpretations in the past have tended to see these developments as primarily the inevitable outcome of long-term historical problems and 'ancient enmities', of the violence that occurred in the period 1920–23 or of partition itself. Here, however, it is argued that, while such matters are of some significance, the changes are primarily the result of contemporary dynamics affecting identities in both states over this whole period. The creation of new states brings special challenges which can influence the formation of identity. A heightened self-consciousness is often exhibited in the early years of recent states, especially when some national or security issue has not yet been resolved.[5] There is usually a strongly felt demand to show that the new state is different both from what has gone before and also from its neighbour. Political leaders are often keen to find issues to distinguish them from their rivals. The necessity for a fledging state to gain stability and legitimacy is often paramount, as is the need to create a uniting sense of community.[6] The development of a strong sense of identity can play an important role in all these matters. In the case of both Northern Ireland and the Irish Free State, these various factors would impact on the dynamics of identity formation.

There are important parallels with elsewhere. In the same years after the First World War, a number of other states were established in Central and Eastern Europe.[7] Most of them – Czechoslovakia, Poland and Yugoslavia are examples – resembled Northern Ireland and the Irish Free State in lacking homogeneity, especially in relation to national identity. In his study of these newly established countries, Rogers Brubaker has stressed the importance for contemporary politics of the continuing conflict over nationality. He has noted how there was often a 'nationalising' state, comprising the majority and dominant national group, which sought to develop the new country in its own image, while there was a minority whose national interest lay elsewhere. He has emphasised the significance of relations both within states and between states, especially when there are national minorities within one state with a strong sense of belonging to the other.[8]

In the case of the two polities in Ireland, what is important is not just the relationship between national majorities and minorities within each state and between north and south, but also the ongoing relationship between both Northern Ireland and the Irish Free State/Éire and Great Britain. In addition, Brubaker has emphasised how the main groups in this conflict often face intra-group as well as inter-group contest, with the result, as Karen Stanbridge puts it, that 'the various representations of nation are modified by their proponents depending on the actions of their rivals'.[9] Such internal rivalries and party politics would influence the development of mainstream political identities in both states in Ireland. It could be argued that a different political settlement in Ireland in 1920–22, perhaps involving a 32-county Irish state or a smaller four-county Northern Ireland, would have made a major difference to future political relations on the island. Regardless of the particular territorial arrangements, the new state or states would still have experienced these contemporary problems, particularly concerning national divisions and minorities.

Background

Origins of various aspects of the identities which became evident in Northern Ireland and the Irish Free State are apparent in the politics of pre-1921 Ireland. The late decades of the nineteenth and the early decades of the twentieth century were a key formative period for politics in many countries in Europe, including Ireland. Extensive political mobilisation and democratisation led to the appearance of modern political movements and parties which reflected the main concerns and divisions/cleavages of each contemporary society.[10] Extension of the franchise in 1885 and 1918 was an important catalyst for these developments.[11] In Ireland, nationalists, based on the majority Catholic community throughout the country, sought some form of independence for Ireland. Unionists, based on the minority Protestant community, centered most strongly in the north east but also found elsewhere in Ireland, wanted to maintain full union with Britain. This confrontation led not only to the emergence of nationalist and unionist parties in Ireland, but also to the formation of armed forces, in the shape of the Ulster Volunteer Force (UVF) on behalf of the northern unionists and the Irish Volunteers, later the Irish Republican Army (IRA), on behalf of nationalists/republicans. Political developments from the time of the 1916 Dublin Rising saw a rise in support for a more advanced form of Irish self-determination that was opposed to any links with Britain. From 1912 northern unionists had come to associate closely with the idea of separate treatment for Ulster. Out of this conflict emerged two new states in Ireland in the form of Northern Ireland, as a result of the Government of Ireland Act of 1920, and the Irish Free State, thanks to the Anglo Irish Treaty of 1921.

The nature of politics and the party system that developed in Ireland in the late nineteenth and late twentieth centuries revealed a strong correlation between denominational attachment and political allegiance. Most unionists were Protestant while most nationalists were Catholic. The character of party politics would change in the sense that the Irish nationalist party would be replaced in 1918 by Sinn Féin as the main party of the Irish nationalist community and the Irish Unionist Party would be superseded by the Ulster Unionist Party, but there would be no change in the main division of unionist and nationalist or in basic denominational support for these two sides. Religion provided an important source of identity for people throughout Ireland in the early twentieth century, as it did subsequently. The late nineteenth and early twentieth centuries also saw the emergence of important cultural dimensions for both political positions and identities. For many nationalists, influenced by the Irish/Ireland movement, the Irish language and a revival of Gaelic culture became an important part of their Irish identity. For many northern unionists there was a growing interest in a regional Ulster identity. All these factors were important for the essential character of politics and society in the two new states which were created in 1920–22. Partition was a result rather than a cause of these divisions.

A number of political scientists, in particular S.M. Lipset and Stein Rokkan, have emphasised the importance of this period for twentieth-century politics in the countries of Western Europe. They have described how the political systems established in these years remained 'frozen' for the next four decades in many cases. The political parties and key divisions in each society by the 1960s still reflected strongly the developments of these years.[12] In the example of Ireland, north and south, this period has proved equally formative and of long-term consequence. In Northern Ireland the unionist and nationalist divide in politics remained central while in the Irish Free State/Irish Republic the dominant party conflict of Fianna Fáil and Fine Gael was based on the intra-nationalist split of these critical years.[13]

Nonetheless, while this background was important for developments post-1921, it was not inevitable that the main identities in both new states should become highly exclusive. In the early 1900s many northern unionists had a sense of Irish identity alongside their attachment to the British crown and their support for the union. Co. Antrim unionist, Ronald McNeill, the author of *Ulster's Stand for Union*, published in 1922, with its endorsement of 'the Ulster movement', responded ten years earlier in parliament to a question about his self-description as an Ulsterman by saying: 'I used the expression "Ulster man" as a more particular phrase. Of course I regard myself as being an Irishman'.[14] In the same period many nationalists were able to accept some British links, in the form of acknowledgement of the crown and the empire, alongside their nationalism and their belief in home rule.[15] Even Arthur Griffith, founder of Sinn Féin, was prepared in the early 1900s to promote the idea of a dual monarchy for Ireland rather than an outright republic. By 1921 political identities had become attached to more rigidly defined senses of Britishness or Irishness, but there were people on both sides who continued to acknowledge broader dimensions. In spite of strong links between religion and politics it should be noted that there were important exceptions, as seen in the election in 1918 of the Catholic Denis Henry as unionist MP for South Londonderry and the Protestant Ernest Blythe as Sinn Féin MP for North Monaghan. We can observe the references to 'civil and religious freedom' in the Ulster Solemn League and Covenant of 1912 and to 'religious and civil liberty' in the Easter Proclamation of 1916.[16]

Given the confrontation between unionists and nationalists/Sinn Féin, there was no realistic alternative to partition in 1920. A 32-county state, run from Dublin, with an oath of allegiance, would almost certainly have found itself facing, as Tom Garvin has written, 'not one but two civil wars, one in Munster and another in Ulster'.[17] As it was, the early years of both Northern Ireland and the Irish Free State were marked by violence and a strong challenge to the legitimacy of the two governments. Politically inspired violence was responsible for the loss of some 600 lives in Northern Ireland, 1920–22, and for the death of over 1500 in the Irish Free State, 1922–23.[18] Both the unionist and the Cumann na nGaedheal governments faced political opponents who initially refused to accept the legitimacy of their respective states and who included those willing to use violence against the authorities. In the south the political conflict was primarily intra-nationalist between supporters of the Treaty and their republican opponents while in the north the conflict was between unionists and nationalists/republicans. Religion would remain important in both societies, but in the north it would continue to be a basic dividing factor in politics because the

Catholic minority constituted a significant one-third of the population, while in the south it would not be a serious source of division because the Protestant minority was under a tenth of the population.

The violence of these early years and the extra-ordinary steps taken by the two governments to defend their legitimacy provided a difficult start for both new states. The Irish Free State government had, what Tom Garvin has called, a 'penchant for emergency legislation', an approach shared by the northern authorities.[19] The government passed a public safety act in 1923 which would be followed by a series of other strong security measures, including the offences against the state act introduced in 1939 by de Valera.[20] In 1922 the Northern Ireland government brought in a special powers act which was renewed annually until 1933 when it was made permanent.[21] The northern government established a police force which was drawn largely from the unionist community: although it was allowed originally that one-third should be Catholic, the figure for Catholics in the Royal Ulster Constabulary (RUC) stood at around 18 per cent in 1925 and would drop thereafter.[22] Over 98 per cent of the original members of the Garda Siochana were Catholic, and drawn largely from IRA ranks, 'carefully screened for their pro-treaty sympathies'.[23]

In the north by June 1922 there were over 500 republican internees while in the south by February 1923 there were around 13,000 republican prisoners and internees.[24] The new army in the south was recruited initially from reliable members of the IRA who supported the Irish Free State government.[25] In response to the civil war, its numbers were expanded rapidly to bring in others, including former experienced British soldiers. To defend its position, in face of IRA attacks, the Northern Ireland government established a special constabulary, under three categories, whose members were drawn exclusively from the Protestant community and often from the former UVF. Eventually, in both states the governments were able to restore public order and their central authority. After hostilities ended, the special constabulary in Northern Ireland was stood down, except for the part time 'B' specials, who were retained as a local defence force, under Belfast rather than London control, and who would continue to provide important support for the police.[26]

Strong measures were introduced to exercise control over local government, north and south. Local government officials were obliged to take oaths of loyalty to their respective states. In Northern Ireland, over 20 councils which refused to recognise the government were dissolved and commissioners appointed to run them. Local government boundaries were redrawn to unionist advantage in certain areas, especially in border regions, owing very largely to concerns about the boundary commission, which was set up as a result of the Anglo-Irish Treaty, and which threatened the borders and territorial integrity of the northern state. Ernest Blythe, minister of local government in the Irish Free State government, disapproved but understood this unionist reaction. In Dáil Éireann in December 1925 he remarked that he 'had no hesitation in saying that things would never have been as bad in the boundary area if there had not been the question of a change in the boundary line. He believed gerrymandering in Tyrone and Fermanagh would not have been carried out to the extent it was if there had not been the question of transfer of territory'.[27] In early 1923 the Irish Free State government enacted legislation which allowed it to dissolve local authorities and appoint commissioners. In May 1923 the county councils of Cork and Leitrim were dissolved, because of their anti-treaty sympathies, and another 20 local authorities were taken over, some for political reasons and some on grounds of inefficiency.[28] Most opposition to the government in the south, however, came from rural district councils. In mid-1923, the central authorities were concerned at allegations that republicans intended to take over some local government bodies and challenge the administration. In July 1923 Ernest Blythe warned the cabinet that the forthcoming local elections would give every 'crank and impossibilist' in the country a platform. His solution was that all rural district councils should be abolished. This was agreed to and their duties were taken over by the county councils.[29]

The consequences of the difficulties and bitterness of these early years, when both governments sought to establish their authority, has been emphasised elsewhere.[30] At the same time, it was not inevitable that the two new political entities would develop narrow and prescriptive identities. By late 1923 a fair degree of stability and peace had been established in both states. Furthermore, there is evidence of some willingness on the part of leading politicians to create inclusive societies and identities. In his 1926 St Patrick's Day broadcast, W.T. Cosgrave stated that the destinies of the country, north and south, were now in the hands of Irishmen: 'if we are to succeed there must be a brotherly toleration of each other's ideas as to how our ambition may be realised, and a brotherly co-operation in every effort towards its realisation'.[31] Cosgrave encouraged his republican opponents to enter fully into parliamentary politics. There is evidence that in the early days of the new Irish Free State government there was some effort by ministers to restrict ecclesiastical influence.[32] The government under Cosgrave sought links with Protestants and the new senate chose a former unionist as chairman.

In the Dáil in December 1925, Major Bryan Cooper, a former unionist MP, declared that 'they had ceased to think in terms of majority and minority'.[33] The Cumann na nGaedheal government showed a willingness to acknowledge a place for commemorations of ex-servicemen and Orange demonstrations were allowed to continue unimpeded during the 1920s in border counties.

In the early years of the new Northern Ireland government some effort was made to maintain a broad basis for the character of the state. In a speech at the Reform Club in Belfast in February 1921, Sir James Craig declared: 'Remember that the rights of the minority must be sacred to the majority, and that it will only be by broad, tolerant ideas and a real desire for liberty of conscience that we here can make an ideal of the parliament and the executive'.[34] The first lord chief justice was a Catholic, and there were efforts initially to keep fair selection procedures for recruitment to the police and civil service.[35] In a speech at a meeting in early 1926 of Belfast Rotary Club, attended by a number of politicians including Joseph Devlin, the nationalist leader, J.M. Andrews, minister of labour, declared that they were 'united in the desire that the better spirit which had been growing in Northern Ireland should continue to grow and to be fostered in their midst'.[36] Devlin responded to this positive approach in a St Patrick's Day speech in March 1926: 'the dominant duty of every true Irishman is to look forward, not to keep gazing back on the past ... not to sulk over misfortunes that are no longer avoidable'.[37] Some cabinet members were determined to oppose sectarianism. In 1927 the minister of education, Lord Charlemont, wrote: 'I cannot say how strongly I object to the idea that a unionist government is brought in not only to maintain the union but also to humour the sectarian prejudices of all unionists'.[38] Such aspirations and instances of tolerance, however, did not materialise in either the north or south. To understand why this happened we must appreciate the new dynamics, discussed at the beginning of this chapter, that affected the fledgling states and their dominant national majorities, in Ireland, as elsewhere.

The Irish Free State/Éire, 1921–49

At the Dublin rising of 1916 the insurgents had proclaimed 'the Irish republic as a sovereign independent state'.[39] Under the terms of the Anglo-Irish Treaty of December 1921, between the British government and Sinn Féin representatives, however, it was agreed that 26 of the Irish counties, to be known as the Irish Free State, would gain self-government, but would remain part of the British Commonwealth.

Irish people became Irish citizens but continued as British subjects. Although this agreement gave the new state virtual complete power, with the British government's authority becoming nominal, it led to sharp divisions over its acceptability among members of Sinn Féin. What mattered most to people was not the question of partition, which was barely discussed in the Dáil debates on the treaty, nor social or economic issues, but matters relating to the question of national status and the fundamental identity of the state. Opponents of the treaty found the continued links with Britain unacceptable, particularly the oath the treaty imposed on members of the new parliament. In Commonwealth countries the oath of allegiance was always first to the crown, but in the Irish case the oath of allegiance was first to the constitution of the new state, followed by an oath of fidelity to the crown.[40] This compromise, however, failed to win over opponents of the treaty. Eventually, the whole dispute led to a civil war in which many more Irish people were killed than during the war of independence. The divisions created at this time provided the basic source of the new party politics in the new state, with the pro-treaty side becoming the Cumann na nGaedheal party and the first Irish government, while their anti-treaty opponents retained the Sinn Féin title until 1926 when most organised under the new Fianna Fáil party which entered government in 1932.

While questions of national identity dominated political life in the first years of the state, relations between the new state and Britain continued to be a vital concern for the main parties. Social and economic issues divided the parties to some extent, but the question of their relationship with Britain remained very important for Irish politicians. In addition, conditions within the fledgling state created special demands on the parties. For the Cumann na nGaedheal government, with a narrow parliamentary majority, there was a necessity to bolster its legitimacy and backing. Fianna Fáil, in order to obtain power, and to maintain it, post-1932 with small majorities, needed to gather extra support. For both parties questions of identity were seen as important to distinguish between them and to strengthen their position among the electors. In addition, these matters of identity served to provide the means to justify the existence of the new state and to show how different it was from its neighbours. In 1923, on the subject of education, Cosgrave spoke of the need for 'the gaelicisation … of our whole culture' and of support for proposals to attempt to make 'our nation separate and distinct and something to be thought of'.[41] In 1931 de Valera declared: 'We are not a British colony. We are not a British dominion. We are a separate people, we are a separate nation. Our rights are inherent'.[42]

The new government took a number of steps, both formal and symbolic, to develop dimensions of Irish identity and reduce elements of British identity. In their dealings with the British government, members of the Cumann na nGaedheal government argued strongly for Ireland's separate political identity and were able to achieve some, although not all, of the changes they wanted. They secured a change in the title of the king but they were not able to achieve a separate Irish citizenship. They went to conferences of the British dominions with the aim, as Patrick McGilligan, minister of external affairs, put it, that the British government 'must be uprooted from the whole system of this state'. At the same time they were willing to accept a role for the British monarch in Irish affairs, 'at the will of the Irish government'.[43] Indeed, in 1926 Kevin O'Higgins proposed an idea of a dual monarchy as a means to promote unification, although this proposal did not proceed far before his death. Irish government representatives played an important part in bringing about the Statute of Westminster of 1931, which meant that dominion parliaments no longer had to refer legislation back to the judicial committee of the privy council in London.

From the state's foundation in 1922, the tricolour was used as the official flag of the Irish Free State, while in 1926 the 'Soldier's Song' was confirmed as the national anthem. The choice of the tricolour and the 'Soldiers Song', both with strong links to the 1916 rising, was important, not only to help define a national identity but also to respond to their opponents. As Ewan Morris has pointed out, the Cumann na nGaedheal government believed that these emblems would not only 'make the state as distinct as possible from Britain', but would also strengthen their own position against criticism that they had failed to achieve a republic. The Irish Free State government sought to use official symbols 'to mark a distinct Irish identity, an identity which had no place for Britishness'.[44]

The accession to power of Eamon de Valera and Fianna Fáil in the early 1930s led to additional expressions of separate identity in relations between the Irish Free State and Great Britain. At a commemoration of the Easter Rising in April 1933, Eamon de Valera declared: 'Let it be made clear that we yield no willing assent to any form or symbol that is out of keeping with Ireland's right as a sovereign nation. Let us remove these forms one by one ...'.[45] Not long after, the Fianna Fáil government abolished the oath of fidelity to the British crown for Dáil members, undermined the position of governor general as the king's representative and ended the right of appeal by Irish residents to the British privy council. Under the External Relations Act of 1936 all references to the crown were excised although the Irish Free State did not leave the Commonwealth nor make the final break with Britain. The 1935 Irish Nationality and Citizenship Act affirmed a separate Irish citizenship.[46] At the same time, we may note that in the 1930s members of Fine Gael continued to advocate membership of the Commonwealth.[47] In 1937 a new constitution was introduced by de Valera which changed the name of the country to Ireland, or Éire, and claimed that 'the national territory consists of the whole island of Ireland, its islands and the territorial seas', but stated that 'pending the reintegration of the national territory' the laws of the Irish parliament would extend only to the 26-county area.[48] While it carried no reference to the crown or the UK, it did not declare Ireland a republic, in keeping with de Valera's idea that there could still be an arrangement whereby Ireland could be linked to the British Commonwealth in some form of external association.[49]

For de Valera and the Irish government, neutrality in the Second World War was not just to do with matters of diplomacy, strategy or self-interest but was related also to views of identity.[50] Joseph Walshe, secretary of the department of external affairs, declared that neutrality 'is just as much a part of the national position as the desire to remain Irish and we can no more abandon it than we can renounce everything that constitutes our national distinctiveness'.[51] This policy of neutrality, however, won wide party and popular support. Nonetheless, we should note the remarks of General Richard Mulcahy in his first speech as leader of Fine Gael in January 1944: 'We stand unequivocally for membership of the British Commonwealth: we believe that the solution of the problem of partition must be brought about by agreement among Irishmen'.[52] In 1948 Fianna Fáil was defeated at the polls over various issues, and a new Fine Gael-led inter-party government was formed under the leadership of J.A. Costello and not Mulcahy, who was unacceptable to other members of this coalition because of his moderate stand on the Commonwealth and partition and his civil war role. In November 1948 the Republic of Ireland Bill was introduced, in Taoiseach Costello's words, to end 'this country's long and tragic association with the institution of the British crown' and to sever all links with the Commonwealth.[53] The introduction and passing of this act represented a strategic move by Costello and Fine Gael to out-manoeuvre de Valera and Fianna Fáil on the issue.[54] At the time, a British diplomat in Dublin observed: 'The fact is that the Fine Gael party had a sudden brainwave that they would steal the "Long Man's" [de Valera's] clothes'.[55] The Fine Gael ministers were also responding to internal pressure in the inter-party government from members of Clann na Poblachta, in particular Sean MacBride, the former IRA leader.[56]

Attitudes towards Northern Ireland changed considerably during this first decade. Initially the new government had been strongly hostile to the Northern Ireland government and state, but the terms of the 1925 Tripartite Agreement declared that the Irish Free State, British and Northern Ireland governments, were 'united in amity ... and resolved mutually to aid one another in a spirit of neighbourly comradeship', confirmed the 1920 boundary and recognised the powers and position of Northern Ireland.[57] At this stage both the Irish Free State and Northern Ireland governments exchanged messages of good will. On 3 December 1925 William Cosgrave declared that 'a new atmosphere of friendship and brotherhood had been created'.[58] Subsequent relations in the later 1920s were limited although not hostile.[59] The southern government continued to express hope for an end to partition but declared its belief, in the words of Ernest Blythe in 1928, 'that the end of that can only come about by consent'.[60] The accession to power of de Valera in 1932 brought change to the government's position, although initially not as radical as northern nationalists expected or unionists feared. At the Fianna Fáil ard fheis in November 1933 de Valera declared that reunification could not be achieved by 'mere words ... neither could they solve it by force'. He then went on to say that the only way the problem of reunification could be solved 'was by having for our people here a livelihood which would be the envy of the north; which would make them say their future lay with their own people and not with strangers'.[61]

At the same time, in interviews and radio broadcasts, de Valera demonstrated his continued strong opposition to partition. He saw the border as 'entirely artificial, fostered by British money and British influence in the alleged interest of "minorities"'.[62] He viewed partition as a fault of Britain and he preferred to deal with the British government to end partition, rather than with the unionists.[63] Eventually, in the second half of the 1930s, he took a more activist role on the north.[64] He was influenced by the need not only to mollify northern nationalists, but also to satisfy his own republican wing, especially after he began to take tough action against the IRA, which had become a threat in the south. The 1937 constitution under articles 2 and 3 claimed all of Ireland for the Irish state. Negotiations with the British government over various defence and trade issues, provided the opportunity for him to pursue the question of partition. Suggestions for concessions on northern imports into the south, which might have improved north–south relations, were rejected by de Valera on the grounds that they would be seen as 'stabilizing' partition.[65]

Criticism of de Valera's approach was raised in February 1938 by Belfast born Sean MacEntee, minister for finance, but to no effect: 'We as the government here have done nothing of ourselves to secure a solution, but on the contrary have done and are doing certain things that have made a solution more difficult. The demand which we make continuously that the British should compel the Craigavonites to come in with us, has only had the effect of stiffening them against us'.[66] At the Fianna Fáil ard fheis in December 1939 de Valera stated his belief that, 'with good will' on behalf of the British government, unity could be achieved, 'even if they had to go to the extent he indicated before of saying that the people who were opposed to unity and who did not want to be Irish, could be transferred out of Ireland if they preferred to be British rather than Irish'.[67] The US minister to Ireland, David Gray, later described de Valera's ideas for expelling the unionists as 'about as practicable as expelling the New Englanders from Massachusetts'.[68]

Besides these political changes, important development also occurred in cultural areas of identity. As Margaret O'Callaghan has written: 'language and religion were the most obvious indicators of separateness'.[69] Gaelicisation was an important part of the new cultural identity. In addition to its role as a 'badge of identity', the Irish language provided a society deeply divided by the civil war with an 'intact cultural ideal' for which there was broad popular support.[70] The 1922 Irish Free State constitution declared Irish as the state's national language. The Irish language was made a compulsory subject in all primary schools in 1922 and in all secondary schools two years later, while it was a required subject for the intermediate examination from 1928 and for the leaving certificate from 1934.[71] Proficiency in the Irish language became an essential qualification in a wide range of state and local authority employments. In 1929 legislation was passed to make a knowledge of the Irish language obligatory for future members of the legal profession. A new school history curriculum was introduced to instil a particular sense of Irish identity among children. Vincent Comerford has written how 'teachers were encouraged to tell the story of Ireland as a story of seven centuries of militant struggle against English domination'.[72]

This enthusiasm for the language was initiated by the Cumann na nGaedheal government, but was continued by Fianna Fáil, when in power. In 1934 the department of education directed that other subjects, in particular English, mathematics and rural science, should be allowed to decline to promote Irish. In February 1939, in response to a call from Frank MacDermot to consider the impact of these policies on northern unionists, de Valera stated: 'I would not tomorrow, for the sake of a united Ireland, give up the policy of trying to make this a really Irish Ireland – not by any means … I believe that as long as the Irish language remains you have a distinguishing characteristic of nationality which will enable the nation to persist'.[73] In 1942, the minister of education, Thomas Derrig, warned how 'we in this country are threatened to be engulfed by the seas of English speech washing our shores …' and declared that 'we are trying to set up these embankments of Irish, these dykes, in order to keep out the tide of anglicization and it is a very urgent matter indeed that we should get these embankments up'.[74]

Government enthusiasm for compulsory Irish peaked in 1943 when Derrig introduced a school attendance bill to make it a criminal offence for parents to send their children to private schools or boarding schools in Northern Ireland or Britain, where they would not learn Irish. De Valera backed this measure on the grounds that Irish was 'part of the equipment necessary for a good citizen'. In the Dáil, General Richard Mulcahy (himself a language enthusiast) protested: 'we are making it a crime for persons to send their children across the border to school without telling the police'.[75] The bill passed the two houses of parliament, but President Hyde referred it to the supreme court whose members rejected it on grounds that it interfered with the constitutional rights of parents in educational matters.

Religion also played an important part in this new identity. Support from the Catholic church helped to provide legitimacy and stability to the new government.[76] While originally not specially deferential to the Catholic church, the Cumann na nGaedheal government became increasingly so.[77] Legislation for film censorship was introduced in 1923 and for book censorship in 1929. Divorce was prohibited in 1925. The Garda Siochana were consecrated to the Sacred Heart of Jesus in 1923 and then to the Blessed Virgin in 1930.[78] Also in 1930 the government arranged the appointment to Ireland of a papal nuncio who was installed, very symbolically, in the former residence of the British under secretary in Phoenix Park in Dublin, at government expense.[79] In this case the members of the government seem to have been driven by the desire to prove their Catholic credentials without involving the Catholic hierarchy, some of whom were annoyed that they had not been involved beforehand.[80] Major public events such as the Catholic Emancipation Centenary Celebrations of 1929 and the Eucharistic Congress of 1932 served to increase 'the identification of the Irish Free State with Catholicism'.[81] All this, of course, reflected the fact that not only was the population predominantly Catholic but that in the new state the Catholic church wielded great influence in a wide range of social, educational and health areas.[82]

De Valera and members of Fianna Fáil were keen to prove their Catholic credentials, on account not only of their own religious beliefs but also of their awareness of the Catholic church as an important and unifying organisation in the country at large. During the late 1920s and early 1930s de Valera sought to rebuild relations which had been damaged during the civil war, and to reassure Catholic clergy about his party's soundness on social and moral issues, all necessary for the party's political success. At the 1931 Fianna Fáil ard fheis, de Valera reminded people of his long-standing religious views: 'I declared that, if all came to all, I was a Catholic first'.[83] At a Dublin election meeting in February 1932 he stated: 'the majority of the people of Ireland are Catholic and we believe in Catholic principles. And as the majority are Catholics, it is right and natural that the principles to be applied by us will be principles consistent with Catholicity'.[84] He repeated this point when, at the Fianna Fáil ard fheis in November 1933, he declared that 'they were a Catholic majority here and they were able to look after their Catholic interests by open methods'.[85] In early 1933, the *Irish Press* had assured its readers that 'there is not a social or economic change Fianna Fáil has proposed or brought about which has not its fullest justification in the encyclicals of either Leo XII or the present pontiff'.[86] At the end of that year, in Geneva, Sean T.O'Kelly, vice-president of the executive council, stated that 'the Free State government was inspired in its every administrative action by Catholic principles and doctrine'.[87] The importation and sale of contraceptives was prohibited by the 1935 Criminal Law Amendment Act.[88] In his 1935 St Patrick's Day speech, de Valera declared that Ireland had been a Christian and Catholic nation since St Patrick: 'she remains a Catholic nation'.[89]

The new constitution of 1937 served to illustrate the denominational character of the new Irish identity.[90] In drawing up the document de Valera sought advice from Catholic clergy, although he refused to make the Catholic church a state church and he introduced a clause which recognised certain other faiths. The constitution declared the 'special position' of the Catholic church, prohibited the introduction of divorce and based some of its social principles on papal encyclicals. Patrick Murray has remarked on how the 1937 constitution contrasted very sharply with the 1922 constitution.[91] Even though the earlier constitution had been drawn up by an administration warmly endorsed by the Catholic bishops, it made no reference to Catholic values or interests, unlike the later one. This change reflected the new, additional importance of religion in national identity, south and north, which had developed since 1922. Ironically, as Murray points out, it was the heirs of republicans who had faced severe episcopal disapproval in 1922 who were responsible for the later constitution with its distinctive Catholic features. Another irony was that in June 1937, in the Northern Ireland parliament, Craigavon stated that he had no objection to the 'special position' of the Catholic church in the new constitution. He declared that he would rather see 'a religious community than a non-religious community'. He then went on to state: 'While the government of the south is carried on along lines which I presume are very suitable to the majority of Roman Catholics in that part ... surely ... the government of the north, with a majority of Protestants, should carry on the administration according to Protestant ideas and Protestant desires'.[92]

A number of commemorative events served as a focus for the new political identity that emerged in these decades. One such event was the annual ceremony in June at Bodenstown, Co. Kildare, at the grave of Wolfe Tone, a Protestant leader of the United Irishmen of 1798 who was commonly regarded as the 'father of Irish republicanism'. From the time of his death until 1921, his burial place attracted fairly small numbers of admirers and this annual commemoration usually passed with little public attention.[93] When it recommenced in 1922, however, the character of the occasion had changed markedly.[94] With the success of the republican movement, the event attracted the leading political figures of the day and became a major public event. On 23 June 1924, for example, the *Irish Independent* described how 'a national tribute to the memory of Wolfe Tone was paid yesterday at Bodenstown. President Cosgrave, the heads of the Irish army and judiciary and eight hundred Irish soldiers assembled to do honour to the great patriot'. At the same time, reflecting the divisions within republicanism, anti-treaty organisations also turned up to commemorate Tone. This pattern of an event marked by the state and other organisations continued. The new Fianna Fáil government maintained this official participation. In the early 1930s, however, units of IRA members and their supporters paraded to Bodenstown and by 1935 the occasion had become the opportunity for a massive public display of IRA strength. By 1936 the government had declared the IRA an illegal organisation and steps were taken to prevent IRA participation at Bodenstown. On 22 June 1936 the *Irish Independent* declared that 'Bodenstown was an armed camp', as some 1000 troops and 500 gardai arrived to stop any republican parade. In subsequent years, and after the war, the event would be marked by a brief official ceremony and also by a small number of republicans.

At Bodenstown, in June 1924, the premier, William Cosgrave, spoke of Tone as the apostle of 'democratic freedom' who devoted himself to 'the cause of Irish freedom'. He then quoted Tone's famous phrase, 'we are to unite the whole people of Ireland, to abolish the memory of all past divisions, and to substitute the common name of Irishmen for that of the denominational Protestant, Catholic or Dissenter'. The term Protestant here is used to refer to members of the Church of Ireland. Cosgrave emphasised the importance of 'unity among all Irishmen'. He even mentioned Tone's education at Trinity College, 'an institution which gave Ireland many illustrious sons'.[95] Very rarely, however, did any Bodenstown speech after 1924, from government or other sources, repeat Tone's call for unity of Protestant and Catholic, or refer favourably to Trinity. In subsequent years the main official speech was given by the defence minister who lauded Tone as the founder of the Irish army. Republicans, such as J.A. Madden, TD, emphasised in 1926 that Tone's object was 'complete separation from England and the establishment of an Irish republic'.[96] Speakers on all sides called for unity, by which they usually meant unity of nationalists or republicans, 'after years of fratricidal strife'. In the 1930s IRA spokesmen cited Tone's example to justify the use of violence and attacked both the British and the Irish governments. In 1934 the republican parade included men from Belfast who were Protestant members of the Republican Congress. Fighting broke out, however, when they refused to lower their flags on republican orders, and they were not able to get to Tone's grave. The following day, the *Irish Times* commented on the irony of Ulster Protestants being prevented by Tipperary Catholics from honouring Wolfe Tone.[97] All accepted Tone as the founder of Irish republicanism, but he was admired by different sections for different reasons concerning matters of legitimacy, separation or the use of violence, which most concerned people post-1921, and not with substituting the common name of Irishmen for 'Protestant, Catholic and Dissenter'.

Northern Ireland, 1921–49

In 1912 Ulster unionists had organised in order to oppose home rule for all of Ireland. Under the terms of the Government of Ireland Act of 1920, however, only six counties of nine counties of Ulster remained fully part of the United Kingdom. Called Northern Ireland, the new state was under the control of the Westminster parliament and government, but was given its own local parliament and government. While the Northern Ireland government in the early 1920s faced considerable opposition from Catholic and nationalist/republican quarters, by the second half of 1923 it had established its authority. Whereas the southern government sought to weaken links between the new state and Britain, the northern government endeavoured to strengthen its connections. After 1921, however, the relationship between unionists and the British government remained problematic. Although the Government of Ireland Act had established Northern Ireland, it left Westminster with complete discretion for future arrangements and the unionist government remained concerned about this relationship. In addition, over the following decades, the unionist government saw itself facing important opposition not only from nationalists, within and outside Northern Ireland, but also from various independent unionist and labour groups. Such pressures would influence how the new government and its supporters came to establish their own form of identity.

Constitutional uncertainties, arising from the 1920 settlement, affected unionist political attitudes. As James Loughlin has written: 'northern unionists were never confident that their membership of the British national family was wholly secure'.[98] The first occasion for unionist concerns came in late 1921, when, against unionist wishes, the Anglo-Irish Treaty laid down that the Northern Ireland government would retain its existing powers, but under an all-Ireland parliament, not Westminster. The Northern Ireland parliament was to be allowed to opt out of this arrangement, which would bring about the establishment of a boundary commission, to investigate redrawing the north–south border. On 7 December 1922 the Northern Ireland parliament voted to opt out of this all-Ireland arrangement and a boundary commission was established eventually.[99] This commission made no difference to Northern Ireland's territorial boundaries in the end, but unionist leaders remained very conscious of the need to keep a watchful eye on British public opinion and Westminster politicians.[100]

In 1936, for example, the Ulster Unionist Council report warned that without a local parliament there would be a 'temptation to certain British politicians to make another bid for a final settlement with Irish republicans'.[101] In 1938 Sir Dawson Bates, minister of home affairs, complained: 'So long as we live there will always be the danger of home rule or merging into the Free State. We will never get rid of it. One has only to go to England to see the extraordinary apathy by people who should be our friends. We do not understand this apathy in England towards us'.[102] This concern became very real again in 1940 when the British cabinet opened negotiations with de Valera to end partition in return for Ireland abandoning neutrality. Nothing materialised from these discussions, although they served to highlight the weakness of the unionist position. During these decades there was debate among unionists on the merits of their own parliament as against the alternatives of integration with Britain or dominion status, but the existing system retained widespread support.[103]

For the new Northern Ireland government in the 1920s another serious problem arose from independent unionist, labour and temperance critics. The unionist government position has sometimes been seen as very strong in terms of its parliamentary numbers, but in fact it faced considerable challenges. The results of the elections to the Northern Ireland parliament in 1924 saw Ulster Unionist Party (UUP) numbers drop from 40 to 32; the second part of the 1920s witnessed a rise in the number of government opponents, especially from within unionist ranks. In January 1927 the Ulster Unionist Council warned that 'there are only seven seats to be won by our opponents to overthrow the government and plunge Ulster into chaos' and that 'our margin of safety' over others is 'deplorably narrow'.[104] During 1927 the normal government majority fell by half in several parliamentary divisions on the intoxicating liquor bill.[105] In February 1928 the *Irish Statesman* remarked that the danger for Craig was 'less absorption by the Free State, than the refusal of an increasing number of his followers to allow this phantom fear to deter them from seeking what they believe to be necessary and urgent social and economic reforms'.[106]

On 12 July 1927 Craig, created Viscount Craigavon of Stormont earlier that year, announced the government's intention to abolish proportional representation in elections to the Northern Ireland parliament. In his speech, he praised the south, 'our friendly neighbours', remarked that 'Mr Devlin and his party are the natural opposition' and concentrated on the need for unionist unity.[107] This effort to abolish proportional representation was directed at preventing the election of independents and members of minor parties formed as a result of unionist splits, and not against nationalists. In fact, the main concern for the UUP party in the first half of 1927 was probably the temperance movement, which threatened to run local option/temperance parliamentary candidates.[108] This presented a special challenge for Craig, given his family whiskey distillery connection. Under the new electoral arrangements, at the 1929 general election, the nationalist numbers actually rose from 9 in 1925 to 10, but, crucially, unionist party numbers increased to 37 compared with 32 in 1925, while the figures for independents and members of small parties fell from 8 to 4.[109] Local option candidates were defeated. Fianna Fáil, when in power, also had concerns that proportional representation helped independents and made it difficult for governments to secure good majorities. In 1935 and 1945 the Fianna Fáil government altered constituencies to restrict the number of independents, but did not try to abolish proportional representation until 1959.[110]

Even after the abolition of proportional representation, the unionist government's position remained vulnerable to attack with the growth of economic and social problems in the 1930s and the activities of organisations such as the Ulster Protestant League, founded in 1931.[111] Writing in early 1936, Lord Charlemont noted the increase in religious issues in speeches by politicians in recent years: 'It's not entirely religious fervour – it's the gradual increase of pressure from independent organisations, leagues, socialism; all the political expressions of Ulster individualism'.[112] In the 1938 general election the Progressive Unionist Party, under the leadership of W.J. Stewart, put forward 11 candidates on a platform of criticism of the government's economic policies and the high unemployment rate. At the same general election there were also 11 independent unionist candidates, including six who combined together in an independent unionist association.[113] This threat of division increased the need for unionist unity, and a heightened sense of identity would play an important part in the approach of the unionist government members to the problem.

Besides the difficulty of internal rivalry the unionist government faced nationalist opposition. After at first boycotting the Northern Ireland parliament, from 1925 onwards nationalists began to enter parliament and take part in debates. After 1932, partly through frustration at the permanent minority position in which they now found themselves, their policy alternated between attendance and abstention. Whereas in the south, the main opposition party, Fianna Fáil, had been able to increase its electoral and parliamentary support, this was not possible in the north because of the strong links between religion and politics and because the abolition of proportional representation had helped to undermine potential labour or independent allies, who could have given the nationalists a stronger role. In spite of their majority position, many unionists continued to see nationalists as a real threat. In January 1930 the annual report of the Ulster Unionist Council declared how 'their political opponents were still striving hard to merge the whole of Ulster in the Irish Free State. Mr Joseph Devlin and other leading nationalists had frequently declared that that was their goal. Nothing short of one parliament for all Ireland would satisfy them, and by every means in their power they were striving to attain their object'.[114] Such unionist concerns explain partly their lack of generosity to their nationalist opponents. A renewed IRA alarmed many unionists. Some IRA activities were absurd, such as the decision in May 1939 in Belfast to burn gas masks, which were described as 'only a form of imperial propaganda'.[115] Nonetheless, in both parts of Ireland, IRA numbers grew from the early 1930s and members were involved in shows of strength and acts of violence. The IRA ran a bombing campaign in Britain during 1939. Both northern and southern governments invoked strong emergency legislation to deal with this threat, before and during the Second World War which broke out on 1 September.[116]

In the years immediately following the 1925 Tripartite Agreement the northern government remained well disposed towards the south. On 12 July 1927 Craigavon referred to the Irish Free State as 'friendly neighbours', while at a meeting of the Ulster Unionist Council on 22 January 1928 he declared that he was glad to say that 'the friendly relations existing between the Free State and themselves had been growing every day'.[117] By 1932, however, with the arrival of the Fianna Fáil government the friendly attitude of the northern government changed. Events in the south were closely followed in the north and politicians were reactive to what happened there.[118] In April 1934, in a speech in the Northern Ireland parliament, Craigavon made his often quoted statement about a 'Protestant parliament and a Protestant state'. His fuller comment read: 'In the south they boasted of a Catholic state. They still boast of Southern Ireland being a Catholic state. All I boast of is that we are a Protestant parliament and a Protestant state'.[119] In 1937, following the passing of the new Irish constitution with its claim to all Ireland, Sir Anthony Babington, attorney general, declared that this constitutional claim could only be meant as 'a warning and a menace to them'.[120] De Valera's new constitution and his efforts to persuade the British government over partition alarmed unionists but Craigavon used the situation to advantage. He called a snap general election in February 1938, declaring that 'Ulster is not for sale' and warning that 'it is only by maintaining a firm and united front that Ulster remains impregnable'.[121] He achieved an electoral triumph, unequalled since 1921, against labour and independent unionist candidates, including the new Progressive Unionist Party.[122]

Post-1921 unionists were able to develop their own identity. This involved an emphasis on links with Britain and the British crown, no doubt partly in response to southern efforts to limit their connections with both.[123] In the early years the unionist government had the opportunity to choose a new flag and anthem for Northern Ireland. They decided, however, to retain the British national anthem and union flag with no official local variation. In 1924, in response to a request to provide a flag for the Northern Ireland pavilion at the British Empire exhibition in London, the Northern Ireland minister of labour rejected the idea of a local flag: 'we should emphasise our union in the United Kingdom by flying the Union Jack without any special symbol'.[124] As Ewan Morris has remarked, the unionist government sought to keep unionists united behind the unionist party, and so emphasised 'those symbols which were honoured by all unionists: the Union Jack and the emblems of the monarchy'.[125] The stress on the union flag not only served to distinguish Britishness for unionists but also helped to forge a common identity among unionists, with their various divisions, in support of the unionist government. In the Northern Ireland House of Commons in 1932, independent unionist Thomas Henderson expressed resentment at what he saw as efforts to exploit the Union Jack as a symbol by the unionist party: 'You never go to any ceremony where there is one of the right hon. gentlemen opposite where you do not see the Union Jack spread on the table, and before they finish their speeches they refer to the glorious flag, the Union Jack ... You have always taken advantage of it, and you are responsible for making political capital out of it'. An official Northern Ireland flag was not adopted until 1953.[126]

In the 1930s the government used a number of public ceremonies and events to stress their British identity and to encourage unity in unionist ranks. The building and opening of parliament buildings at Stormont had great symbolism for many unionists. In 1932 Lord Craigavon declared: 'It is indeed a noble building and will stand on its base of granite from the Mourne mountains, as a symbol of the link between Great Britain and Northern Ireland'.[127] Royal visits served as occasions to emphasise loyalty to the Crown of the United Kingdom. In addition, as Gillian McIntosh has remarked, these visits were seen not only 'as occasions of affirmation for the state', but also as 'an embodiment of shared consensus among Protestants and unionists'.[128] Speeches by Craigavon in the 1930s showed a renewed emphasis on the importance of the links with Britain, partly due to developments in the south and partly due to concerns about Protestant disunity arising from severe economic and social hardship.[129] On 12 July 1933 Craigavon stated: 'British we are and British we remain'.[130] There was also additional stress on links with the empire, especially with Canada, Australia and New Zealand. In July 1938 Craigavon declared that 'The British Empire, and all it stands for, is the sun and air of our existence'.[131]

In a broadcast in 1940 Craigavon gave strong support to the allied war effort with the words: 'we are king's men and we will be with you to the end'.[132] As Tom Hennessey has written: 'for Ulster unionists the strategic and material role of Northern Ireland reinforced their sense of Britishness and difference from nationalists'.[133] For many there was also a strong personal sense of involvement and sacrifice. There is the case of Sir Basil Brooke, a nephew of the Chief of the Imperial General Staff, Field Marshall Alan Brooke: his three sons served and two were killed in action. The local contribution to the war effort encouraged new support for Northern Ireland in Britain. In 1943 Winston Churchill wrote to J.M. Andrews, following his resignation as Northern Ireland prime minister after Craigavon: 'during your premiership the bonds of affection between Great Britain and the people of Northern Ireland have been tempered by fire and are now, I believe, unbreakable'.[134] In 1947 the possibility of seeking dominion status was considered briefly, partly in response to a new labour government in Britain, but rejected, owing partly to economic considerations. The labour government proved well disposed towards Northern Ireland, thanks to this war record. In 1948, in a debate on the southern decision to become a republic, Sir Basil Brooke, now the Northern Ireland prime minister, declared: 'Here we look upon the crown as a symbol of freedom; in the Free State the crown is said to be a symbol of aggression'.[135] The next year, in response to Ireland's declaration of a republic, and reflecting the new level of support for Northern Ireland at Westminster, the UK parliament passed the Ireland Act which removed much of the uncertainty, contained in the 1920 settlement, concerning the constitutional status of Northern Ireland. The act stated that 'in no event will Northern Ireland or any part thereof cease to be part ... of the United Kingdom without the consent of the parliament of Northern Ireland'.[136]

At the same time as maintaining this British aspect of their identity, there developed what J.C. Beckett described in 1972 as a kind of 'Ulster patriotism'.[137] He wrote how the use of the term 'Ulster' served to give 'the new state a kind of continuity with the past; it implied that it represented a recognised and well-established territorial division; and it associated Northern Ireland with those stirring seventeenth-century events that were always alive in the folk-memory of Ulster Protestants'. A number of times the government gave consideration to changing the name of the state from Northern Ireland to Ulster, partly out of concern to promote the idea of Ulster and partly out of resentment over how the term Ireland was used by the southern government.[138] There was a possibility that this Ulster identity could have embraced nationalists. In a speech in the Northern Ireland parliament on 9 March 1926, Joseph Devlin declared: 'We are all Ulstermen and proud to be Ulstermen. We want to further the welfare of our province. We are all Irishmen and want to see North and South working harmoniously together'.[139] Three years later, however, Devlin objected that 'there is an ever-growing tendency here in the north of Ireland to draw us away ... from our national attachments; to tell us that we are not Irishmen but Ulstermen, that we belong to something that is apart from Ireland'.[140] This Ulster identity became associated primarily with the unionist population.

The new emphasis given to an Ulster identity can be seen in part as an effort to emphasise differences with the south and to diminish an Irish identity among unionists, although we should note that some retained a sense of Irishness and links with the rest of Ireland. In 1925, in protest at a decision to set up a separate medical register for the south, an editorial in the Belfast unionist paper, the *Northern Whig* declared: 'when Ulster declined to join the south in separating from Great Britain it did not surrender its title as part of Ireland, nor renounce its share in those Irish traditions in art, in learning, in arms, in song, in sport and in science that were worth preserving in a united form'.[141] In some areas for some unionists a sense of Irish identity survived and there were those who still regarded themselves as Irish. Even on 5 March 1929, in a parliamentary debate, Lord Craigavon declared: 'We are Irishmen ... I always hold that Ulstermen are Irishmen and the best of Irishmen – much the best'.[142] When Craigavon died his successor as prime minister, J.M. Andrews, said of him that he was 'a great Ulsterman, a great Irishman, a great imperialist'.[143] The idea of an Ulster identity, however, was already strong by the 1920s, and for many unionists this led increasingly to the rejection of any sense of Irish identity or concern for Ireland.[144] This development can be seen as partly an effort to create a distinct Ulster/British identity and partly a response to changing ideas of Irishness in the south.[145] The war and the final break between the UK and the south, after the declaration of an Irish republic in 1949, was another important stage in this divergence of identity.[146]

During the 1920s the Irish language continued as an optional subject in Catholic schools despite some strong unionist and Orange opposition. In 1928 Lord Charlemont, minister of education, sought to justify to his colleagues continued support for Irish: 'the fact that some recognition is given to Irish by the ministry has greatly disarmed criticism on the part of anti-British elements in the population, while the actual results in spreading a knowledge of the language are insignificant'.[147] In 1933, however, a campaign against the Irish language led by a number of unionist and independent unionist MPs succeeded in ending the government payment of grants for the teaching of Irish as an extra subject in secondary schools. Some unionists were very antagonistic towards the Irish language. In 1933 Sir John Davison, MP, declared that 'the teaching of Irish has been largely a matter of political propaganda, and of disloyal propaganda at that'.[148] In the early 1940s Davison pressed Prime Minister J.M. Andrews, who in turn pressed J.H. Robb, minister of education, to prohibit the Irish language in all schools. Robb refused, on grounds which he explained to Andrews: 'the choice is for them, and is part of that freedom of the individual for which we profess to be fighting this war'.[149] As regards history teaching in schools, David Fitzpatrick has noted how 'the curriculum concentrated on Britain rather than any part of Ireland'. At the same time, the government resisted demands from unionist MPs that Ulster history should be taught, partly because it would have caused controversy and partly because 'while promoting a sense of Ulster, the Northern Ireland government took care not to allow it to go too far in case it weakened the British dimension'.[150]

This British/Ulster identity was not directed at the whole of the population of Northern Ireland but primarily at the Protestant majority. What emerged was a clear public identification of the government and state with the Protestant and unionist community. In the early years, however, it is worth noting that there was an effort to avoid such close links. Sir James Craig was an enthusiastic Orangeman, but in 1922 he rejected a request in the Northern Ireland parliament to make the 12th of July a public holiday. Subsequently it did become a public holiday but from 1923 to 1926 Craig did not attend the annual July parades.[151] On 12 July 1927 the editorial in the nationalist *Irish News* observed that the Orange resolutions for that year were moderate and that the 12th occasion was under 'happier auspices than in the past'. It remarked: 'A broader toleration is spreading, a kindlier feeling is growing up, a better understanding is helping to remove the ancient antagonisms and assuage the bitterness of years of conflict and controversy'. The editorial even declared: 'the great dividing lines are fading away, and Orangemen and nationalists are being brought to recognise their common bond as Irishmen'. When Craig returned on that same day in 1927 to the 'field' (a name used in reference to the field to which the Orangemen march on their parades every July), the main topic of his speech was not the south or northern nationalists, but the threat to unionism from independents and splits within unionist ranks, which necessitated the removal of proportional representation in elections to the Northern Ireland parliament. From this time onwards Craig and other cabinet colleagues began to develop strong public links between members of the government and the Orange Order. In 1929 it was announced that in future Craig would attend the 12th of July demonstration in a different county every year.[152] All this served to maximise Protestant unity and support for the unionist party and government.

In the 1930s links between the unionist government and the Orange Order continued to grow, in face of a new nationalist challenge, especially from the south, and also continuing divisions. An editorial in the *Belfast Telegraph*, 12 July 1932 observed: 'Divided as they are into different churches, it is necessary that Protestants should have some common rallying ground, and a bond of union which will enable them to face assaults from any and every quarter. Such a bond is provided by the Orange Institution'. Speeches and resolutions at 12th demonstrations now became more strident. On 12 July 1932 at Drumbanagher in Co. Armagh, Lord Craigavon declared: 'Ours is a Protestant government and I am an Orangeman' (reported in the nationalist *Irish News*, 13 July 1932, but not in the unionist *Northern Whig* or *Belfast News Letter*). On 12 July 1933, at Newtownbutler, Co. Fermanagh, Sir Basil Brooke urged loyalists, 'wherever possible, to employ Protestant lads and lassies'.[153] In April 1934, in the Northern Ireland parliament, when Brooke's speech was debated, Craigavon defended him and went on to speak of a 'Protestant parliament and a Protestant state'. He also declared that he was 'an Orangeman first and a politician and member of this parliament afterwards' and that he was very proud to be 'grand master of the loyal county of Down ... I prize that far more than I do being prime minister'.[154] The public links between members of the unionist party and government and the Orange Order brought criticism. In 1938 a British Home Office report warned: 'It is everywhere inimical to good and impartial administration where government and party are as closely united as in Northern Ireland' and that 'the government of Northern Ireland have not been able to throw off their dependence on the Orange lodges', but to no effect.[155]

The Protestant churches were an important influence in society in Northern Ireland, especially over educational matters, where they were able to alter government plans on a number of occasions.[156] Sabbatarianism and the temperance movement were significant forces. A licensing act of 1923 prohibited the opening of public houses on Sundays.[157] There were restrictions by local and central authorities on various activities on a Sunday. In 1937, for example, Belfast Corporation Police Committee refused a request to allow a Sunday concert that involved the London Symphony Orchestra.[158] In May 1945 Rev. C.W. Maguire, Orange Order County Grand Chaplain, declared that 'not only was there the link with Britain to be preserved, and not only were the people of Ulster entitled to freedom from want and poverty, but the Ulster way of life would need to be upheld against those who preached a false liberty. The Ulster Sabbath Day would need to be safeguarded from secularisation'.[159] In 1934, after complaints from various quarters, including Craig, the BBC stopped broadcasting Gaelic football results in Northern Ireland on a Sunday 'on the grounds that they were hurting the feelings of the large majority of people in Northern Ireland'. It recommenced in 1946, although initially the results of matches were broadcast on Monday.[160] The government banned some republican publications and also the pamphlet, *Orange Terror*, printed in 1943, which was very critical of the Northern Ireland state. Not all unionists agreed with the banning of *Orange Terror*. In the Northern Ireland senate, on 25 January 1944, Sir Roland Nugent warned, unsuccesfully but presciently: 'Members of this house may remember a certain book called "Lady Chatterley's love," [*sic*] by, I think, Lawrence, that was banned in England. That was one of the dullest books ever written, and no one would have bothered to read it if it had not been banned. I commend that to the attention of the government'.[161]

Post-1920 various commemorative events served as a focus for the new identity that developed among members of the Protestant and unionist community. One such event was the annual commemoration of the siege of Derry, 1688–89, when Protestant defenders of Derry held out against the Catholic forces of James II. This event is marked annually by parades in Derry by clubs of the Apprentice Boys of Derry, a Protestant fraternal organisation. In 1788, at the centenary of the siege, it was commemorated in Derry with an interdenominational procession, including the Catholic bishop and clergy, to the Church of Ireland cathedral where the event was celebrated as a blow against tyranny which brought liberty to people of all religious denominations: 'on earth, peace, goodwill towards men' was the message from the siege, according to the preacher on that day.[162] From early in the nineteenth century, however, this commemoration became an exclusively Protestant event. The Apprentice Boys organisation and parades were restricted mainly to Derry Protestants until the 1880s when branch clubs of the Apprentice Boys were set up in other parts of Ulster. In August 1912 a total of six parent clubs and 17 branch clubs paraded in Derry. In 1923 similar numbers were present and in that year more than 300 new members were initiated. From this time on rapid expansion occurred. By 1930 there were 51 branch clubs, while by 1939 there were 93 branch clubs, not only from all parts of Northern Ireland, but also from Counties Donegal, Monaghan and Cavan, as well as Scotland and England, plus visitors from Canada. By the late 1940s there were regularly on parade over 100 branch clubs, numbering some 7000 Apprentice Boys and 90 bands, while numbers initiated annually into the organisation were often over a thousand.[163]

Increased support for the Derry parades can be seen as evidence of a growth in popular Protestantism, uniting different denominations, as well as a spread in a heightened political identity based around the siege of Derry story. By the 1920s the August siege commemorations in Derry centered largely on a parade and a religious service held in the Church of Ireland cathedral. In 1924, for the first time, a Presbyterian minister preached in the cathedral. The next day the Belfast *Northern Whig* (read mainly by Presbyterians) devoted an editorial column to the celebrations, declaring that 'every loyalist in the province loves and claims a patriotic interest in the stones of Derry', reflecting concerns that in the threatened redrawing of the border, the city could be lost to the Free State.[164] This threat did not materialise, but clearly the story of the city's past siege took on a modern relevance for many unionists, as reflected in the rise in support for the commemorations. Sometimes sermons on these occasions included political messages. In August 1939 the preacher, Dr James Little, a Presbyterian minister and a unionist MP, referred to threats from the southern government and militant republicans: 'we send today this message from the historic walls of Derry, that neither to politician nor terrorist will we ever consent to surrender any portion of the inheritance which God has entrusted to us'.[165] In August 1947 the Rev. J.G. MacManaway, a Church of Ireland clergyman and also a unionist MP, declared: 'We in Ulster have our own holy place, our own religious shrine to which our history as Protestants forever joins us. The Protestant shrine of Protestant Ulster is forever Derry'.[166] This rise in interest in Derry and the siege helped to reinforce unionist identity: it also made it difficult for the unionist government to deal dispassionately with the problems of contemporary Derry.

Comparative dimensions

By 1949 two new states were well established in Ireland. In spite of initial difficulties, both managed to create stable structures and democratic societies, at a time when many other recently formed states had collapsed from both internal and external forces. The new mainstream identities which developed over this period up to 1949 played a vital role in providing an important sense of solidarity and community for the two fledgling polities. During these decades, however, Irish and British/ Ulster identities became prescriptive, exclusive and confrontational in a number of important ways. A problem was that most people in the main groups in each polity were, as Tom Garvin has put it, 'majoritarian rather than pluralist democrats'.[167] These majority identities largely excluded the nationalist and Catholic minority community in Northern Ireland and the Protestant and former unionist minority community in the Irish Free State, officially called Éire after 1937. Both these communities are investigated in depth in our next chapter. At the same time, there were other individuals and sections of society who fell outside or challenged the identities of these main groups.

In the new southern state, tens of thousands of veterans of the First World War, a majority of them nationalists, faced isolation. As Jane Leonard has pointed out: 'They matured into middle age and retirement, aware that they were excluded from the national cultural identity forged after independence in 1922. This identity declared that: "twas better to die neath an Irish sky/Than at Suvla or Sud el Bahr'.[168] Another type of exclusion was described by Gerry Fitt, a merchant seaman on the convoys to Russia and later a member of the two houses of Westminster, whose brother, George, an Irish Guardsman, died in Normandy in 1944. In 1995 he recalled being spotted by some people from unionist York Street in Belfast while he was on his way to VJ celebrations at the Belfast City Hall in 1945: 'They weren't too friendly and shouted insults about me being a Catholic and Irish neutrality. I remember looking at Union Jacks that were being waved about. I had served under it during the war and had been glad to do so but I realised here that it was a Protestant unionist flag and it looked different then'.[169]

In the case of both Northern Ireland and the Irish Free State the position of women in the new dominant political identity in each state diminished over this period. In the decade before 1921 women had played an active part in both unionist and nationalist/republican politics. The Ulster Women's Unionist Council, formed in 1911, became the largest women's political organisation in Ireland and organised their own signed 'covenant' against home rule in 1912. The Cumann na nBan was established in 1914 as a women's auxiliary corps to the Irish Volunteers and played an active role in the 1916 Rising. Subsequently, however, their influence declined, reflecting conservative and religious attitudes, both north and south. In spite of a rise in interest in this previous period in women's rights, the new states put in place a number of restrictions in relations to women's employment, as in the civil service and teaching, and to their public role, as in serving on juries in the Irish Free State.[170] The 1937 Irish constitution emphasised the place of women in the family and home rather than the political and economic equality of the sexes promised by the 1922 constitution.[171] Over the whole period from 1921 to 1972 just 17 women stood as candidates to the Northern Ireland parliament and only nine were elected. In the case of Dáil Éireann, five women deputies were elected in 1923, but subsequently this figure was rarely achieved and in 1969 only three women deputies were returned.[172]

There were other members of the mainstream groups who did not share all aspects of these new identities. In the south, changes in Irish identity meant the eventual removal of all connections with the crown or Great Britain and the growth of a strongly separate identity. Nonetheless, there were those who rejected an isolationist position. In April 1995, at a ceremony at Islandbridge in Dublin to mark the fiftieth anniversary of the end of the Second World War, Taoiseach John Bruton paid tribute to the 150,000 Irish people who had 'volunteered to fight against Nazi tyranny in Europe, at least 10,000 of whom were killed while serving in British uniforms'.[173] In the north, there was a decided reduction in Irish identity among members of the unionist community, but there were those who retained a sense of Irishness. In 1949, in one of his first public speeches, Brian Faulkner, unionist MP, objected to the way in which the south had now adopted the title of republic of Ireland: 'They have no right to the title Ireland, a name of which we are just as proud as they'.[174] Subsequently, he would continue to argue that he was Irish as well as British. When it was suggested to the Northern Ireland cabinet in 1959 that the name of Ireland in the title of the state should be dropped, Faulkner objected on the grounds that he was not prepared to concede to the south a monopoly of the term 'Irish': he saw nothing incompatible between being Northern Irish and British.[175] A decade later, Richard Rose's survey noted that some 20 per cent of Northern Ireland Protestants (very few of whom were nationalist) still saw themselves as Irish. At the same time, a similar 20 per cent of Catholics (very few of whom supported the unionist party) identified themselves as British or Ulster.[176]

It should be noted that the churches, various sports organisations and certain cultural bodies retained an all-Ireland dimension. In some sports, such as hockey, cricket, Gaelic football and rugby, there continued to be all-Ireland associations. A number of Irish national sports teams drew members from both sides of the border. In the case of soccer, however, political disputes after 1921 saw southern teams withdraw from the Irish Football Association, based in Belfast, and set up the Football Association of Ireland, based in Dublin: there would now be two separate national teams, for Northern Ireland and the Irish Free State/Republic of Ireland.[177] Some cultural bodies, such as the Royal Irish Academy, continued to draw members from all parts of Ireland. *Irish Historical Studies*, established in 1938 to publish material embodying original research in Irish history, was run as a joint journal of the Irish Historical Society, based in Dublin, and the Ulster Society for Irish Historical Studies, based in Belfast. In late 1938 the Irish Association was founded, with influential public figures from north and south. Its aim was, through debate and publications, to 'make reason and good-will take the place of passion and prejudice in determining the character of the relationship between north and south, no less than between each part of Ireland and Great Britain'.[178] During this period, we can also observe the attempts of organisations, such as the Northern Ireland Labour Party, to raise social issues in defiance of national and denominational issues.[179] There were individuals, such as Protestant nationalists, like Denis Ireland, or liberals, like R.N. Boyd (later Albert McElroy, Claude Wilton and Sheelagh Murnaghan), who adopted independent positions, outside the usual political/religious lines.[180]

Nonetheless, such efforts to maintain north–south links and to challenge existing divisions and identities had limited effect. The reasons for the deep polarisation in the two states lie partly in the pre-1921 divisions, which continued to be important, and the violence of 1920–23. More significantly, however, the situation reflected developments that had occurred since 1921. In a radio broadcast in April 1949 the editor of the *Belfast Telegraph*, Jack Sayers, surveyed changes in identities in the two parts of Ireland over the previous three decades. He observed that: 'what has happened is that some differences have been accentuated, but others have sprung up that can hardly have been thought of when partition was first put forward as a remedy. And taking them all in all, I fear that by now they amount to a formidable total'.[181] After 1920 the dominant political groups in both states sought to develop their own identities. Some evidence of exclusive aspects of these identities can be detected in the first decade, but one can also see here efforts to curtail such trends. Over the next two decades, however, identities in both states became highly prescriptive and exclusive. Crucial for all these developments from 1920 were the new dynamics to do with the establishment and running of the two new polities. Relations of both with Britain and with each other remained important, as did the presence of minorities. Internal conflict within the dominant groups and party rivalries were significant. Contemporary needs to create a sense of community, to strengthen stability, and to bolster legitimacy, were influential as was the concern to prove that these new states were different from what had gone before and from their neighbours. Even if alternative arrangements to the existing partition division of 1921 had been enacted, such as a larger 32-county Irish state or a smaller Northern Ireland, any new state would still have been subject to these tensions. Whether they possessed a large or a small religious/political minority, the experience of these two states showed the difficulties of creating a pluralist society and identity.

In a British Home Office report of the late 1930s Sir Harry Batterbee was critical of both northern and southern governments: 'If the government of Northern Ireland wish partition to continue, they must make greater efforts than they have made at present to win over the Catholic minority, just as on his side Mr de Valera if he wishes to end partition can only do so by winning over the northern Protestants. At present both sides are showing a lamentable lack of statesmanship and foresight'.[182] A major difficulty for the two governments, however, in pursuing what would rationally have been a sensible approach on these matters was that their actions were now heavily restricted by the mainstream identities in each state, which involved a range of dimensions, not only political but also religious and cultural. As regards the south, the comments of Malcolm MacDonald in 1939 were pertinent. He commented how 'the two barriers to a united Ireland at the moment are Éire and Northern Ireland', drawing attention to how southern attitudes were critical in maintaining partition.[183] Around the same time, in 1938, Lord Dufferin told the Dominions Office in London that Northern Ireland government policies damaged the union. He described how many Protestants were 'uneasy about the attitude of their government which had the effect of perpetuating a division which a more enlightened policy might close – that is, treating Catholics as "a part of the nation to be incorporated" rather than a "a minority to be kept under"'.[184] Of all the unionist politicians, James Craig understood the value of generosity to one's opponents. His family motto, acquired in the early 1900s and inscribed on his tomb in the grounds of Parliament House at Stormont, was 'charity provokes charity'. There is evidence that in the 1920s he made some effort to accommodate his opponents, but by the 1930s any such moderation had ended, owing to the deep polarisation of attitudes.

Throughout this period the character of identities in both polities was influenced by their political relationship with Britain which reached a new stage by 1949. The position of the south in relation to Britain was substantially settled with the 1949 declaration of a republic, while Northern Ireland's relationship with Britain was significantly improved with the 1949 guarantee of its place within the UK. The resolution of these matters, however, did not lead to a change in the exclusive and confrontational nature of the identities in both states, which, if anything, became more strident. This was partly because there was still no satisfactory resolution of north–south relations, and partly because the various other political, religious and cultural dimensions of these identities remained not only strong but, in many areas, the antithesis of each other. Internal divisions influenced politics in both states. In addition we may note how changes in the identity in one society often impacted on the other. It has been observed, in particular, how what happened in the north was influenced by what occurred in the south.[185] Writing in 1948 on cultural, religious and political differences between north and south, Hugh Shearman noted, caustically but accurately: 'Reaction in Éire will produce and seem to justify a counterbalancing reaction in Northern Ireland'.[186] Developments in both states over the next decade would illustrate how these mainstream identities remained highly polarised, although some changes would begin to occur in the late 1950s.

Republic of Ireland, 1949–60

In early September 1948, in Canada, J.A. Costello, head of the inter-party coalition, announced the government's intention to repeal the External Relations Act and to declare a republic. He also stated that he considered himself prime minister of all Ireland, 'no matter what the Irish in the north say'.[187] This led to an added focus on partition as all parties sought to prove their republican credentials. At an anti-partition rally in Scotland in October 1948 de Valera warned unionists that they would have to choose to be Irish or British, and, if their choice was not the former, he urged: 'In God's name will you go to the country that your affections lie in'.[188] The opposition to partition became even more strident, after the British government announced its intention of introducing an Ireland Act, giving new guarantees to northern union-ists, even though this act was a direct outcome of the Irish decision to declare a republic.[189] Lord Rugby, British ambassador to Dublin, observed in early December 1948: 'each party must now outdo its rivals in a passionate crusade for Irish unity ... no leading politician dare to appear reluctant to join the anti-partition bandwagon or to seem doubtful about the wisdom of giving it a shove'.[190]

On his own initiative, on 27 January 1949 Taoiseach Costello organised a public meeting of the leaders of all the southern Irish parties, plus northern nationalist representatives, to protest against partition and to provide support for anti-partition candidates at the forthcoming elections to the Northern Ireland parliament.[191] It was agreed to establish a new anti-partition body to be known as the Mansion House Committee and to raise funds to help these candidates with a country-wide collection outside churches on the following Sunday. This intervention proved unsuccessful and the Mansion House Committee and Irish government then organised a propaganda campaign in Britain and America against partition, which lasted some years. This campaign also proved unsuccessful, although it served to raise both unrealistic expectations among northern nationalists and undue fears among northern unionists.

After the return of Eamon de Valera and a Fianna Fáil government in 1952, the Mansion House Committee became virtually moribund. The issue of the north continued as an issue to be debated at Fianna Fáil ard fheis, but largely as a ritualistic gesture.[192] At the same time, de Valera continued to state his opposition to the use of force to achieve reunification and after 1957 his government took strong action against the IRA, including imprisonment without trial. At the 1957 Fianna Fáil ard fheis, de Valera discussed partition and declared that 'he had done everything humanly possible ... to try to solve this problem'.[193] In one of his final speeches to the Dáil, in July 1958, he stated that 'anybody who would get the solution would be regarded as one of the greatest men in Irish history'.[194] Curiously, however, in a speech at Ennis, Co. Clare, on 23 June 1957, the fortieth anniversary of his first election in 1917, he described one approach that he had not tried and which might have made some difference: 'the unity of our country had to be achieved now by cultivating good relations with our fellow-countrymen in the north. There was no other way to do it.'[195] The problem was that the way Irish national identity had developed under de Valera and the other party leaders made such an approach very difficult for them either to understand or promote. At a personal level, however, de Valera's new insight was still only partial. Later, in an interview in the *New York Times* in 1962, when he was Irish president, he repeated his suggestion that if 'in the north there are people who spiritually want to be English rather than Irish, they can go and we will see that they get the adequate, right compensation for their property'.[196]

Religious aspects of this identity remained important. In a private letter in 1949 to Ernest Blythe, Thomas Johnson, the Protestant former leader of the Irish labour party, remarked that the 'revival of militant Catholicism' lent credence to the 'Rome Rule' doubts of unionists, a charge he would have denied 'at any time up to 15 or 20 years ago'. He was concerned about the effect on northern labour voters when, in the south, 'a labour leader states that the labour party's policy is based on the papal encyclicals and they proudly acknowledge the authority of the Catholic church on all matters which related to public policy and public welfare'.[197] This attitude affected not just the labour party but the other parties in the inter-party government, as was revealed in the controversy in 1950–51 over the 'mother and child scheme', when the government accepted Catholic episcopal intervention in the minister for health's scheme to provide state funding for maternal care.[198] Fianna Fáil politicians fully endorsed this religious ethos in Irish public life. In 1950 Dublin corporation passed a resolution tendering 'our filial homage and devotion' to the pope, prompting Robert Briscoe, Fianna Fáil TD and a Jewish member, to declare that Ireland was a Catholic country and the more Catholic the people became, the more he liked it.[199] Not long after his return to power in 1951 de Valera attended a ceremony in Dublin at which 'Our Lady, Queen of the Most Holy Rosary' was named as the patroness of the Irish army.[200] This close church–state relationship, it should be noted, reflected not just the special influence of the bishops but also the wide support among politicians and the public for this affinity.

At the end of the 1950s we can observe the start of change. In mid-1959 Sean Lemass became taoiseach and began to challenge the whole nationalist way of thinking, in a wide range of areas, from economics and social policies to attitudes towards Northern Ireland.[201] On 21 July 1959, in Dáil Éireann, he urged practical co-operation between the two parts of Ireland. He reiterated his belief in a united Ireland, but stated that the north should consider 'possibilities of concerting activities for the practical economic advantages that may result'. Then, in language rarely used since the 1920s, he declared: 'Ireland without its people means nothing to us – no more than it did to James Connolly – and if it is in our power to contribute to the welfare of Irishmen anywhere, we would want to do it'.[202] On 15 October 1959 Lemass spoke at a debate in the Oxford Union, supporting Irish reunification. Opposed to Lemass was a young lawyer, whose mother's family had been prominent in both unionist and nationalist politics in Ireland, pre-1921.[203] His name was Patrick Mayhew, and he was to become secretary of state for Northern Ireland, from 1992 to 1997. Lemass emphasised that the goal of the republic was 'reunification of Ireland by agreement'. Despite familiar anti-partition language, he did not demand that the British government end partition, but urged that they should say that 'there is no British interest in preventing ... you from seeking agreement'. He addressed directly the northern unionists on what he said were the advantages of reunification, and stated that, while he believed their 'fears' that they would 'suffer disadvantages' because of their religion in a new state were 'groundless', arrangements would be made to protect their rights. These speeches revealed the beginning of new thinking by Lemass. Nonetheless, in that same year, he proved unwilling to question church–state relations, when he accepted a veto of Dr John Charles Mc Quaid, Catholic archbishop of Dublin, against a proposed union of the National Library of Ireland and the library of Trinity College Dublin.[204]

Northern Ireland, 1949–60

By early 1949 the unionist government faced strong challenges not only from the heightened anti-partition campaign, run by both the Anti-Partition League and the southern political parties and government, but also from a revived labour movement. At the elections to the Northern Ireland parliament in 1945, labour candidates had won 113,413 votes and four seats. On 21 January 1949 Sir Basil Brooke, the northern prime minister, called a fresh general election. In his manifesto, he attacked Costello's decision to declare a republic: 'we have now on our southern border a foreign nation ... Today we fight to defend our very existence and the heritage of our children'.[205] Labour candidates urged that voters should concentrate on economic and social matters.[206] On 27 January 1949, however, the meeting of the all-party Mansion House Committee in Dublin denounced partition and declared its intention to support anti-partition candidates in the north, including 'the holding of a national collection in all parishes on Sunday'.[207] An *Irish Times* reporter on 29 January 1949 warned that this southern move was probably 'worth 60,000 votes to unionists' and quoted an anonymous northern nationalist who stated: 'Those fellows in Dublin are playing party politics, and that is not going to help us'. This prediction proved correct. The following Monday, a banner headline of the *Belfast Telegraph* read 'The chapel gate collections. Dublin. Limerick. Donnybrook lead ...'.[208] This direct southern intervention with such clerical undertones had considerable impact, but not as intended. It failed to help northern nationalists of whom fewer were returned to the Northern Ireland parliament than in 1945. It became the focus of the unionist campaign and helped lead to the withdrawal of some independent unionist candidates and to the collapse of the labour vote. The unionist party increased its representation to 37, while the NILP failed to hold on to a single seat, which meant that apart from two independent unionists the opposition at Stormont was entirely Catholic for the first time since 1921.[209]

In a subsequent victory speech, Brooke dealt very largely with what he saw as the threat from the south.[210] After referring to the recent southern intervention, he went on to state that the southern minority had been 'almost completely squeezed out'. 'That' he declared, 'is the sort of treatment Ulster unionists would get if they allowed themselves to be swallowed up in the Éire republic'. Elsewhere he referred to the 35 per cent drop in the number of Protestants in the south over the previous 40 years.[211] In speeches in the early months of 1950 at anti-partition rallies in the north, Noel Browne and Sean MacBride, both Clann na Poblachta ministers in the Irish government, sought to deal with this religious issue.[212] They asserted that southern Protestants were well treated, referred to the high number of Protestants in key positions in southern economic life, and stated that they 'played their full share in national life'. MacBride declared his belief that 'certain fears and prejudices' that existed in the north about a united Ireland could be overcome and promised safeguards. By the end of the year, however, both Browne and MacBride had become embroiled in the controversy with the Catholic bishops over the mother and child scheme. In response to this, the Ulster Unionist Council published and distributed widely a report of Dáil proceedings and Browne's correspondence on the matter. The introduction to this pamphlet, called *Southern Ireland – Church or State?*, remarked that the incident served as a 'final revelation of the dominating influence' of the Catholic church in Ireland.[213] It specifically mentioned MacBride's earlier assurances and stated that 'the fears of the northern loyalists regarding their civil and religious liberty have been justified'. Concerns about the influence of the Catholic church and the decline in southern Protestant numbers would continue to feature prominently during this decade in the speeches of leading northern unionists, such as Brian Faulkner.[214]

While unionists criticised the close religious-political links in the south, religious-political links were also close in the north. On earlier occasions Protestant church leaders had exercised considerable influence over education legislation. Between 1945 and 1947, the Northern Ireland minister of education, Lt Col. Samuel Hall-Thompson, sought to introduce a new education bill, in face of strong opposition, especially from some Protestant church organisations and the Orange Order, which were greatly concerned about his proposals for religious instruction in state schools, as well as increased grants for Catholic schools. He faced criticism in a stormy debate in the Northern Ireland parliament, one MP, Lord Glentoran, remarking: 'The trouble about us here in Ulster is that we get excited by religion and drink'.[215] His bill was passed but he incurred Orange and Protestant outrage again in 1949 when he proposed some changes in a new bill, including the payment of Catholic teachers' national insurance and superannuation. Following Hall-Thompson's proposals, Prime Minister Sir Basil Brooke was obliged to attend a meeting of the Grand Lodge of Ireland, the head body of the Orange Order, to explain government actions. He sought to convince the Orange leaders that the government had to be fair to all sections and that if the minority 'were treated unfairly as an 'oppressed people' it would create a bad impression in England'.[216] Brooke was able to save the new bill in an amended form, but only after he persuaded Hall-Thompson to resign and he appointed in his place the Protestant populist and former labour leader Harry Midgley. Unionist politicians continued to emphasise and justify unionist–Orange links, with their great value for Protestant and unionist unity. On 12 July 1960, Brian Faulkner, MP, declared that 'until the Roman Catholic hierarchy renounces its influence in politics, the Orange institution cannot renounce its influence in the unionist party', while W.M. May, MP, stated that the unionist party was the only party that 'accepts the aims and objects of the Orange Order'.[217]

After the 1949 general election the Irish government stepped up its campaign abroad against partition but to no lasting effect, given the international situation. By the end of 1953 the Fianna Fáil government allowed the matter mostly to drop, while the Anti-Partition League in the north had become largely ineffective. Subsequently, however, there was a revival of republicanism in the north which led to Sinn Féin candidates contesting all 12 Northern Ireland seats in the British House of Commons at the 1955 and 1958 general elections, with their protest against 'the foreign occupation of Irish territory'.[218] In 1956 the IRA started an armed campaign against the northern state which lasted until 1962 and resulted in 18 deaths. These developments served to help keep the unionist party together in spite of internal conflict over various social, religious and economic issues.[219] Government spokesmen emphasised the need for unionists to be continually united and vigilant against their enemies, external and internal. In 1957 the minister of education, Harry Midgley, declared: 'all the minority are traitors and have always been traitors to the government of Northern Ireland'.[220] In 1953 a controversy arose over the flying of flags when enthusiastic loyalists put up the union flag in contentious areas where they had not been flown previously, and the police took them down to avoid trouble.[221] Strong unionist criticism followed which led to the passing of the Flags and Emblems (Display) Act, 1954. This act made it illegal to prevent the flying of a union flag anywhere in Northern Ireland, and also imposed a ban on the display of the Irish tricolour, which George Hanna, the minister of home affairs, described as 'very close to an act of treason'.[222]

The late 1950s witnessed the beginning of new challenges to unionists, but their response showed how exclusive and prescriptive their identity had become. At a Catholic social studies conference summer school at St McNissi's College, Garron Tower, Carnlough, Co. Antrim in August 1958, G.B. Newe appealed to Catholics to 'co-operate with the de facto authority that controls ... life and welfare' and to take a more active part in public life in Northern Ireland.[223] This speech caused great controversy. For Jack Sayers, editor of the *Belfast Telegraph*, the conference represented 'a public examination of the Catholic conscience in relation to life in Northern Ireland, the community in Northern Ireland'.[224] Many unionists, however, were suspicious. Shortly afterwards, Brian Faulkner, unionist chief whip, and acting deputy prime minister, declared that this offer of co-operation by nationalists was an effort to 'penetrate the machinery of government', so that they could achieve their ultimate aim of 'national unity'.[225] Later, on 25 October 1958, he stated that the 'neo-nationalist policy was policy of the fifth column'.[226] Remarks by Sean Lemass in 1959 about north–south co-operation also raised mistrust in unionist ranks.

In late October 1959, however, W.B. Maginess, Northern Ireland attorney general, spoke to the Young Unionist Council.[227] He called for toleration and co-operation: 'We must look on those who do not agree with us, not as enemies but as fellow members of the community ...'. In reply to a question on this occasion, Sir Clarence Graham, chairman of the Ulster Unionist Council, declared that he saw no reason why they should not select a Catholic as a parliamentary candidate. A week later Sir George Clark, head of the Orange Order, publicly rebuked Maginess and Graham for their comments and the implication that Catholics could become unionist party members: 'under no circumstances would such a suggestion be countenanced or accepted by our institution'.[228] The Prime Minister, Lord Brookeborough (Brooke had been ennobled in 1952), fully endorsed this stance. He declared that it would be difficult for Catholics 'to discard the political conceptions, the influence and impressions acquired from religious and educational instruction by those whose aims are openly declared to be an all-Ireland republic'. He stated: 'There is no change in the fundamental character of the unionist party and the loyalties it observes and preserves'.[229]

Final observations

In the case of both new states the development of identities over this 40-year period helped the creation and survival of stable, democratic governments and societies, in contrast to the fate of many other states established in the early 1920s. Among other things, these identities served to provide legitimacy, a common purpose and sufficient unity. At the same time, however, the restrictive nature of these identities brought certain problems which would be very damaging in the long run. In the Irish Free State/Republic of Ireland the nature of the new identity served to marginalise the Protestant minority, whose percentage of the population would continue to fall, but, because their numbers were small, this caused little direct damage to the viability of the state. Mainstream nationalist identity became strongly irredentist and the approach of southern politicians to Northern Ireland managed both to deepen the fears of northern unionists and to fail to help northern nationalists.

For the south, however, the most serious problem was how important elements of this identity also affected economic, cultural and social policies. This particular form of Irish political nationalism led to economic nationalism. As Patrick O'Mahony and Gerard Delanty have pointed out, Fianna Fáil's economic policies in the 1930s, particularly protectionism, illustrated how 'moral and evaluative components of national identity continued to be given precedence over functional considerations'.[230] After the war, the policies of successive southern governments, consisting of not just Fianna Fáil but also the other main parties, continued to back economic protectionism. Other dimensions of this identity included extensive censorship and clericalism, leading to a strong sense of isolationism. By the 1950s the result of this situation was a massive rise in Irish emigration, a fall in population and a great concern about the survival of the state.[231] Only with the premiership of Sean Lemass would serious efforts begin to challenge the 'existing national identity code' and to seek to tackle all these problems.[232]

In the instance of Northern Ireland, the difficulty created in the long run by the new dominant identity was of a different nature. Here the mainstream political identity had not such a detrimental effect on the society or economy. Although there were internal critics, Northern Ireland by the early 1960s, in social and economic areas, as seen in matters such as funding for education and social welfare, and in the growth of its population, had performed well compared to the Republic of Ireland. In 1961 the north, with half the population of the south, spent double, in absolute terms, the south's total in education.[233] Over the period 1926–61 the northern population rose by 168,481 while the southern population fell by 153,650.[234] A symbolic measure of such differences was the introduction of a television service in Northern Ireland in 1953 but not in the Irish Republic until 1961.[235]

There was failure, however, to deal effectively with the national and religious divisions which remained central to politics in Northern Ireland. Here the nationalist and Catholic minority made up one-third of the population. As Nicholas Mansergh pointed in his 1936 book, *The Government of Northern Ireland*, there was 'close identification of the unionist party and the northern state' and 'almost complete identification of political with sectarian divisions'. He acknowledged that the government faced a serious difficulty in reconciling nationalists to its rule, but he declared that it had not given 'that positive leadership which is so needed if a spirit of common citizenship is to be established', and he criticised its public links with Orangeism, as well as its failure to seek to break down 'the traditional hostility between the respective creeds'.[236]

Subsequently, matters did not improve. The exclusive and prescriptive elements of the new British/Ulster identity that emerged in these decades helped to reinforce these problems. The outcome was that government existed without adequate consensus and society remained deeply divided. Relations between north and south remained highly confrontational. At this stage concepts of power sharing or a shared community had not yet emerged in a significant manner, but existing identities would not have permitted such innovative approaches. The arrival of the 1960s would see significant efforts, from within and outside unionism, to seek to challenge this mainstream unionist identity.

2
Parallel universes: minority identities, 1921–60

The political changes in Ireland of 1921–22 meant not only the establishment of new polities in Ireland but also the creation of two important minorities. The outcome of these arrangements left a Protestant and predominantly unionist minority in the Irish Free State and a Catholic and very largely nationalist minority in Northern Ireland, both in states not of their own choosing. The subsequent fate of these minorities has been the subject of considerable debate among both historians and political commentators, past and present. In this comparative study of the two groups, we seek first to describe the position in which the two minorities found themselves after 1921. How did they respond to their novel and unwanted situations and what were the immediate consequences? Next, the political and social fortunes of these minorities over the following half century must be investigated. Attention focuses then on some key aspects of both communities. What can we say about the particular identity of these two important minorities? How did their identities relate to the mainstream identities in each state? From this study it may be possible to arrive at a better judgement about their treatment and fate.

There have been strong divisions of opinion about how the two groups fared in the 40 years after 1921. In the case of Northern Ireland, critics have claimed that the Catholic and nationalist minority was treated badly, facing discrimination in employment and public housing, and political marginalisation. This has been contested by others who have pointed out that the numbers of the northern Catholic minority increased over these decades, proportionally more than any of the other main communities in Ireland, north or south, a fact that has been seen as contradicting this picture of poor treatment. As regards the Irish Free State/Republic of Ireland, critics have argued that the

Protestant and unionist minority fared poorly, as seen in the reduction of southern Protestant numbers from some 10 per cent of the population pre-independence to 5 per cent in 1961. On the other side, commentators have drawn attention to the election of southern Protestants to high office, namely Lord Glenavy as the first chairman of the Irish senate and Douglas Hyde as the first president of Ireland, to provide evidence of the fair treatment of the minority. This debate has concerned not just academics but also politicians who have seen the fate of these minorities as important for their contemporary nationalist or unionist positions.

The situation in which these two minorities found themselves after 1921 was not unique to Ireland. Elsewhere, in Central and Eastern Europe, in many of the new polities established after the First World War, significant groups found themselves in states where they felt that they did not belong: at the same time they looked to elsewhere as their national 'homeland'.[1] Often religious, language or cultural divisions were involved originally in this national conflict and these would continue to be important.[2] Only two-thirds of the inhabitants of Poland spoke Polish, while Czechoslovakia contained large numbers of Sudeten Germans. In Yugoslavia, where religious and cultural differences were very important, the population was sharply divided between Croats, Serbs and Bosnian Muslims. There was a large Magyar (Hungarian) minority in Southern Slovakia. Such inherent problems between the majority and minority groups in each country tended to become more difficult over time as the majority 'nationalising' section sought to develop the mainstream national identity and to strengthen the new state in its own liking. In many of these countries, therefore, the position of these national minorities was not just a matter of their social and economic situation but also of their place in the new societies and of their identity in relation to the increasingly exclusive dominant identities. In Ireland, both north and south, differences in identity, embracing a wide range of political, religious and cultural dimensions, remained critical for the relations between majority and minority communities.

Early days

The two new states that were established in the early 1920s contained substantial minorities whose national and religious identities differed greatly from those of the majority of the inhabitants of the societies in which now they found themselves, against their wishes. In Northern Ireland there was a significant Catholic and nationalist minority while in the Irish Free State there was an influential Protestant and unionist minority. There were still some important exceptions to these general alignments of politics and religion. On the one side, there were individuals such as A.G. Bonaparte Wyse, Limerick born Catholic, who joined the Northern Ireland ministry of education in 1921, and became permanent secretary in 1929, commuting weekly from his home in Blackrock, Co. Dublin.[3] There were also Catholic members of the Royal Irish Constabulary (RIC), such as Major Jack Gorman, the Co. Tipperary born army officer and RIC inspector, who was the last adjutant of the RIC depot at Phoenix Park, Dublin. Following the Anglo-Irish Treaty, he then moved north to join the Royal Ulster Constabulary (RUC), because of his 'loyalty to the crown', as his son later put it.[4] On the other side, there were people such as Ernest Blythe, a Lisburn born member of the Church of Ireland, who became a Sinn Féin MP for Co. Monaghan and then a minister in the Irish Free State government.[5] Dr Kathleen Lynn, daughter of a southern Church of Ireland rector, served in the Irish Citizen Army during the Easter Rising of 1916 and was elected a Sinn Féin TD, 1923–27.[6] Nonetheless, in the new Northern Ireland most Catholics were nationalist while in the new Irish Free State most Protestants were unionist or former unionist.

There were important differences in the numbers and distribution of these two groups, and also in what happened to them over this early period. In 1911, according to the census of that year, Protestants in the 26 counties, which later became the Irish Free State, numbered 327,179 and 10.4 per cent of the total population of 3,139,688.[7] Their presence was strongest in the three Ulster counties of Cavan, Donegal and Monaghan, and in parts of Dublin city and Co. Dublin, and Counties Wicklow and Cork, although nowhere were they a majority, apart from certain small areas such as the Laggan district of Co. Donegal and Pembroke Township. Elsewhere they were widely distributed in small numbers. By 1926, when the next census was recorded, their numbers had fallen substantially to 220,723 and 7.4 per cent of the southern population of 2,971,992. Of this Protestant population in 1926, 164,215 were members of the Church of Ireland, 32,429 Presbyterian, 10,663 Methodist and 13,416 others (including a Jewish population of 3686). In 1911, Catholics in the six counties which later became Northern Ireland numbered 430,161 and 34.4 per cent of the population of 1,250,541. Their numbers were greatest in the west, and they were a small majority in Counties Fermanagh and Tyrone and Derry city. In some parts of the east their numbers were substantial, in areas such as south Down and west Belfast, but elsewhere they were more thinly distributed. By 1926 their numbers had fallen marginally to 420,428 and 33.5 per cent of the northern population of 1,256,561.[8]

In spite of the overwhelming support for Sinn Féin at the 1918 general election throughout Ireland outside Ulster, most members of the southern unionist and Protestant community continued to support the union with Britain, although many were also opposed to partition, as it would weaken them politically. It was clear, however, that now they played a minor role in public affairs which were dominated by the continuing conflict between Sinn Féin and the British government. The first formal meeting of representatives of southern unionists and Sinn Féin, after the start of the war of independence, occurred only on 4 July 1921 when four leading southern unionists attended a peace conference in Dublin, organised by Sinn Féin, which led to a truce between the IRA and crown forces and the start of British government and Sinn Féin negotiations.[9] The main participants at these talks paid little attention to the concerns of southern unionists, although, at a very late stage, Arthur Griffith, in a published letter to Lloyd George, gave a general reassurance to them about their future.[10] The terms of the Anglo-Irish Treaty of December 1921 were more extensive and contained fewer formal safeguards than most southern unionists had wanted. For many, the treaty was seen as a betrayal. Lady Alice Howard of Co. Wicklow recorded in her diary on 10 December 1921: 'The government have given over everything to the rebels and they are to govern Ireland entirely ... too dreadful – with only a nominal oath of allegiance to the king'.[11] A week later the leading Co. Cavan unionist, Lord Farnham, stated that southern unionists felt that they 'were being shamelessly betrayed and abandoned'.[12]

Nonetheless, in spite of deep reservations held by many, the majority of the Protestant and unionist community accepted the treaty as a *fait accompli* and agreed to work with it.[13] In a sermon delivered in Dublin on 11 December 1921, Dr John Gregg, the Church of Ireland archbishop of Dublin, declared: 'We may not like the facts; many of us had no desire for a change of constitution. But it will be our wisdom to acknowledge them and reckon with them ... it concerns us all that we should have a strong, capable and wise government ... it concerns us all to offer to the Irish state so shortly to be constituted our loyalty and good-will ...'.[14] A meeting of the board of Trinity College Dublin on 10 December 1921 supported the new settlement and declared its belief that in the building up of happier conditions in Ireland, 'Trinity men should take an active and sympathetic part'.[15] On 19 January 1922 a meeting of unionist leaders in Dublin passed a resolution that 'we the unionists of the south and west, recognising that a provisional government has been formed, desire to support our fellow countrymen in this government in order that peace may be brought about and the welfare of the community secured'.[16]

Hopes that the settlement would bring peace and stability proved to be short lived. Divisions among republicans over the terms of the treaty led to widespread unrest and violence, and eventually to civil war. A meeting of members of the Church of Ireland synod, resident in the 26 counties, was held in Dublin on 9 May 1922, after a series of attacks on Protestants, including the murder of 13 civilians in Dunmanway, Co. Cork, in late April. A delegation was authorised to interview members of the provisional government 'in order to lay before them the dangers to which Protestants in the twenty-six counties are daily exposed' and to assure them of the support of Church of Ireland members in the cause of law and order.[17] At a meeting with Michael Collins three days later, the Church of Ireland delegation asked Collins whether the government was 'desirous of retaining them, or whether, in the alternative, it was desirous that they should leave the country.' The *Irish Times* reported that Collins declared that 'Ireland required the services of all her sons of every class and creed in the country, and they took hope from that statement'.[18] Also, he condemned the recent outrages against members of their community and promised to take action to prevent such occurrences.

This reaction by Collins, and later comments by William Cosgrave and Kevin O'Higgins, seems to have given some confidence to members of the Protestant community of the government's intentions, but many continued to suffer attacks and intimidation. During the first half of 1922, meetings took place also between leading unionist figures and members of the government in relation to the new Irish Free State constitution.[19] The unionist representatives were not happy about the outcome of these discussions, particularly because any future role for them in the proposed senate was not formally laid down, apart from a general undertaking that the head of the government would nominate members to 'represent minorities or interests not represented in the dáil'.[20] At the end of the year, however, fears were allayed considerably when Cosgrave exercised his right to nominate members to appoint a sizeable number of former unionists to the first senate, and one, Lord Glenavy, was elected chairman. Glenavy was proposed by Donegal Senator John McLoughlin on the grounds that his election would serve as a guarantee of fair play in the south, which would encourage northern unionists towards a united Ireland.[21] Some republicans were strongly opposed to this choice and during the 1923 election campaign, Joseph Connolly, then chairman of the reorganised Sinn Féin, condemned it 'as an outrageous insult to our people', on grounds of Campbell's unionist background.[22]

In this early period, members of the unionist and Protestant community in the south faced widespread violence. During the war of independence, 1918–21, and the following civil war, 1922–23, considerable numbers of them suffered political and sectarian attacks.[23] Such incidents sometimes involved murder, but more commonly intimidation and burning of homes, which led large numbers to flee.[24] Members of this community, often labelled as 'loyalists', were targeted in reprisal for actions of the British army, as described by Tom Barry, IRA commander in West Cork, in his later account: 'our only fear was that, as time went on, there would be no more loyalist homes to destroy'.[25] Sometimes these attacks happened in response to events in the north. After the Dunmanway murders in late April 1922, Church of Ireland archbishop of Dublin, Dr John Gregg denounced such reasoning: 'I fail to see what is the connection between these residents in the west of County Cork and the troubles in the north. I cannot see any intelligible cause for this declaration of war upon a defenceless community', and called on the government to 'protect a grievously-wounded minority'.[26] In early May 1922, Gregg recorded in his diary: 'A week of v.great anxiety as to the church's future. News of evictions, ejections and intimidations everywhere. Where is it all to end? Is it beginning of end, or a short storm? Prol. Govt. so far seems powerless to intervene'.[27]

During the Civil War, many homes of former unionists, including those of new senators, were destroyed by republicans. At the May 1923 general synod of the Church of Ireland, the primate, Dr Charles D'Arcy, declared how over the previous year 'tens of thousands of all classes and creeds had fled from the land ... households were broken up and the members scattered. Their church had suffered especially, although all churches had been impoverished'.[28] By mid-1923, however, the government had established its authority over the whole state. At the Leighlin Church of Ireland Diocesan Synod, in July 1924, Bishop Fitzmaurice Day reported: 'in looking over the past year they could surely find much cause for thankfulness and encouragement ... The country was now settled and peaceful'. He declared that the government 'had won the admiration of all classes by the way they had done their work'.[29]

At the 1918 general election, the Catholic and nationalist community in Ulster had shown itself united in support of Irish self-government, although divided between supporters of Sinn Féin and the Irish nationalist parliamentary party. Both wings of Irish nationalism in the north were strongly opposed to the Government of Ireland Act which received royal assent in December 1920, and which provided for separate governments and parliaments in Northern Ireland and Southern Ireland. In March 1921, Joseph Devlin, leader of the northern nationalists, denounced the proposed northern parliament: 'The highest service to render to Ireland would be to make it impossible'.[30] Sinn Féin opposition to these arrangements meant that in the south they never came into operation and so led to new terms under the Anglo-Irish Treaty of December 1921. In the north, however, the proposed structures under the 1920 act were established. Following a general election at which 40 unionists, six Sinn Féin and six nationalists were elected, the new government under Sir James Craig was formed on 7 June 1921. Three weeks later the new Northern Ireland parliament was formally opened. The nationalist and Sinn Féin MPs stayed away from this event and subsequently declined to take their seats in the new assembly. In the coming months a number of nationalist controlled local authorities declared their loyalty to Dáil Éireann. In December 1921 the Fermanagh County Council resolved that: 'We ... do not recognise the partition parliament in Belfast and do hereby direct our secretary to hold no further communications with either Belfast or British local government departments, and we pledge our allegiance to Dáil Éireann'.[31]

The Anglo-Irish Treaty of December 1921 marked an important stage of agreement between the Sinn Féin leadership and the British authorities, but it also led to profound disagreement and difficulties within Ireland, north and south, leaving both governments, with, as Michael Laffan has described, 'the task of overcoming resistance by the large minorities which rejected their authority'.[32] In the south, of course, this opposition came from the republican minority and not the former unionist and Protestant community. In the north, most republicans and nationalists accepted the treaty and the pro-treaty side in this dispute, but they remained opposed to partition and the new Northern Ireland government. A critical element in all this was article 12 in the Anglo-Irish treaty which promised a boundary commission to deal with the question of the frontier between the two states. Among many northern nationalists and republicans there was a belief, encouraged by the southern government, that such boundary changes would lead to substantial loss of territory from the northern state which would make it unviable.[33] This proposed boundary commission raised nationalist and republican expectations: of course, it also heightened unionist fears. During early 1922 more northern local authorities pledged allegiance to Dáil Éireann.[34] Efforts in January 1922 in dialogue between James Craig and Michael Collins were a failure. Subsequently, Collins authorised

IRA activities to destabilise the northern government.[35] On 2 February 1922 a cabinet meeting of the southern provisional government resolved that 'the Belfast parliament is to be hampered in every possible way'.[36] The northern authorities faced a concerted IRA campaign. Many Catholic teachers refused to recognise the new Northern Ireland ministry of education and from late February 1922 they received their salaries from Dublin, rather than the northern ministry.

The Northern Ireland government took various steps to establish its authority which directly affected the nationalist and Catholic minority. In December 1921 it introduced legislation allowing it to take over local councils that declared allegiance to Dáil Éireann and replace them with commissioners. By April 1922 21 local authorities had been dissolved.[37] Proportional representation in local government elections was abolished in an effort not only to counter a labour threat and to strengthen the unionist position in various councils, but, as Michael Collins observed, 'to paint the counties of Tyrone and Fermanagh with a deep Orange tint', in anticipation of the boundary commission's work.[38] In 1923 the Leech commission was appointed to draw up new local government boundaries. Nationalists contributed to the commission in only two places (where they were able to affect its findings), but otherwise boycotted the whole proceedings. In their absence, unionists were able to influence the commission's findings so as to obtain control of a number of nationalist councils, partly in order to seek to influence the boundary commission.[39]

From September 1922 an oath of allegiance was imposed on all those holding local government offices, a test extended to civil servants and teachers in 1923.[40] By late 1921 the Northern Ireland government authorities had assumed responsibility for policing and security and in April 1922 the Civil Authorities (Special Powers) Act gave it additional powers. By late 1922 it had been able to establish its authority to a considerable degree and to achieve relative peace and stability. The IRA offensive earlier in the year had failed, not only because of tough government security policies and the outbreak of civil war in the south, but also because of growing Catholic criticism of IRA violence.[41] In August the Irish Free State cabinet adopted 'a peace policy ... with North East Ulster' which moderated its approach towards the northern state.[42] On 31 October 1922 it ended its payment to northern teachers, and encouraged them to deal with the Northern Ireland ministry of education.

The question of 'recognition' of the Northern Ireland parliament and state remained a divisive one for members of the nationalist and Catholic community. Nationalists in border areas continued to pin their hopes on the boundary commission and remained opposed to participation in the northern parliament. In the east, however, there was a greater willingness to recognise the new structures, and eventually, after the 1925 general election, Joseph Devlin and a nationalist MP for Co. Antrim, T.S. McAllister, took their seats in the northern parliament on 28 April 1925. The Northern Ireland parliament contained a senate, as did the southern parliament, but during this period it did not provide a voice for minorities, as did its southern counterpart. Members of the House of Commons in the Northern Ireland parliament elected all the senators, apart from two ex-officio members, namely the mayors of Belfast and Derry. In 1921, however, nationalist MPs boycotted the parliament and all its proceedings, while the nationalist mayor of Derry, Hugh O'Doherty, rejected a senate seat, declaring in February 1922 that he would 'rather be reduced to the gutter' than take his seat.[43] After the 1925 general election, Devlin and McAllister proposed a nationalist candidate for the senate, but their votes arrived late by post and were rejected.[44]

In late 1924 the boundary commission began its work. Its report was ready by the end of 1925, but was shelved amid great controversy when it was revealed that its proposed changes would be minimal. The British, Northern Ireland and Irish Free State governments now signed an accord which accepted the existing boundary of the six counties of Northern Ireland. This outcome produced great shock in northern nationalist and republican circles, and many felt badly let down by the southern government. The *Frontier Sentinel*, published at Newry, near the border, stated: 'The nationalists of the border have been callously betrayed. Nationalists never clamoured for good government from Belfast but struggled instead for the unity of Ireland: they have been so unblushingly betrayed by the latest bargain'.[45] Nonetheless, it now meant that the idea of recognition of the northern institutions gained much greater support. In early January 1926 Devlin declared that the reasons for nationalists not attending the Northern Ireland parliament had disappeared and that they must 'recognise that parliament as a sacrosanct institution of democracy'.[46] Canon Frank O'Hare, parish priest of Banbridge, Co. Down, urged northern nationalists to look to their own efforts for the future and 'not the gymnasts of the Free State'.[47] Following nationalist conventions, three more nationalist MPs took their seats at the opening of parliament in March 1926. After de Valera and Fianna Fáil entered Dáil Éireann in 1927, the remaining nationalist MPs in border areas decided to attend the northern parliament, leaving only two republicans (including de Valera, elected for Down) to continue an abstentionist policy.

During these early years, members of the Catholic and nationalist community in the north endured considerable violence.[48] In the Belfast area, in particular, large numbers faced political and sectarian attack. During July and August 1920 most Catholic employees in the Belfast shipyards and other engineering works, often labelled as 'Sinn Feiners', had been expelled. In August 1920 Dr Joseph MacRory, Catholic bishop of Down and Connor, wrote; 'I am pained to say that thousands of our Catholic workers are already in distress. Nor is there the slightest sign at present that they will be permitted to return to their work'.[49] Rioting in 1920 and 1921 led to the expulsion from their homes of thousands of Catholic residents of Belfast, many of whom fled south. Intimidation of Catholic families occurred elsewhere, such as in Lisburn. Often attacks on members of the Catholic community were in response to actions of the IRA and attacks on southern Protestants.[50] Renewed violence in Belfast in the first half of 1922 led to greatly increased fatalities, including the incident on 23 March 1922 when five members of the Catholic MacMahon family were murdered. It was widely believed that RUC District Inspector J.W. Nixon and other policemen were involved in the MacMahon murders: Nixon was later dismissed from the police, and became an independent MP and critic of the government.[51] Bishop MacRory challenged this outbreak of violence as an 'expression of vicarious punishment, according to which Catholics of Belfast are made to suffer for the sins of their brethren elsewhere'.[52] Speaking at the Presbyterian General Assembly in June 1922 the moderator, Dr W.J. Lowe, attacked the actions of 'some nominal Protestants' who had engaged in 'reprisals and counter-reprisals' with 'the most deplorable results', condemned the murders they had committed, and urged citizens to 'discountenance these outrages in every possible way'.[53]

A joint statement issued by all the Irish Catholic bishops on 26 April 1922 expressed their deep anxiety about 'the terrible state of things prevailing in the North East Corner' and declared that 'if that government is to be judged by results, it must rank more nearly with the government of the Turk in his worst days than with anything to be found anywhere in a Christian state'.[54] The northern bishops believed that the authorities and security forces had failed to protect the Catholic community. Members of the Protestant community also suffered violence in this period, such as the six Presbyterians murdered by the IRA at Altnaveigh near Newry on 19 June 1922.[55] Nonetheless, the violence in the north bore most heavily on members of the nationalist and Catholic community. In the six counties of Northern Ireland, over the period July 1920–July 1923, the death toll has been estimated at 557, of whom there were 303 Catholics, 172 Protestants and 82 members of the security forces. Catholics were only a quarter of the population in Belfast, but over a two-year period they suffered 257 deaths out of a total of 416.[56]

The violence and changes of these years brought marked displacement of populations, north and south. In the north a majority of those Catholics who fled from Belfast to the south seem to have returned to their city. Between 1911 and 1926 the percentage of Catholics in Belfast fell only from 24.10 to 23.0 per cent, while their numbers went up from 93,243 to 95,682. In the south there was a much greater permanent loss of members of the Protestant community, whose numbers declined by 106,456, nearly one-third, over the same period.[57] This drop in the southern Protestant population, given its magnitude, requires special explanation.[58] Following the publication of the 1926 census, it was estimated that around 20 per cent of the Protestant loss over this census period could be put down to departure of British forces and members of the RIC from the 26 counties.[59] Also, while all sections endured losses during the war, it is probable that, because of their strong connections to the British crown, the members of the Protestant and unionist community suffered proportionally greater losses than others.[60] Most Protestant churches contain memorials to those who died. A brass plaque in Waterford Cathedral records that Colonel E. Roberts lost five grandsons, four in France and one in Gallipoli.[61] A stained glass window in the First Presbyterian church in Monaghan town commemorates two sons of the Black family, aged 18 and 22, who were killed at Gallipoli. Also, there were those who departed in 1921 because they were not happy with the new political arrangements for the future.[62]

At the same time it is evident that many left because of violence and intimidation in the years 1918–23, especially from July 1921 to May 1923, and most did not return. On 23 June 1922, for example, the *Church of Ireland Gazette* reported how 'in certain districts in southern Ireland inoffensive Protestants of all classes are being driven from their homes, their shops and their farms in such numbers that many of our small communities are in danger of being entirely wiped out'. Reports from Church of Ireland diocesan synods across the country during this period reveal the loss very starkly. On 13 June 1923, at the Cork diocesan synod, the bishop, Dr C.B. Dowse, described how during the previous two and a half years: 'Many of our people have gone ... Their houses have been burned. Destruction has marched through the land'.[63] On 5 July 1923, at the Kilmore diocesan synod, the local bishop, Dr W.R. Moore, declared that: 'One of the saddest features of the situation is that so many of our communion have been driven from this country. By their expulsion such citizens ... are now much fewer than they were'.[64] These events brought condemnation from Catholic sources. In February 1923 the Catholic bishop of Cork, Dr Daniel Cohalan, described how 'Protestants have suffered severely during the period of the civil war in the south' and urged that 'charity knows no exclusion of creed', while in May 1923, the Catholic bishop of Killaloe, Dr Michael Fogarty, appealed to a higher sense of patriotism, noting that 'their Protestant fellow countrymen – he regretted to have to say it – were persecuted and dealt with in a cruel and coarse manner'.[65]

Displacement of populations and violence against minorities occurred not just in Ireland at this time but also in parts of Central and Eastern Europe and on a much greater scale. In spite of such terrible events in Ireland, however, there seems to have been a widespread and determined effort to move on and to build for the future. Perhaps the two minorities, north and south, believed that to raise these matters later might only have provoked further hardship for them. In 1923 an historian at Trinity College Dublin, W. Alison Phillips, wrote strongly about the suffering of southern unionists over the previous four years, but in the preface to the second edition of his book in 1926 he gave credit and support to the efforts of the Irish Free State government: 'for me, so far as practical politics are concerned, the dead past may bury its dead'.[66] Even in July 1923, at the Killaloe diocesan synod, after remarking that there had been 'much suffering and loss', the bishop, Dr Sterling Berry, declared that 'it is better to think of the present and of the future than of the past'.[67] The desire not to dwell on the suffering of these years is reflected in the three-volume history of the Church of Ireland, edited by Phillips and published in 1934 and 1935. In the chapter on the modern period it was stated that 'it could give no pleasure to the present writer to recall for others the dark and terrible deeds done in Ireland during one of the darkest periods in her history' and instead simply recalled the 'courage and patience' of church members.[68] A 1953 history of the Church of Ireland covered all these events and losses in one line.[69]

In 1922 Father John Hassan compiled a book on the sufferings of Belfast Catholics over the two previous years but, apart from the printing of some 18 copies at the time, the book was not published until the 1990s, apparently in an effort not to provoke controversy.[70] In fact, there were very few other accounts by contemporaries or historians until recently of the events of this period which have been called a 'forgotten war'.[71] When in 1925 Joseph Devlin justified his decision to attend the Northern Ireland parliament, he declared: 'at such a hopeful juncture as this, it would be cruelly wrong to revive old controversies,

stir up forgotten feuds, or renew bitter memories of a past that had
better be buried and forgotten'.[72] The Catholic primate, Cardinal Patrick
O'Donnell, in February 1926, urged efforts to achieve accommodation
in the north: 'What would have happened had the [nationalist] members taken their seats from the beginning I am unable to conjecture. But
what matters now is that the case be made in such a way as to be thor-
oughly understood, and that can be pressed by every legitimate means,
with nothing but good feeling for our neighbours'.[73]

Political representation

After the violence and political turmoil of the early 1920s, it seemed
that minorities in both parts of Ireland would play important political
roles in their respective societies. Forty years later, however, the evidence of their part in parliamentary politics showed that prospects for
such involvement had not materialised. At the 1921 general election
to the Northern Ireland parliament, the non-unionist seats were split
equally between six nationalists and six Sinn Féin members, reflecting
divisions between followers of the former constitutional Irish parliamentary party and the republican Sinn Féin. The following general
election in 1925 saw not only a shift to ten nationalists and two Sinn
Féin members, but also the appearance of four independent unionists,
three members of the Northern Ireland Labour Party and one independent. In response to the rise of these independents and labour, and in
fear of others, the unionist government in 1929 abolished proportional
representation and created single member constituencies at elections
to the Northern Ireland parliament. This was not aimed at nationalists,
and indeed at the 1929 general election their seats rose from 10 to 11,
although the republican seats fell from two to none. As intended, the
number of independents and others was reduced from eight to four.
After the 1929 general election three nationalists were elected to the
northern senate for the first time, while at the elections to the British
House of Commons in the same year, two nationalists were successful
out of a 13 MP representation, including a university seat.[74]

At first every nationalist and republican elected to the Northern
Ireland parliament refused to attend. In 1924 nationalists Joseph Devlin
and Thomas McAllister took their seats to be followed by three others
in early 1926 and finally by the remaining five in late 1927. During
the late 1920s the nationalist and Catholic representatives provided a
'constructive opposition', alongside the labour party members.[75] For
a period they hoped to be in a position to challenge effectively and even

to replace the government with labour and independent allies, just as the Fianna Fáil party did later in the Irish Free State with support from independent and labour allies. In late 1927 Cahir Healy, nationalist MP for Fermanagh and Tyrone, wrote: 'we must not forget that the opposition in the northern parliament numbers 19 elected members to the government's 33. If we win 7 seats, the fort is ours. With the growing dissatisfaction amongst the farming and industrial classes, that is possible if we handle the situation tactfully, and we can secure a little money to finance independent unionist candidates in Belfast city – not much will be needed'.[76] Nationalists were critical of the abolition of proportional representation in 1929. This change did not reduce their numbers of MPs, but it served to remove the possibility of effective labour or independent MP allies. The loss of such support at the 1929 general election weakened the opportunity for nationalists to make an impact in parliament, and caused Devlin and his colleagues to feel frustrated by their minority position, with little influence in political affairs. By the early 1930s the nationalists had withdrawn from the Northern Ireland parliament. Devlin, elected also to the British parliament, believed that concerns of northern nationalists were not taken seriously in that parliament, owing in part to a convention that internal Northern Ireland affairs were not discussed at Westminster.[77]

From the late 1920s, after becoming disillusioned with the southern government over the Anglo-Irish treaty and the boundary commission, many northern nationalists began to view with great hope the rise of Eamon de Valera and Fianna Fáil. In 1933, on a northern nationalist initiative, de Valera was nominated and duly elected for Down South at the Northern Ireland parliament. He did not however take his seat.[78] His election led to the government bringing in legislation requiring candidates to undertake to take their seats if elected. Nationalist hopes of new southern assistance, however, were considerably dashed, when the Fianna Fáil government under de Valera failed to honour an earlier pledge to allow northern representatives to sit in the Dáil and refused to refund to northern teachers the pension premiums deducted by the Irish government during the campaign of 1922 of non-recognition of the northern ministry of education.[79] Fianna Fáil declined requests to set itself up as a party in Northern Ireland. In addition, the Irish citizenship act of 1935 placed restrictions on the eligibility of northerners to claim Irish citizenship, and during the 1938 Anglo-Irish negotiations de Valera failed to achieve any concessions for northern nationalists.[80] De Valera continued to denounce partition, even in his St Patrick's Day broadcast at the beginning of the Second World War on 17 March 1940.

Nonetheless, a year later, during the bombing of Belfast by the German air force de Valera agreed without hesitation to a request from the northern government to send southern fire engines there.[81]

Nationalist MPs remained divided over the question of abstention from the Northern Ireland parliament. By 1934 some, including their new leader, T.J. Campbell, had returned, but they had only minor influence on legislation.[82] Others, affected by a rise in republican opposition, attended rarely or not at all. After the Second World War there was a strong effort by Catholic politicians to create new unity and purpose among northern nationalists under the Anti-Partition League, founded in November 1945.[83] Besides seeking to bring together northern nationalists, its primary aim was to end partition through putting pressure on the British government, by propaganda at home and abroad and by seeking outside allies. The league won strong support from the southern government and the party leaders. This effort, however, failed completely and led to disillusionment with constitutional means of protest. The problem, of course, was that the policy of concentrating on ending partition through outside intervention was ill conceived and ill timed. As John Bowman has remarked, 'no juncture in European history could have been less propitious to seek sympathy for Irish grievances on partition'.[84] Owing to the role of Northern Ireland during the Second World War and its strategic importance in the new 'cold war', neither Washington nor London paid any attention to these nationalist demands.[85] The campaign gave primacy to ending partition, rather than dealing with specific grievances within Northern Ireland which might have been more achievable.[86] Northern nationalist expectations were dashed again when the southern parties proved once more unwilling to meet their demands over issues such as better north–south nationalist co-operation or places in the Dáil.[87]

The 1950s witnessed a significant revival of republicanism in the north. At the 1955 and 1958 general elections to Westminster, nationalist candidates withdrew from the contest while there were Sinn Féin candidates in every constituency, seeking to 'unite the people in the demand that the British occupation forces must leave Ireland'.[88] Two Sinn Féin candidates, T.J. Mitchell and P.C. Clarke, were elected in 1955 for Mid-Ulster and Fermanagh and South Tyrone, respectively, but were disqualified because they were convicted felons. From 1956 to 1962 the IRA mounted a campaign of violence, called 'Operation Harvest' against the northern state. This achieved little headway, owing mainly to northern government security measures but also to southern government security efforts and denunciation of violence by the Catholic bishops.[89]

In his Lenten pastoral of March 1957, Dr Eugene O'Callaghan, Bishop of Clogher, not only condemned republican violence as morally wrong, but, in a departure from the traditional nationalist view on partition, went on to describe the border as 'not merely a geographical division' but 'a spiritual division of minds and hearts which physical force cannot heal'.[90]

After an initial rise in electoral backing for republicanism, such support in Northern Ireland fell from 152,310 to 63,415 between the 1955 and 1959 general elections.[91] At the elections to the British parliament in 1959 and 1964, all 12 seats were won by unionists, owing to republican/nationalist divisions. By the late 1950s the Anti-Partition League had collapsed and a loose grouping of nationalist MPs was elected to the Northern Ireland parliament. At the 1962 general election nine nationalist, one Irish labour and one republican labour candidates were elected, along with four members of the Northern Ireland Labour Party. During this period of the 1940s and 1950s, a number of independent Catholic candidates (Dr Eileen Hickey, Dr Frederick McSorley and Charles Stewart) were among the candidates returned for Queen's University.

In the south, members of the Protestant and former unionist community played a major part in parliamentary politics in the early days of the new Irish Free State. From the beginning, they ceased describing themselves as unionist, an acknowledgement that unionism was now irrelevant in their new situation.[92] An editorial in *The Church of Ireland Gazette* on 13 January 1922 declared: 'Unionism, as such, has ceased to exist in practical politics'. A few former unionists, such as Major Bryan Cooper, joined one of the main parties. Nonetheless, while some were members of one of the main pro-treaty or anti-treaty wings of Sinn Féin (later Cumann na nGaedheal and Fianna Fáil respectively), most Protestant members of Dáil Éireann (TDs) were members of newly-formed and short-lived farmers' or business parties, or independents. In 1922 Protestant TDs numbered nine, and as late as June 1927 the figure stood at 14, including nine independents, out of a total 153.[93] These Protestant TDs tended to be found in areas with a significant Protestant presence such as the three Ulster counties, and parts of Dublin city and county. While Protestant TDs were usually independents, a small number were influential members in the main parties, such as Ernest Blythe in Cumann na nGaedhael and Thomas Johnson in Labour. Of the 60 senators in the first senate (1922–5), 23 were Protestant, including 15 nominated originally by William Cosgrave (there was also one Jewish senator). Subsequent senate elections saw the number of Protestant senators drop, but by 1930 they numbered still over a dozen.[94]

Later decades witnessed a rapid decline in the role of members of the Protestant community in parliamentary affairs. The number of Protestant TDs shrank from 12 in 1932 to seven in 1937 and three in 1948.[95] The fall in the 1930s was affected in part by the electoral act of 1935 which reduced the size and redrew the boundaries of a number of constituencies, some of them in Counties Dublin and Donegal where significant numbers of Protestant voters were split between the new constituencies.[96] Probably more important was the fall in numbers of Protestant electors and a paucity of Protestants among the membership of the main parties. After the new parliamentary arrangements provided for in the 1937 constitution came into effect, the four Dublin University seats in the Dáil were abolished and three such seats created in the new senate. In 1948 there were three Protestant TDs, namely Maurice Dockrell, Fine Gael (Dublin South Central), Erskine Childers, Fianna Fáil (Longford Westmeath), and an independent, William Sheldon (Donegal East).[97]

Ironically, it was the last of the independent Protestant TDs, William Sheldon, who had the greatest parliamentary influence. Originally, he supported Fine Gael and the inter-party government, but after their decision to declare a republic he withdrew his support to show his strong objections. His vote, along with those of a few other independent TDs, was crucial in supporting a minority Fianna Fáil government after the 1951 general election. Still an independent, he was appointed a vice-chairman of Dáil Éireann and chairman of the important Dáil public accounts committee.[98] It is possible that the toning down in anti-partition rhetoric by the new Fianna Fáil government was due to their reliance on Sheldon's support. Sheldon continued to hold his East Donegal seat until he retired from it in 1961. A change in the Donegal boundaries in 1961 (described in the *Irish Times*, 14 October 1961 as a 'jerrymander'), as part of constituency changes organised by Neil Blaney, minister for local government and another Donegal TD, ended his career in the Dáil. At the 1957 general election, Sheldon had won 6011 votes, which was higher than the quota required to be elected in both new Donegal constituencies at the 1961 general election, but because of the altered boundaries he did not even stand.[99] In 1961 there were four Protestant TDs, Maurice Dockrell, Fine Gael (Dublin South Central), Henry Dockrell, Fine Gael (Dún Laoghaire), Lionel Booth, Fianna Fáil (also Dún Laoghaire), and Erskine Childers, Fianna Fáil (Monaghan).[100]

The original senate had included a large proportion of members of the Protestant and former unionist community but from the first triennial elections in 1925 their numbers fell, in large part because of growing polarisation of voting for senate seats between the chief parties, in which few Protestants were involved. In 1925, indeed, Douglas Hyde failed to get elected, owing very largely to allegations that he was 'pro-divorce', in spite of his protest that it was 'not likely' that 'the writer of two volumes of the *Religious Songs of Connacht* would be in favour of divorce. He is not, and never was'.[101] Some mainly ex-unionists formed an 'Independent Group', dropping from 12 in 1928 to seven in 1934.[102] There were also a few independent Protestant senators outside this group. Conflict arose in the 1930s between the new Fianna Fáil government and the senate, where a pro-treaty majority, including these independents, challenged the government over a number of issues, including the abolition of the oath. This confrontation led to the abolition by the government of the entire senate in 1936. In the new senate, under the 1937 constitution, Dublin University (as well as the National University of Ireland) elected three senators, and until the 1960s all were Protestant, except for Owen Sheehy Skeffington.

Under the new arrangements, the taoiseach nominated 11 members and another 43 were elected by a number of electoral bodies which in practice operated on mainly party lines and which very rarely elected Protestant senators. The taoiseach's nominees occasionally included one or two Protestants, but often of a strong nationalist persuasion. One of these, nominated by de Valera in 1938, was David Lubbock Robinson, whose father had been dean of St Ann's Church of Ireland cathedral, Belfast. *Flynn's Irish Parliamentary Handbook, 1939*, noted that Robinson served with distinction in the British army during the First World War, and then, 'joined IRA. 1919. Served 18 months in Mountjoy and elsewhere, 1922–3–4'.[103] Despite, or perhaps because of, this background, Robinson was selected to represent de Valera and the Irish government at the funeral of Craigavon in 1940. In the event Robinson was so well received by the unionists, in particular by the prime minister, J.M. Andrews, that he asked that the Irish government send a message of thanks for his reception to the secretary of the Northern Ireland government. De Valera refused to allow this on the grounds that 'a letter from the secretary of this department [of the taoiseach] would be too formal' and he told Robinson to send the letter himself.[104] Unusually, in 1961 Sean Lemass nominated an independent Protestant senator, a graduate of the Queen's University of Belfast, who advocated stronger north–south relations and was very critical of the compulsory Irish language policy. This person was William Sheldon, who had lost his Donegal Dáil Éireann seat the same year, due to a Fianna Fáil led redrawing of constituency boundaries, but who had given vital support to Fianna Fáil in the past. He continued as a senator until 1973.

Social and economic conditions

The social and economic profile of the southern Protestant community during this period showed both change and diversity. The most obvious development was the sharp decline in numbers. Between 1911 and 1926, numbers of Protestants fell from 327,179 and 10.4 per cent of the total to 220,723 and 7.4 per cent.[105] These figures continued to decline and were 144,868 and 5.1 per cent in 1961. In 1911 in the three Ulster counties of Donegal, Cavan and Monaghan, Protestants numbered 70,500 and 21.7 per cent of the total population of these counties: fifty years later, in 1961, their numbers stood at 28,885 and 13.3 percent.[106] The census returns for 1926 show how most of the Protestant community was widely dispersed, and even where Protestant numbers were greatest they still measured relatively low percentages of their locality. By 1926, the small town of Greystones, Co. Wicklow, was the only urban area in which Protestants were a majority, while even in Co. Monaghan, where their numbers were the highest proportion in any county, the figure was just over 20 per cent.[107] As numbers continued to fall, it became difficult for this minority to retain its own social or community structures. Information from the decades immediately after independence also reveals a lower birth rate than for the rest of society and an increasing percentage of older people. In common with others, the Protestant community suffered from emigration.[108]

By the middle of the century, however, the most important factor in Protestant decline was loss due to inter-church or mixed marriages as regulated under the Catholic church's *Ne Temere* decree of 1908, which stipulated that the children of mixed marriages had to be brought up as Catholics. By the early 1960s it was reckoned that at least 16 per cent of marriages of Protestants were to Catholic partners. Since most children of these marriages were brought up as Catholics, this had adverse consequences for Protestant numbers.[109] In 1950 the Catholic church ruling was given state legal backing by the Tilson case. This dispute over a mixed marriage and the religious upbringing of children, went finally to the Supreme Court, where, surprisingly, the Catholic wife was represented by the Irish attorney-general, C.F. Casey. The judgment found in favour of the wife, under a pre-nuptial agreement arising from the *Ne Temere* decree, in a departure from common law practice. The one Protestant Supreme Court judge, Justice William Black, dissented from this finding.[110] On a later occasion in early 1951, explaining the government's opposition to introducing legal adoption, which was deemed to be against Catholic church teaching, Casey stated that: 'this was a Catholic country – this did not mean that parliament should be expected to penalise other creeds. It did mean that parliament could not be asked to introduce legislation contrary to the teaching of that great church'.[111] It is probable that his intervention in the Tilson case was to help prevent the courts from over-riding Catholic church law on mixed marriages.

In 1957 there was widespread public controversy when members of the Protestant community in Fethard-on-Sea in Co.Wexford suffered boycott called by the local Catholic priest following a family dispute over the education of children of a mixed marriage. De Valera, then taoiseach again, criticised the boycott, which had caused the government embarrassment internationally. At the same time, the Catholic stance on mixed marriages received little public criticism, even from leading Church of Ireland figures. The arrangements which helped end the boycott eventually included a private undertaking by Dr G.O. Simms, Church of Ireland archbishop of Dublin, that he would not mention the incident again, as well as an agreement between Protestant and Catholic representatives by which, in effect, blame for the original dispute was shouldered by local Protestants, even though they had been the victims. In 1998, Dr Brendan Comiskey, Catholic bishop of Ferns, expressed a 'deep sorrow' at what had happened and asked for forgiveness from the Church of Ireland community.[112]

How did members of the Protestant community fare in terms of employment and opportunities under the new regime? The 1926 census recorded that 2 per cent of the civic guards/police and 7 per cent of the army were Protestant. By 1961, however, Protestants were only 0.7 per cent of garda sergeants and lower ranks, and 2.2 per cent of the defence forces.[113] As regards the judiciary, there was always a Protestant on the bench of the Supreme Court in this period. Justice Gerald Fitzgibbon, who served from 1924 to 1938, was a former unionist. Later Protestant members were from demonstrably nationalist backgrounds: Justice James Meredith (1936–42) had helped to set up early Sinn Féin courts, and Justice William Black (1942–51) 'took part in the 1918 Sinn Féin election and did important work in the reconstruction of Sinn Féin'.[114] The early 1950s, however, saw the appointment of the former independent Trinity senator, Justice Theodore Kingsmill Moore (1951–66). In 1926 Protestants comprised nearly 13 per cent of those employed by the civil service or local authorities, including many from the former British civil service.[115] Similar information is not available for 1961, but we can note that in that year, Protestants were 4.5 per cent of senior officials in the civil service and local authorities. One was Thekla Beere, daughter of a southern Church of Ireland rector, who became secretary of the department of transport and power, 1959–66.[116] Lack of political control in any important council area minimised the opportunities for job patronage which usually went with such control. At a demonstration of members of the Royal Black Institution in Co. Monaghan in June 1926 a resolution was passed in protest against 'the continued exclusion of Protestants from any share in local appointments just because they are Protestants'.[117] The absence of Protestants in council jobs in Co. Monaghan was raised on a number of occasions in subsequent decades.[118]

In late 1930 controversy arose over the employment of a Protestant graduate of Trinity College Dublin, Letitia Dunbar Harrison, as Mayo county librarian.[119] Her appointment by the Local Appointments Commission was rejected by the county council on the grounds of her lack of Irish and also her Trinity and Protestant background. The Irish government, under William Cosgrave, took initially a firm stand against the actions of the council, but various politicians and Catholic clergy opposed strongly her appointment. Eventually, the government backed down and she was obliged to resign in early 1932 and was given another job as librarian of the department of defence's military library. At the same time, the question of the suitability of Protestant and Trinity graduates for public medical appointments such as dispensary doctors had been raised by certain influential Catholics, most notably by Dr Thomas Gilmartin, Catholic archbishop of Tuam, in his 1931 Lenten pastoral.[120] On this matter, however, Cosgrave declined to budge and in correspondence with the Catholic hierarchy he refused to agree to a religious test for these medical appointments.[121]

In a debate in the Dáil in June 1931 on the appointment of the Mayo county librarian, Eamon de Valera expressed his views. He declared his belief 'that every citizen in this country is entitled to his share of public appointments and that there should not be discrimination on the grounds of religion'. Then he proceeded to say that where there were Catholic communities, positions of doctors as well as librarians should be filled only by Catholics. He stated: 'I say that if I had a vote on a local body, and if there were two qualified people who had to deal with a Catholic community, and if one was a Catholic and the other a Protestant, I would unhesitatingly vote for the Catholic'.[122] For Miss Dunbar Harrison, at least, her sojourn in Co. Mayo had one happy outcome. She met Rev. Robert Crawford, Methodist minister at Castlebar. Subsequently, they married and moved to Whitehead in Co. Antrim, where she played a leading role in the 1950s in promoting the ordination of women in the Methodist church.[123]

In the 1940s two pamphlets on the position of members of the Church of Ireland in the south were produced by W.B. Stanford, regius professor of Greek at Trinity College Dublin. In both he emphasised the role of prominent Protestant nationalists, such as Theobald Wolfe Tone. In the first, published in 1944, he rejected the idea of persecution, but declared that members of his church suffered from 'political and religious pressure'.[124] He listed matters affecting them, such as exclusion from 'public and private appointments', and referred to their fall in numbers. In his second pamphlet, printed in 1946, he criticised exclusive attitudes in both north and south. He argued that in the north there were more government statements defending northern exclusivism compared to the 'official discretion in the south'.[125] He praised the southern government as impartial, which he attributed to the liberal tradition started by people such as Davis, and also to the small numbers and lack of a political threat of the southern minority in contrast to the larger numbers and political threat of northern Catholics. At the same time, he attacked Gaelic exclusivism and jobbery in the south. Also in 1946, an Ulster Unionist MP, Edmund Warnock, claimed that southern Protestants 'did not prosper' or 'were not happy' in the south. This led to a public response from Protestant Fianna Fáil TD Erskine Childers. He declared that this was 'an entirely baseless allegation' and that 'the Protestants of the 26 counties lived in an atmosphere of complete tolerance'.[126] At the same time, however, in private correspondence to Sean McEntee, Childers expressed deep concern about anti-Protestantism and described how there was 'a general feeling on the part of Protestants that in regard to government appointments and the local authorities, they had better not apply'.[127] Brian Girvin has remarked how the willingness of Childers to conceal his real views 'attests to the strength of nationalism and the pressure on Protestants to conform to nationalism's public image'.[128]

Nonetheless, the Protestant community in the south enjoyed some considerable advantages. For the first time, the census of 1926 included ownership of land by religious denomination. It recorded that 5189 Protestant farmers held land of over 100 acres, representing around 22 per cent of farmers in this category. Also, there were another 19,459 Protestant farmers with smaller farms as well as 3615 Protestant farm labourers.[129] By 1961 there were still some 3812 Protestant farmers with over 100 acres, a figure of 15.33 per cent of the total.[130] In 1926 and 1961 the Protestant community was well represented among the professions and financial and commercial occupations, although their numbers and proportions fell, especially among doctors and dentists.[131]

Of the 10,469 directors, managers, and company secretaries in 1961, Protestants were nearly 30 per cent. During these years, a number of the biggest firms, such as the Guinness Brewery and Jacobs, the biscuit firm, were Protestant owned. Protestants were strongly placed in the banking and legal sectors. It has been pointed out how in the horse-racing world, all the 17 men who were stewards of the Irish Turf Club, in the years 1914–45, were either 'peers, officers in the British army or former landlords or their representatives'.[132]

In the early decades of the new state, the prominence of Protestants among the professions and business caused resentment in some Catholic circles, which led to action by a number of organisations to restrict the Protestant presence in these areas.[133] By the 1960s, however, there was less concern about this Protestant role, partly because of the fall in Protestant numbers and partly, as Kurt Bowen has pointed out, because of the many new opportunities for Catholics, not only in the expanding professions but also in the businesses and semi-state bodies established from the 1920s onwards.[134] At the same time we should note that there had been a sizeable Protestant working class in Dublin city in the early twentieth century (including the playwright Sean O'Casey), but post-1921 their numbers dropped very considerably as did Protestant numbers in other urban centres.[135] In some of the Dublin townships, such as Pembroke and Blackrock, there were substantial Protestant middle-class communities, and although their numbers fell after 1921 they remained significant.

After 1921 the fortunes of Trinity College Dublin were reduced, not only by the decline in the number of southern Protestants, but also by the continued ban on Catholic students attending the college, imposed by the Catholic bishops. In his 1961 Lenten pastoral, the Catholic archbishop of Dublin, Dr John Charles McQuaid, reiterated that Catholics were forbidden 'under pain of mortal sin ... to frequent that college'.[136] Nonetheless, Trinity survived, thanks to being able to draw students and staff (such as the historian T.W. Moody) from the north and elsewhere and to the willingness of some Catholics to attend, in spite of the ban. The government gave a very small grant to the university until the 1950s when better funding was provided. The bishops' ban was lifted only in 1970, by which time many Catholics were attending the college. After 1921, Trinity graduates were able to make only a limited contribution to the politics and public life of the new state, compared to graduates of the National University of Ireland. Not until Noel Browne became minister of health in 1948, did a Trinity graduate serve in the Irish cabinet. At the same time many Trinity graduates were prominent in northern political and public life, such as MPs J.H. Robb and Brian Magennis, Lord Chief Justice Sir William Moore and Sir Robert Kidd, head of the Northern Ireland Civil Service, 1976–79. In an obituary on Kidd in 2004, it was remarked that when he joined the Northern Ireland Civil Service in 1947 it was 'normally headed by Englishmen, Scotsmen and Trinity graduates'.[137] Trinity continued to train most of the northern clergy of the Church of Ireland and students of the Presbyterian divinity school, Magee College, Derry, still completed their degrees at Trinity.

The social and economic profile of the Catholic and nationalist community in the north was very different from that of the Protestant and former unionist community in the south. In 1911, in the six counties which later became Northern Ireland, Catholics numbered 430,161 and 34.4 per cent of the total population, while in 1926 they numbered 420,428 and 33.5 per cent.[138] By 1961, however, their numbers had grown to 497,547 and 34.9 per cent: by 1971 they were estimated at 559,800 and 36.8 per cent.[139] This meant that, proportionally speaking, northern Catholic numbers had increased not only more than northern Protestants but also more than southern Catholics, whose numbers fell by 77,796 between 1926 and 1961. In contrast to southern Protestants, northern Catholics were not only a higher proportion of the population, but also they were heavily concentrated in certain areas. In 1926 they were a majority in Co. Fermanagh (56 per cent), Co. Tyrone (55.5 per cent) and Derry city (59.9 per cent): by 1961 their numbers and proportions of the population were only slightly lower in Co. Fermanagh (53.2 per cent) and Co. Tyrone (54.8 per cent), but slightly higher in Derry city (67.1 per cent). In Counties Armagh, Tyrone and Fermanagh, the Catholic population in 1926 numbered 155,928 while in 1961 it numbered 156,437: this contrasted sharply with Counties Monaghan, Cavan and Donegal where Catholic numbers fell from 250,454 in 1926 to 188,639 in 1961.[140] Catholics were also a majority in south Down, south Armagh and west Belfast. Their substantial numbers and heavy concentration in some areas gave significant cohesion to their communities and made it easier to maintain their social and community structures. Mixed marriages in this period in the north were rare and so had no significant effect on the numbers of the various denominations.

How did members of the Catholic community fare in areas of state and public employment in Northern Ireland? The Constabulary Act (Northern Ireland) 1922 included a one-third quota for Catholics in the new police force to be called the Royal Ulster Constabulary (RUC).

By the beginning of 1925, however, the RUC was 2990 strong of whom there were 2449 Protestant and 541 Catholic members.[141] Many of the Catholic officers had previously served in the Royal Irish Constabulary. This proportion for Catholics of around 18 per cent would fall only marginally to 17 per cent by 1936, but by 1969 it stood at approximately 11 per cent.[142] The proportion of Catholics at county or district inspector level stood at 24 per cent in 1925, but had reduced to 16 per cent by 1936 and to a lower level subsequently.[143] Still, we should note that in the late 1950s a Catholic, John Gorman, son of Major Jack Gorman who came north in 1922, was appointed district inspector in Armagh. Subsequently, he was elected in the late 1990s as an Ulster Unionist Party assembly member and deputy speaker of the Northern Ireland Assembly. In the early 1960s he was succeeded in Armagh as district inspector by another Catholic, Brendan Durkan, whose son, Mark Durkan, later became head of the SDLP.[144] Besides the RUC, throughout this period there was also a reserve force, the RUC Special Constabulary, known as the 'B' Specials, and it was entirely Protestant in composition. The Cameron Commission of 1969 noted that among Catholics there was resentment against the existence of the 'B' Specials as 'a partisan and paramilitary force recruited exclusively from Protestants'.[145]

As regards the judiciary, we may observe that the first lord chief justice of Northern Ireland was a Catholic, Sir Denis Henry, a former unionist MP. After Henry's death in 1925, his successor, Sir William Moore, was another former unionist politician, as were the other Supreme Court members in this early period, except for Judge James Andrews, brother of J.M. Andrews, later prime minister of Northern Ireland.[146] Lack of Catholics in the judiciary was a subject of concern for nationalists, including the nationalist leader, a leading barrister and KC, T.J. Campbell, who referred to it in his book *Fifty Years of Ulster, 1890–1940*, published in 1941.[147] Four years later, however, considerable controversy arose over the appointment of a county court judge for Co. Tyrone. It was announced that the new judge would be not only a Catholic but T.J. Campbell himself. This appointment caused deep division among nationalists over the question of accepting positions under the crown. It earned for Campbell the opprobrious title of 'Judas Campbell' in some nationalist circles.[148] Republican Labour MP Harry Diamond accused Campbell of 'posing as a patriot' and accepting 'a commission from his majesty King George VI'.[149] Nonetheless, in 1949 Catholic Judge Charles Leo Sheil was appointed to the bench of the Supreme Court, to be followed in the 1960s by Catholic Judge Ambrose McGonigal.

In the Northern Ireland Civil Service during this period Catholics were neither numerous nor influential, although it seemed at first that this would not be so. Shortly after the establishment of the service, the first chairman of the selection board in 1924 wrote that the board had not regarded 'the question of religious belief of essential importance in interviewing candidates and deciding upon appointments to the service'.[150] Figures for the number of Catholic civil servants in these early years are not available, but it is clear that they declined until by the mid-1930s the proportion of Catholics in the lower ranks of the civil service was estimated at about 10 per cent.[151] Statistics for 1943 showed that Catholics comprised just 5.8 per cent of the administrative class and analogous technical grades.[152] A.N. Bonaparte Wyse, permanent secretary of the ministry of education, 1927–39, was the only Catholic to achieve such high office until the appointment of Patrick Shea to the same position in 1969. By the 1960s Catholics were still under-represented throughout the Northern Ireland Civil Service, especially among senior officers, although in posts in the 'Imperial' civil service, under the control of London, such as the Post Office and the Inland Revenue and Customs, the proportion of Catholics employed was higher.[153] Catholic representation on the academic staff of Queen's University of Belfast was small and a subject of complaint among Catholics.[154] During this period, however, the university employed few local academic staff, either Catholic or Protestant. In 1949, out of 24 non-medical professors only two were local and just one held a Queen's degree: of 11 medical professors there were five locals, all in areas of clinical medicine attached to the main teaching hospitals (established and governed very largely by members of the Protestant community), which effectively kept these positions for locals. All these seven local professors were Protestant.[155]

In local government, council employment, especially at the higher level, was greatly influenced by the dominant party in each local authority. Maurice Hayes, who succeeded his father as town clerk of Downpatrick in 1955, has written how 'there were very few cases of a council appointing an officer who did not 'dig with the right foot' or who was not drawn from the supporters of the majority party'.[156] In areas controlled by nationalists, in particular Downpatrick, Newry and Strabane, most council jobs went to Catholic candidates.[157] Overall, however, Catholics were at a disadvantage, because, as David Harkness has pointed out, 'there were not only more unionist authorities, but more than there ought to have been'.[158] Thanks to electoral redistribution of the early 1920s, owing to the Leech local government commission, unionists were able to regain control of a number of areas, in particular Counties Tyrone and Fermanagh and Derry city, which they had previously lost. These factors limited opportunities for Catholics in local government employment, which was a source of nationalist complaint.[159] In the 1950s the nationalist critic Frank Gallagher estimated that 32 per cent of all workers but only 12 per cent of executive, administrative, and clerical staff in local government in Northern Ireland were Catholic.[160] Nationalists were concerned that some of the health, education and welfare committees employed low numbers of Catholics. Later, in September 1969, the Cameron Commission reported that 'only thirty per cent of Derry corporation's administrative, clerical and technical employees were Catholics. Out of the ten best-paid jobs only one was a Catholic'. It also reported very low figures for Catholic council employment at senior level in other places, particularly in the west, such as Co. Fermanagh and Dungannon.[161]

Public statements by some unionist politicians served to support discrimination against Catholics in employment. On 12 July 1933, at Newtownbutler, Co. Fermanagh, Sir Basil Brooke declared that: 'There were a great number of Protestants and Orangemen who employed Roman Catholics. He felt he could speak freely on this subject as he had not a Roman Catholic about his place ... He would point out that the Roman Catholics were endeavouring to get in everywhere and were out with all their might to destroy the power and constitution of the north ... He would appeal to loyalists, therefore, wherever possible, to employ Protestant lads and lassies'.[162] While Brooke's speech revealed how in fact Protestants did employ Catholics, his comments, which he would later repeat and defend, were widely seen as an effort to discourage such practice.[163] In the Northern Ireland parliament on 21 November 1934, Lord Craigavon rejected the idea that religion should matter for appointments and then proceeded to state: 'It is undoubtedly our duty and privilege ... to see that those appointed by us possess the most unimpeachable loyalty to the King and Constitution. That is my whole object in carrying on a Protestant government for a Protestant people'.[164] This carried the clear implication that 'loyal' meant 'Protestant'. In spite of Craigavon's statement that religion was not relevant for matters of employment, his viewpoint about a 'Protestant government for a Protestant people' helped to strengthen the links between religion and politics. It meant that in practice many unionists regarded all Catholics automatically as 'disloyalists' and therefore not suitable for state or public employment. An extreme example of such attitudes was seen in Orange Order criticism in the 1930s of a Catholic employee on the Stormont estate, although he was an ex-serviceman and known personally to the Prince of Wales: only the intervention of the head of the civil service prevented his dismissal.[165]

Unlike southern Protestants, northern Catholics did not have the advantage of major land or business ownership. As David Kennedy pointed out in a 1962 radio broadcast on the subject of Catholics in Northern Ireland during the years 1926–39: 'this Catholic community was, and still is, composed mainly of small farmers, shopkeepers and unskilled labourers'. He described how it 'has a measurable share in the professions of medicine and law … it plays a not unimportant part in the commercial life of Northern Ireland but it controls none of the heavy engineering and textile industries which are the basis of our economy'.[166] In their 1962 study of group relations in Northern Ireland, Denis Barritt and Charles Carter drew attention to Catholic disadvantage in private employment, caused in part by discrimination, but also by other factors such as geographical location and lower Catholic educational attainment.[167] By the end of the 1960s, however, the Cameron Commission recorded that in recent years 'a much larger Catholic middle-class has emerged'.[168] Important in this change was the improvement in educational opportunities for Catholics. In the early 1920s, Lord Londonderry, first minister of education, had sought to introduce an improved, non-denominational, system of education for all children, but this was strongly opposed by the Protestant and Catholic churches. New arrangements in 1923 and 1930 gained Protestant but not Catholic backing, because the Catholic bishops and clergy were not willing to diminish control of their church schools. By 1930 Catholic schools received full staff teaching costs but only 50 per cent capital funding for buildings.

This disparity between Catholic and state schools in capital funding was an important source of grievance for the Catholic community. The government argued its funding for church schools was as generous as most other countries, but Catholics pointed to the case of Scotland where full capital funding for Catholic schools had been in place since the early 1920s. The 1947 education act, modelled on acts passed for England, resulted in an increase to 65 per cent in funding for buildings and also extra support for grammar and secondary school education. Catholics remained responsible for some school costs, and educational standards were not yet equal to those in the Protestant and state sector, affecting job opportunities for working class Catholics.[169] Nonetheless, the Catholic community benefited significantly from the additional resources available for education, post-1947. At the opening in November 1959 at Omagh, Co. Tyrone of St Patrick's secondary intermediate school, one of five new schools built or under construction that year in his diocese, the Catholic bishop of Derry, Dr Neil Farren, praised the northern ministry of education.[170] As bishop of a cross-border diocese, he was aware of the much greater funding for education in Northern Ireland compared to in the Irish Republic. Tom Garvin has pointed out that by 1961 the spend on education per head of population in the north was approximately four times that in the south. Of course, southern schools had the benefit of virtually free educational input from Catholic clergy and orders, as did some northern Catholic schools.[171] The 1947 act increased the numbers of Catholic pupils entering grammar schools and led to a rise in the Catholic student population in Queen's University by the 1960s.[172] The 1968 education act increased capital funding for Catholic schools to 80 per cent.

Allocation of public housing was a matter of concern for members of the Catholic community. In the early period there was limited public house building, but after the Second World War there was a great increase, provided by both local councils and the Northern Ireland Housing Trust, an autonomous public authority. Figures from the late 1960s and the early 1970s show that around one-third of public housing in Northern Ireland was occupied by Catholic families, which approximates to their proportion of the population.[173] In many parts, public housing allocation was uncontroversial. Indeed, nationalist MP Cahir Healy praised local authorities in Belfast and Counties Down and Antrim, as well as the Housing Trust, for their fair housing practices.[174] Elsewhere, however, particularly in the west, there was considerable controversy. Allocation of council housing was controlled by councillors and in a number of unionist controlled areas housing policy was influenced primarily by concerns to maintain or strengthen unionist electoral advantage and not by need.[175] By the 1960s there were strong nationalist complaints about public housing in some western areas, such as Dungannon and Omagh, but especially Derry.

The Cameron Commission of 1969 reported on housing policies in Derry. It acknowledged that there had been (from 1947 until the early 1960s) what it called a 'vast programme' of new public housing in the city's south ward, which included the Bogside and Creggan areas and which benefited greatly Derry's Catholic population.[176] It also noted, however, that in 'recent years', the unionist controlled corporation had curtailed any new building to maintain its already weak electoral position. This created a serious housing crisis in the city, particularly affecting needy Catholic families, which led to efforts by John Hume and others in the mid-1960s to challenge existing housing policies. By the mid-1960s unemployment was also a serious problem in Derry, although this had not been such a pressing matter during the previous decade. Indeed, on 14 November 1955, a report in the *Irish News* had noted an 'employment boom' and 'abundant work' in the city. This was due not only to the presence of 30 thriving shirt factories but also to the success of government economic policies in attracting to Derry a number of overseas industries, such as BSR (Birmingham Sound Reproducers) and, later, Du Pont.[177] In early 1967, however, BSR, now called Monarch Electric, which had employed over 2000 male workers six months previously, relocated its factory out of the country, causing severe unemployment and dashing expectations. Many in Derry were also aggrieved by the decision in 1965 to locate the new university in Coleraine rather than in Derry. All these new factors, plus an ongoing controversy over the city's electoral arrangements, meant that by the late 1960s the social and political situation in Derry was a highly volatile one.

Electoral practices were a subject of concern to nationalists in Northern Ireland. In the case of elections to both Stormont and Westminster, there was virtually no complaint about either constituency boundaries or the franchise.[178] At these parliamentary elections from the late 1920s there was full universal suffrage, or, as it was later called, 'one man, one vote'. There remained a second vote for owners of business premises in elections to Stormont but this involved small numbers and steps were taken in 1967 to abolish this business vote, in advance of civil rights protests. The abolition of PR in 1929 for elections to the Stormont parliament had very little effect on nationalist parliamentary representation. Where problems arose was in the area of local government. Throughout this period, the local government electorate was based mainly on rated occupiers and their spouses (including owner occupiers and tenants), but not their adult children, a system used in Britain until 1945. Catholics were over-represented among those disenfranchised, owing to this property franchise, although a majority of the total numbers disenfranchised were Protestants.[179] There was also a business franchise which created extra votes, but it did not involve significant numbers. This ratepayers' franchise was criticised by nationalists and defended by unionists, often because it was regarded as influential for the political balance in a number of councils. In fact, an investigation in 1969 concluded that a change in the franchise would probably affect political control in only one local authority.[180] Nonetheless, the call for 'one man, one vote' in local government elections took on symbolic importance for both sides in the 1960s. The property franchise was less important than the way in which ward boundaries were drawn.

Thanks to the redrawing of local government constituency boundaries in the early 1920s, as John Whyte has pointed out, 'nationalists were manipulated out of control in a number of areas where they had a majority of electors'.[181] Unionists controlled a majority of council areas because they were clear majorities in these areas, but gerrymandering of boundaries lost nationalists the control of a number of councils, especially in the west, where they had a majority of the population. Nationalists controlled only some 15 per cent of local authorities even though they were one-third of the population.[182] In 1936, when it seemed that unionists would lose control of Derry city, the wards were redrawn again under a scheme which meant 9961 nationalist electors returned eight councillors, while 7444 unionists returned 12.[183] For many local Derry unionists, whose Stormont MP, 1951–68, was the Dublin born and Trinity educated Protestant, E.W. Jones, minority control of the city corporation and jobs was justified. They saw themselves as under threat from nationalists and were very aware of the sharp decline in southern Protestant numbers, as Victor Griffin, later dean of St Patrick's Cathedral, Dublin, observed when he came as a curate to the city in 1947.[184] They witnessed the situation of Protestants in neighbouring Co. Donegal, where in 1934 over 5000 had petitioned to be moved to Northern Ireland, where their numbers fell throughout this period and where they lost their last elected independent Dáil representative through a redrawing of constituency boundaries in 1961.[185] In a speech in November 1959 Jones spoke of how 'in the border areas the real issue was before the people at all times' and of unionist determination to 'keep the house we lived in'.[186] Nonetheless, in 1965 Dr R.S. Nixon, unionist MP for North Down, warned his colleagues: 'You cannot run away ... from Derry City where the population is 60 per cent nationalist and 34 per cent unionist. You cannot maintain Ulster this way'.[187] Indeed, by 1961, the population of Derry was actually 67 per cent Catholic and 33 per cent Protestant.[188]

The subject of the treatment of the Catholic minority in the north and the Protestant minority in the south during this period from the 1920s until the 1960s is complex and controversial. In recent decades opinion on the situation in both cases has ranged from those who have argued that discrimination in one form or another was very harmful to others who have claimed that such claims are greatly exaggerated.[189] In his judicious 1983 study of the position of the northern Catholic minority over these years, John Whyte declared: 'the consensus among those who have looked at the evidence dispassionately is that the picture is neither black nor white, but a shade of grey'.[190] In the case of the southern Protestant minority, the evidence we have seen points to a similar conclusion. Furthermore, while economic and social factors were part of the picture that affected the position of these two minorities, more important was the gulf between majority and minority identities in each case.

Community interests

In both north and south the two main minority groups faced dominant groups who imposed their identity on each society. In reaction to this the minorities developed further their own senses of identity, based around their particular communities which took on new importance. In the new Irish Free State, as Marianne Elliott has described, most members of the Protestant and former unionist community 'felt isolated in a country whose ethos was now so demonstrably Catholic and whose national narrative bore so little relationship to their own'.[191] They withdrew into what has been called a kind of 'ghetto' or 'parallel universe'.[192] They had their own churches, schools, sports clubs and, in Dublin and Cork, hospitals. In Dublin their views were represented in the *Irish Times* and the *Evening Mail*. They continued to regard themselves as Irish Protestants or, preferably, as Irish, but found that they were often called 'Anglo-Irish', a term the Trinity College historian Edmund Curtis, in a lecture in 1933, rejected because it 'seemed to separate them in some way from the Irish nation', which implied they were not wholly Irish.[193] Stephen Gwynn, a former Protestant nationalist MP, remarked in 1926: 'I was brought up to think myself Irish without question or qualification, but the new nationalism prefers to describe me and the like of me as Anglo-Irish'.[194]

Some deliberately isolated themselves from the broader Irish society, such as the so-called 'West Britons' of Malahide, described by Brian Inglis.[195] Most others, however, found that their minority position made it difficult to be involved fully in the new nation. In 1939, in comments on the fall in Protestant numbers, Archbishop John Gregg described how the Protestant and Catholic communities were 'outside one another', and 'we are outside the close-knit spiritual entity which the majority constitutes'. Nonetheless, he insisted that 'our smaller community ... is yet conscious of an identity of its own, an identity genuinely Irish, which is more natural to it than the identity it recognises in the majority'. He spoke of the danger of 'the wholesale adoption of the culture of the majority, with the consequent loss of our distinctive identity as a community' and stated that it was 'not necessary to be Gaelic in order to be Irish'. He warned particularly of the danger of 'Gaelicisation' which, 'added to other factors in our environment, would involve our absorption ...'.[196]

The role of the Irish language was a matter of concern for many Protestants. The early years of the Irish language revival had involved a number of Protestants, including Douglas Hyde, son of a Church of Ireland rector and first leader of the Gaelic League, who in 1938 was elected president of Ireland. His election was viewed widely as an important gesture to the Protestant community. Nonetheless, many in that community objected strongly to how the Irish language was made compulsory in schools and for all government positions, public appointments, some professions, such as law, and cultural bodies.[197] At the Church of Ireland general synod in May 1926, the bishop of Limerick, Dr H.V. White, declared: 'We have no wish to discourage the teaching of Irish, but we have every wish to discourage the compulsion placed upon our people'.[198] An editorial in the *Irish Times*, 9 June 1929, described how many Protestants regarded the state policy of compulsory Irish as not only a substantial material burden, but also a 'denial of intellectual freedom'. At the same time, it must be noted that some individuals, such as Donald Caird, a Church of Ireland clergyman and later archbishop of Dublin, and Terence McCaughey, Presbyterian minister and lecturer in Irish at Trinity, were enthusiastic supporters of the Irish language. Founded in 1914, Cumann Gaelach na hEaglaise (the Irish Guild of the Church), sought to encourage Irish among people in the Church of Ireland community.

For many Protestants, however, 'Gaelicisation', which Gregg had raised concern over, involved not just the language, but also much of the new culture which imposed a strong 'Gaelic' and nationalist narrative, and ignored the contribution made by their community in the past and present. For example, enthusiasm for Gaelic games meant that sports such as cricket and rugby, played by the minority, were regarded by many as 'foreign', while the school curriculum disregarded any British heritage.[199] An editorial in the *Irish Times*, 18 June 1934, expressed concern that those who declared pride in Irish involvement in British armed forces in the First World War and before were represented as 'West Britons' and 'anti-Irish', and complained: 'the heirs of their tradition are regarded as aliens in Ireland today'. In the second half of 1934, a series of memorials, signed by over 5000 East Donegal Protestants, was sent to both the Northern Ireland and British governments to ask that they be moved into Northern Ireland, either through a transfer of territory, as envisaged in the boundary commission, or by an exchange of farms. This effort, which came to nothing in the end, was driven partly by the effects of the new trade barriers on the border. It was also the result of concern that certain measures for their protection under the Treaty, such as the right of appeal to the privy council, had been removed, and de Valera's proposed changes over citizenship threatened their status as British subjects. They complained of compulsory Irish, lack of influence on Donegal county council and discrimination over cattle export and fishing licences.[200]

The religious dimension was a significant aspect of the identity of southern Protestants. Church involvement and religious commitment were important for many.[201] At the same time, the small numbers of Protestants in a predominantly Catholic state where nationalism and Catholicism were often closely linked, meant that many felt isolated from mainstream society. In March 1957, Rev. J.C.M. Anderson, moderator of the Presbyterian synod of Armagh and Monaghan, attributed the recent emigration of Presbyterians from Co. Monaghan not only to better economic and educational opportunities elsewhere but also to 'a sense of not being wanted – a type of ideological and spiritual loneliness'.[202] Many Protestants were conscious of a widespread belief that to be Irish one had to be Catholic. The statements and actions of some Catholic churchmen and politicians, as well as the promotion of Catholic social policies and values by the state, served to reinforce this point.

Incidents such as the Fethard-on-Sea boycott case alarmed many Protestants, but the common reaction was to say little publicly, influenced no doubt by their numerically weak minority position. In his account of growing up in Co. Wicklow and Dublin in the 1930s and 1940s, Victor Griffin, later dean of St Patrick's Cathedral, Dublin, has described how 'Protestants felt vulnerable and kept a low profile'. His mother's advice to him was to 'steer clear of religion and politics'.[203] Indeed, it was more common for prominent Protestants to declare, as Erskine Childers did in 1945, despite personal reservations, that southern Protestants fared well in the new state.[204] In 2010, Martin Mansergh, a Protestant Fianna Fáil TD, spoke of how 'post independence ... notwithstanding vestiges of a more idealistic and inclusive republicanism, there was a concerted effort to create a homogeneous 26-county society, in which there would be no challenge to the hegemony of the Church'. In this early period, however, few Protestant spokesmen expressed publicly such views or challenged this hegemony.[205] One notable exception was Hubert Butler, the essayist and antiquarian, who fell into public disfavour in 1952 over criticism of Catholic clerical involvement in events in wartime Yugoslavia. Later, however, he organised a series of annual debates between northern unionists and southern nationalists, and he urged southern Protestants to adopt a higher public profile.[206]

Many members of the Protestant community shared their own particular political perspective. At the start of 1922, an editorial in the *Church of Ireland Gazette* declared that unionists would now give 'their whole-hearted and active support to the Irish Free State', and went on to say: 'they are good Irishmen, but they are also good Britons, loyal to the throne and person of their king, and to the glorious traditions of centuries which are woven round Great Britain's name. They have never been, and never will be republicans'.[207] Legally speaking, of course, links between Britain and the new Irish state survived until 1949. In 1933, in response to an appeal by Eamon de Valera to those who 'had formerly been known as old unionists', an editorial in the *Irish Times* promised to support his new government and then declared: 'The "old unionists", and probably a still greater number of "old nationalists", can have no sympathy with an independence which would discard the British empire'.[208] Some did adopt a more republican stance. Countess Constance Markevicz, an Easter Rising veteran and Fianna Fáil TD, came originally from a Protestant and unionist background. More typical of her family and community, however, were her two nephews who are commemorated in a memorial window in Lissadell church, Co. Sligo. Neither lies buried in his native Sligo. They were Sub-Lieutenant Brian Gore-Booth, RN, who drowned when his ship, HMS Exmouth, was sunk during convoy duty in the Atlantic in 1940, and Lieutenant Hugh Gore-Booth of the Royal Irish Fusiliers, who died in action on the island of Leros in the Aegean Sea in 1943.[209] Most members of the Protestant community accepted that the government's policy of neutrality during the Second World War was unavoidable. At the same time, many volunteered to serve with British and allied forces.[210] Of course, we should note that this was also true about very many Catholics.[211]

The decision of the inter-party government in 1948 to break the last links with the British crown and commonwealth brought important change in the political attitudes of most members of the southern Protestant community. In Dublin on 10 May 1949, at the first general synod of the Church of Ireland after the formal declaration of a republic at Easter 1949, the Church of Ireland primate, Dr John Gregg, described the sadness of many at this decision, but declared that 'above all, there must be reality', which meant they must adapt 'what we know as the state prayers, to the republican form of government in this part of the land'.[212] An *Irish Times* editorial on 14 May 1949 declared that 'facts ... must be faced' and 'Irish Protestants must make up their minds that they can have only one political allegiance: they must be unconditionally loyal to the republic'. Most southern Protestants accepted these changes and adjusted accordingly. Subsequent years witnessed the disappearance of any sense of a British dimension as part of their identity, although in the border counties such attitudes remained important, perhaps because of the close proximity of Northern Ireland and because of how from the early 1930s southern Orangemen were unable to hold their annual demonstrations in the south, except for Rossnowlagh, Co. Donegal.[213]

Besides such political change in identity, we can witness new efforts among members of the Protestant community to become more involved in the broader society. Individuals, such as the writer Hubert Butler and W.B. Stanford, who was elected a Trinity senator in 1951, urged that Protestants should adopt a higher public profile, as did the columns of the Church of Ireland journal, *Focus*.[214] In January 1957, after his enthronement as the new Church of Ireland archbishop of Dublin, Dr George Otto Simms, a fluent Irish speaker, spoke both of the isolation of his church members and a new determination to become involved. He said: 'It is all too easy for a church to feel fearful, and to live a life apart from public and civic concerns'. He continued: 'After today let us remind ourselves that our church allegiance, or beliefs, and our way of worship will not hinder, but will rather help, anything we can contribute in public service, in the field of education, in matters cultural and communal'.[215] In his history of the Church of Ireland Alan Acheson has commented how, after 1949, 'tacit acceptance of the state gave way to positive support, and southern church members, particularly in the cities, became more confident in their citizenship'.[216]

As regards the Catholic community in Northern Ireland in this period, Marianne Elliott has described how 'after partition northern Catholic society turned in on itself and, like the Protestant minority in the south, developed a parallel universe to the majority one'.[217] In the 1990s Cardinal Cahal Daly recalled that in his early days in the 1930s he thought of the state of Northern Ireland as 'something other, separate, not our state'.[218] This led to what has been described as a 'state within a state'.[219] The Catholic church offered an effective organisation that provided not only local churches and parishes, but also schools, church societies, such as the St Vincent de Paul Society, and a hospital, the Mater Infirmorium, in Belfast. The Catholic and nationalist community was served by a number of weekly regional newspapers, as well as the daily Belfast *Irish News*, with its editorial banner, *Pro fide et patria*. The most important sporting organisation was the Gaelic Athletic Association, which was run on a parish, county and all-Ireland basis. The Ancient

Order of Hibernians continued to provide a nationalist and Catholic fraternal organisation for many, especially in rural parts. People in the north regarded themselves as Irish Catholics, or, preferably, Irish. For many, the Irish language was viewed not just as an important cultural asset, but as evidence of a separate identity. Recalling his schooling in Newry in the 1930s Denis Donoghue described how 'learning Irish ... was a sign that one's kingdom was not of the Protestant, unionist world: we lived elsewhere'.[220] Lack of Irish history on the school curriculum was a matter of concern for nationalist MPs.[221]

For many northern Catholics, their religion was not only an important part of their daily lives, but it served to bolster their sense of national identity. Events such as the Eucharistic Congress in 1932 helped to provide 'all-Ireland demonstrations of Catholic power'.[222] When the Catholic Truth Society of Ireland conference met in Belfast in 1934, the editorial in the *Irish News* declared: 'North and south are forever tied by the unbreakable bonds of their common faith, which is their proudest heritage. The ceremonies which will take place in Belfast tomorrow ... will have a northern setting ... but the glory will belong to the Catholic Irish nation ...'.[223] In addition, Catholics were alienated from the Northern Ireland state by the way in which the state and government were often associated with Protestantism and Orangeism. From the 1930s concern was also strongly expressed by leading Catholic spokesmen that all Catholics were being labelled as 'disloyalists' by Sir Basil Brooke and others and this was treated as a reason why they should be discriminated against in employment and denied other political and educational rights. Nationalist spokesmen refused to accept the defending argument that the term 'disloyalist' was used purely in a political sense, but believed, as nationalist MP J.J. McCarroll asserted in 1934, that it was 'directed absolutely and entirely against our people because of their faith'.[224] An *Irish News* editorial, in August 1935, acknowledged that the political goal of northern Catholics was a united Ireland, but stated that the great majority sought this end by constitutional means, and 'while they abide by the rules, no one is entitled to reproach them with disloyalty, even to "Ulster"'.[225]

Most members of the Catholic community shared a general nationalist political outlook, although there were differences in emphasis between nationalist and republican perspectives, often over matters such as abstention or recognition of the state and state institutions. An editorial in the Co. Tyrone paper, the *Ulster Herald*, 25 June 1921 declared: 'No matter how they [the unionists] ... fulminate and demonstrate, the nationalists of Ulster are resolved to march steadily and unitedly along the high road of allegiance to Irish nationhood'.[226] The basic nationalist and republican argument was that the results of the 1918 general election had served to justify self-determination for all of Ireland and, therefore, partition was inherently wrong. Another argument, favoured by those in the west but not in the east, was that Counties Fermanagh and Tyrone, with their Catholic majority populations, should be moved to the southern state.

In 1943 J.J. Campbell, under the pseudonym, Ultach, wrote a highly critical article on the treatment of Catholics in Northern Ireland in the *Capuchin Annual*, which was reprinted as a book with comments by many public and church figures, mostly from nationalist or republican backgrounds. Campbell did not blame partition as such for their treatment which he saw as a 'necessary part of the administration'. Despite Campbell's approach, however, most of the writers insisted that partition was the main problem and its abolition the only answer. The influential Dr Daniel Mageean, Catholic bishop of Down and Connor, wrote: 'Remember this, the very existence of the six counties parliament is intensely resented by more than 400,000 people. Even were its regime one of justice and equality, of liberty and fair play – and it is not – we should still oppose the dismemberment of our fatherland.' He continued: 'For we are Irish and until we are united with our brethren of the rest of Ireland, not only are we deprived of our rights as Irishmen but the historic Irish nation, unnaturally divisioned, is robbed of its glory and greatness. Partition is an evil which only its removal can remedy'.[227]

Divisions within the Catholic and nationalist community over the question of recognition of and involvement in the northern state were highlighted again in late 1945. Controversy arose because T.J. Campbell, the nationalist leader, was appointed as a county court judge and also because the nationalist MP, Cahir Healy, pledged support to the government to withhold some of its imperial contribution to the London exchequer in order to improve local living conditions. In the *Derry Journal*, Campbell was criticised because he had accepted a 'Stormont judgeship' and Healy was attacked because he was accused of seeking to 'bolster up Stormont's partition policy by British grants'.[228] This internal dissension was eventually overcome, and nationalist energies were channelled into the new Anti-Partition League with its aim of seeking outside help to end partition. The 1950s saw the rise of support for republicans, who rejected completely the northern state, and an IRA campaign lasting from 1956 to 1962.

The chief emphasis for both nationalists and republicans remained the ending of partition. This position also meant opposition to some early efforts at north–south official co-operation. In the early 1950s Eddie McAteer, chairman of the Anti-Partition League, and his Derry colleagues, were critical of what they called the 'fraternisation policy' of the Dublin government and believed that co-operation in matters such as electricity was 'helping partition to work'.[229] They even boycotted a lunch in Derry for officials of the republic's Electricity Supply Board to meet their Northern Ireland counterparts.[230] During 1955 two Irish government representatives visited the north to consult various nationalist groups and spokesmen to encourage links between them and the Dublin government. They reported that such a policy of co-operation had strong support, the only exception being the 'Sinn Féin IRA group which, in any event, automatically disapproves of all actions of the Irish government in this matter'. Despite this favourable reception, however, they also noted that some nationalists 'may never publicly welcome various forms of economic co-operation between the six and twenty-six counties on the official plane, because they are afraid of being accused of collaborationism'.[231]

The late 1950s witnessed the beginning of a new approach among members of the Catholic and nationalist community to their situation, but existing attitudes, reflecting restrictive ideas of identity, proved too dominant to allow significant change. After the 1958 general election to the Northern Ireland parliament, it seemed for a time that the nationalists might become the official opposition in the Northern Ireland parliament. The new nationalist leader, Joseph Stewart, MP, proposed such a policy but was strongly opposed by others, including Roderick O'Connor, MP, who told Stewart that he would 'go to his grave like T.J. Campbell [who had accepted a judgeship], a discredited nationalist, and his children would bear the stigma of his actions to their dying day'.[232] The proposal was rejected. In August 1958 the summer school of the Catholic Social Study Conference was held at St McNissi's College, Garron Tower, Carnlough, Co. Antrim. The theme of the conference was 'The citizen and the community'. Speakers urged that Catholics should accept the existing constitutional arrangements and seek to participate more in public affairs. In his address, G.B. Newe, a Catholic and secretary of the Northern Ireland Council of Social Services, stated that they had a duty to 'co-operate with the *de facto* authority that controls ... life and welfare'.[233] He declared that the attitude of Catholics 'towards the government of Northern Ireland over the past 30 years has been, generally speaking, anything but in keeping with the precept of charity, or, indeed, with many other precepts governing our duties and responsibilities as Catholic citizens. It may be argued that Catholics, as such, have had much provocation, but so have non-Catholics'. Newe went on to question the 'suggestion that the ending of partition is the most important political objective in Ireland today, and that only he who works assiduously, by any and every means, to that end is a true patriot'.[234]

Most of the nationalist reaction to this conference was very hostile. The *Irish News* condemned it as giving a 'false picture' of the Catholic community, and various nationalist MPs denounced the arguments put forward at Garron Tower. In response to the conference, Eddie McAteer, nationalist MP for Foyle, declared, with mixed historical allusions, that: 'Dermot McMurrough was a co-operator, those who "took the soup" would be high on the list of co-operators'.[235] The election of Sean Lemass in 1959 as taoiseach and the announcement of his intention to seek economic co-operation with the Northern Ireland government raised additional concerns among some leading nationalists about 'recognition' of Northern Ireland and partition. At a St Patrick's Day parade in Dungannon in March 1960, nationalist spokesmen rejected 'the path of compromise'. The nationalist party leader, Joseph Stewart, denounced as 'utterly unacceptable' the suggestion that the nationalist minority should acquiesce in the 'constitutional rights' of the 'six county system'. Cahir Healy, MP, stated that any declaration of accepting the 'present partition position' would be 'tantamount to saying they were traitors to their country'.[236]

Final observations

How do we rate the fortunes and treatment of these two minorities over this period? Both faced mixed social and economic conditions, the effects of which were more nuanced than has been usually understood. Also, both experienced key differences in identity with their dominant groups which related to national political issues as well as to religious and cultural matters. In November 1962, Charles J. Haughey, TD and Irish justice minister, addressed a student audience at Queen's University Belfast on the subject of 'the Protestant minority in a united Ireland'. He claimed that a united Ireland would correspond to what is now the republic of Ireland, adding that it would be 'difficult to conceive of a structure in which individual liberty and religious freedom would be more adequately safeguarded'. He referred to the good treatment of southern Protestants. 'What is really important' he declared, 'is not that there is no unfair treatment of minorities – but the fact that there couldn't be. There is no longer any argument about it'.[237]

It was true that southern Protestants enjoyed freedom of worship, held important positions in business and commerce and were well represented among those who owned the larger farms. What was also true, however, was that their numbers had dropped considerably, not only in the years 1911–26, but in the following decades also. In part, their difficulty was that they experienced discrimination in some areas, but, more importantly, they were marginalised in a society where the dominant ethos was Catholic, Gaelic and republican. Born into Protestant working-class Dublin in the 1920s, and later provost of Trinity, William Watts recounted how 'most Protestants kept their heads down but it was easy to feel that we were not seen as really belonging in the country'.[238] After 1921, southern Irish Protestants accepted the new state and government, but retained their own Irish identity with its British dimension, while after 1949 most accepted the new exclusive republican identity. The 1950s saw the beginning of additional efforts among this minority community to integrate into the broader society. The outcome of such actions, of course, would depend not just on their own efforts but on the response of the majority section.

At Westminster in late March 1962, a debate took place on Northern Ireland affairs. Henry Clarke, MP for Co. Londonderry, declared: 'In my opinion, the north of Ireland is completely guiltless in this matter of discrimination. In fact, those concerned have fallen over backwards to help [the minority]'. He also stated: 'It is remarkable that the minority in Northern Ireland is steadily increasing and has every appearance of being a healthy community. On the other hand, the minority in Southern Ireland ... has steadily decreased'.[239] It was correct that the numbers of northern Catholics and nationalists had grown, proportionally more than any other community in Ireland, north or south, that they enjoyed freedom of worship and that their total allocation of public housing was fair in relation to their percentage of the population. At the same time, they faced discrimination in employment, unfair electoral arrangements and unjust public housing allocation in some areas.

More significantly, however, members of the Catholic and nationalist community were peripheral to a society that was Protestant, unionist and British/Ulster in ethos. At the opening of the 1958 Garron Tower social study conference, the headmaster, Father William Tumelty, had described how the 'attitude on the part of the majority has produced in us a feeling of frustration, in that we are excluded from taking any effective part in the affairs of the community at large' and noted that 'the inclination is to isolate ourselves in self-defence'.[240] At the same time, unlike southern Protestants, most members of the northern Catholic and nationalist community had afforded limited or no acceptance of the northern state. This conference raised key questions about their role in the public life of Northern Ireland. Following decades would involve members of this community not only challenging the dominant unionist ethos, but also redefining their position within Northern Ireland.

3
Remembering and forgetting: commemorations and identity, 1921–60

Public holidays and commemorations of important anniversaries often reflect the values, secular or religious, of a society. Christmas Day and Easter, for example, have special Christian significance in many countries of the world. May Day is also reserved as a holiday in honour of workers in a number of countries. Some public holidays, however, are specific to particular countries, such as Bastille Day on 14 July in France and Independence Day on 4 July in the United States of America, and often refer to events of significance in the history of these countries. Indeed, most countries mark by way of annual commemoration the anniversaries of important episodes, events or people in their history. Whether celebrating the early or recent history of a society, these occasions often help to engender a sense of common purpose and identity, even though there may be differences of opinion about the exact significance of the events being celebrated. In Ireland, however, while Christmas Day and Easter have been celebrated by the vast bulk of the population, this has not been the case with some of the other principal public holidays and acts of annual commemoration which have been associated strongly with particular communities. A study of these commemorations can help provide us with an insight into different and changing identities.

This chapter looks at how four public holidays or annual commemorative events have been marked in some form or other in both political states in Ireland during the period, 1921–60. The special dates on which these events or persons are recalled are as follows: 17 March, when St Patrick, Ireland's patron saint, is remembered; Easter (usually Easter Sunday), when the Easter Rising led by republicans in Dublin in 1916 is commemorated; 12 July, when the Battle of the Boyne of 1690 that saw the Protestant King William defeat the Catholic King James, is celebrated; 11 November, or a Sunday nearest to that date, when those who died in the British forces during two world wars are remembered. Two of these dates mark an historical episode or personality of antiquity, while the other two commemorate more recent historical events. We explore what these commemorations tell us about people's identity and sense of history and how these changed over this period. Particular attention is paid to the way in which the respective governments viewed the four commemorations, to the way in which the commemorations were claimed by various groups and to how dominant groups within each state viewed minority groups and opinions. Two of the events commemorated, the Battle of the Boyne and the Easter Rising, are single identity concerns relating to unionists and nationalists/republicans, respectively. St Patrick's Day and Armistice Day/Remembrance Sunday, however, were both originally part of widespread shared identity in Ireland but this ceased to be the case and each became monopolised very largely by one or the other side.

St Patrick's Day

In the early twentieth century St Patrick's Day was celebrated in many parts of Ireland. All the main churches regarded St Patrick as the patron saint of Ireland. Many church and cathedral buildings of both the Catholic church and the Church of Ireland are named in his honour. In 1903 a bill was introduced at Westminster to make St Patrick's Day a bank holiday and it quickly passed into law with the support of all the MPs from Ireland – an outcome which, as the *Belfast News Letter* commented, was 'rare good fortune' for an Irish bill.[1] That same year the paper also remarked: 'The anniversary helps to create a spirit of mutual tolerance and good will amongst Irishmen and this year perhaps the spirit is more evident than before'.[2] The rise in political controversy over the next decade did not dent this wide support for St Patrick's Day. On 18 March 1914, an editorial of the Belfast *Northern Whig* noted: 'Irishmen, whatever their creed or politics have an affectionate regard for St Patrick's day and yesterday the shamrock was worn in honour of the festival by fully nine tenths of the population of the country'. After 1921, however, important differences would emerge between north and south in how St Patrick's Day was celebrated.

In the new Irish Free State St Patrick's Day quickly took on special significance. In 1922 it was made a general holiday and from 1925, thanks to the Irish Free State licensing act, all public houses were closed on that day. In Dublin, an annual army parade now replaced the processions organised previously by the lord lieutenant and lord mayor. Throughout the country there were also parades, often involving army marches to church for mass. Dances, sporting activities, theatrical events and excursions were run on the day. The Irish language was specially promoted, frequently with events organised by the Gaelic League. In 1926 the southern premier W.T. Cosgrave made the first official radio broadcast on St Patrick's Day. He called for mutual understanding and harmony and declared: 'The destinies of the country, north and south, are now in the hands of Irishmen, and the responsibility for success or failure will rest with ourselves. If we are to succeed there must be a brotherly toleration of each other's ideas as to how our ambition may be realised, and a brotherly co-operation in every effort towards its realisation'.[3] In his 1930 St Patrick's Day's speech Cosgrave declared that 'as we have been Irish and Roman, so it will remain', but he took care to preface his statement with the remarks that he was speaking for the majority of people in the state.[4] In 1931 in a St Patrick's Day broadcast to the Irish in America, and reported in the Irish press, Cosgrave again sought to make a reconciliatory gesture 'whatever be your creed in religion or politics, you are of the same blood – the healing process must go on'.[5]

With the accession to power of Eamon de Valera and Fianna Fáil in 1932, however, St Patrick's Day took on added importance. Links between church and state were stressed publicly with the annual procession on St Patrick's Day of de Valera and his executive council, complete with a cavalry troop, to the Dublin pro-cathedral for mass.[6] Marking the anniversary of St Patrick's arrival in Ireland, the Patrician Year of 1932, which included the Eucharistic Congress, gave an opportunity for large demonstrations, with considerable official involvement, emphasising connections between Ireland and Rome.[7] This religious aspect was taken up again by de Valera in his St Patrick's Day broadcast of 1935 in which he reminded people that Ireland had been a Christian and Catholic nation since St Patrick's time: 'She remains a Catholic nation' he declared.[8] De Valera now used the St Patrick's Day broadcasts, which were transmitted to the USA and Australia, to launch vigorous attacks on the British government and partition. These speeches reached a peak in 1939 when de Valera broadcast on St Patrick's Day from Rome where he had attended the inauguration of Pope Pius XII. He declared how he had made a pledge beside the grave of Hugh O'Neill that he would never rest until 'that land which the Almighty so clearly designed as one shall belong undivided to the Irish people'. He urged his listeners to do likewise.[9] At the same time, however, the links between Catholicism and Irish identity as expressed on St Patrick's Day were not absolute. In 1939 too, the Protestant president of Ireland, Douglas Hyde, attended a St Patrick's Day service in the Church of Ireland cathedral of St Patrick's in Dublin.[10]

During the Second World War celebrations on St Patrick's Day were restrained, although de Valera continued to make his annual broadcast. In 1943 he spoke of the restoration of the national territory and the national language as the greatest of the state's uncompleted tasks. He also talked of his dream of a land 'whose fields and villages would be joyous with the sounds of industry, the romping of sturdy children, the contests of athletic youths and the laughter of comely maidens'.[11] After the war St Patrick's Day became a major national holiday once again. In 1950 the military parade in Dublin was replaced by a trade and industries parade. In their St Patrick's Day speeches in the1950s, heads of government, Eamon de Valera and J.A. Costello, continued to use the event to make strong denunciations of partition. In his St Patrick's Day broadcast in 1950 Costello declared that 'our country is divided by foreign interference'.[12] By the 1950s, government ministers and spokesmen, such as Sean MacEntee, were also making public speeches on the day at a range of venues in Britain and the USA, usually concentrating on attacking partition.[13] In 1955 a rare discordant note was struck by Bishop Cornelius Lucy of Cork when in his St Patrick's Day address he suggested that emigration was a greater evil than partition.[14] Irish leaders in their speeches continued to emphasise links between Ireland and Rome. By the mid-1950s it was common for either the president or the taoiseach to be in Rome on St Patrick's Day. The 1961 Patrician celebrations marked a high point in this religious aspect of the festival. It began with the arrival on 13 March of a papal legate, Cardinal MacIntyre, who, in the words of the *Capuchin Annual*, was 'welcomed with the protocol reception given only to a head of state'. This included a welcome at the airport from the taoiseach and a full military guard.[15]

In Northern Ireland after 1921, St Patrick's Day was still observed, but in a more understated way than in the south. During the 1920s and 1930s the shamrock continued to be worn widely and the day remained a bank holiday when banks, government and municipal offices and schools were closed, although most shops and factories seem to have been unaffected.[16] In Catholic churches St Patrick's Day was an important feast day that was well attended. The Ancient Order of Hibernians continued to organise demonstrations on this date and nationalist politicians often used the occasion to make speeches. From 1925 the BBC in Northern Ireland commenced an annual series of special broadcasts on St Patrick's Day.[17] The Patrician Year of 1932 was marked by all the churches. At Saul, the site of St Patrick's first church, the Church of Ireland built a new church while the Catholic church erected a statue of St Patrick on a nearby hill top. Each of the main denominations took advantage of the occasion to reaffirm its belief that St Patrick belonged exclusively to its tradition.[18]

Sporting activities took place on St Patrick's Day, including the Ulster schools rugby and Gaelic football cup finals, and special theatrical events, dances and dinners were well attended in the 1920s and 1930s. On 18 March 1939 the *Belfast News Letter* reported that 'in Belfast and all over the province Ulster folk said goodbye to St Patrick's Day with dances and other entertainments'. Special ceremonies of the trooping of the colour and presentation of the shamrock to Irish regiments remained a tradition (begun by Queen Victoria at the end of her reign). There was, however, no official involvement in or recognition of St Patrick's Day, apart from a number of dinners or dances on the day, organised by the Duke of Abercorn as governor of Northern Ireland.[19] On the unionist and government side there was no attempt to hold parades or make speeches on 17 March. The speeches of southern politicians on the day denouncing partition or declaring Ireland's attachment to Rome were reported regularly in the northern press and sometimes criticised in editorials but there was no attempt by the government in this period to respond.

After the Second World War banks and government offices continued to close on St Patrick's Day, while the wearing of the shamrock remained popular and the tradition of presenting it to Irish regiments abroad continued. Catholic churches still observed it as a special feast day and the Ancient Order of Hibernians organised parades and demonstrations as before. In the late 1940s and early 1950s the Northern Ireland premier, Lord Brookeborough, used the occasion of St Patrick's Day to issue public addresses to Ulster people abroad, while members of his cabinet spoke at dinners organised by Ulster associations in Great Britain.[20] By the mid-1950s, however, these attempts to match the political use made of St Patrick's Day by the southern government had mostly ceased. In the late 1950s a government information officer urged the Northern Ireland cabinet that it might be wise to 'quietly forget' St Patrick's Day and abolish it as a bank holiday.[21] The suggestion was rejected, but it is clear from newspaper reports in the 1950s that for many people St Patrick's Day was 'business as usual'. Many schools dropped it as a holiday and shops and businesses remained open.[22] Correspondents in the unionist press denounced the political overtones of the day in the south and elsewhere. One letter on 17 March 1961 in the *Belfast News Letter* stated that 'the day is now chiefly memorable to the average Ulsterman as the day on which repeated threats against his stand for constitutional liberty are pronounced in the republic and on which Ulster's position is vilified throughout the English speaking world'.[23]

Nonetheless, it should be noted that there were some in unionist and Protestant church circles who believed that more attention should be given to the event. From the mid-1950s the editorial in the *Belfast Telegraph* often urged that the day should be a full public holiday, a request backed by the Church of Ireland diocesan synod of Down and Dromore.[24] In 1961 a resolution of the Young Unionists' Conference deplored the apathy in Northern Ireland towards St Patrick's Day.[25] We may note that Dr Ian Paisley chose to open his first Free Presbyterian church at Crossgar, Co. Down, on St Patrick's Day, 1951. In the 1950s the Church of Ireland inaugurated an annual St Patrick's Day pilgrimage and special service at Downpatrick and Saul, which was well attended. Such events were still strongly limited by denominational barriers although small elements of change were occurring. In 1956 the nationalist members of Downpatrick council refused an invitation to participate in a joint wreath-laying ceremony at what was believed to be St Patrick's grave, on the grounds that the Catholic church 'had arranged adequate celebrations for the Feast and they could not add anything to them'. Eight years later, however, when the Archbishop of Canterbury was the special guest at the St Patrick's Day service at the Church of Ireland cathedral in Downpatrick, nationalist councillors turned up to greet the archbishop at the entrance to the cathedral, although they felt unable to enter the building.[26]

Armistice Day/Remembrance Sunday

During the First World War some 200,000 men (of whom it is reckoned at least three-fifths were Catholic) volunteered from Ireland for service in the British armed forces.[27] The total Irish death toll has been put at around 50,000. It has been calculated that in the Second World War 52,147 British service personnel were from Northern Ireland. The Irish state was neutral during the Second World War, but it is reckoned that 78,826 individuals from the south served in the British armed services. Of the war dead, 2241 were from the north and 2302 from the south.[28] During the war some 4800 members of the Irish armed services are estimated to have deserted or left legally to join British forces.[29] After 1945, the annual act of commemoration of the war dead changed from Armistice Day on 11 November to Remembrance Sunday on the Sunday nearest 11 November. The first Armistice Day on 11 November 1919 was marked throughout Ireland. Thereafter, significant differences would emerge in how this occasion was marked, north and south.

The day after Armistice Day, 1919 the *Irish News* reported how: 'the two minute pause was generally observed in Belfast yesterday ... on the lines suggested by the King, all work in the shops and factories and all traffic in the streets being stopped at 11 o'clock for the space of two minutes'. Services were held in churches of all denominations. From the early 1920s the event was commemorated not only with a two-minute silence and church services, but also with parades to new war memorials. There is evidence that in the early days there were efforts to keep these events open to all sections of the community. At the unveiling of the Enniskillen war memorial in 1922, for example, Protestant and Catholic war orphans laid wreaths.[30] At a ceremony in Ballymena on 11 November 1924 Major General Sir Oliver Nugent, who had commanded the 36th (Ulster) division at the Somme, declared that 'the service given by the Ulstermen in the war was not confined to one creed or one denomination; it was given by Ulstermen of all denominations and all classes'.[31] The ceremony for the unveiling of the Portadown war memorial in 1924 involved the Catholic parish priest along with the other clergy, and wreaths were laid by representatives of the Orange Order and the Ancient Order of Hibernians.[32] On 12 November 1924 the *Irish News* reported commemorations in both Northern Ireland and the Irish Free State with the headline 'Brotherhood of bereavement – north and south pause to salute the dead'.

In spite of these comments and inclusive incidents, however, the Armistice Day commemorations in Northern Ireland became largely linked with unionism. To some extent this arose because of a reluctance in certain Catholic and nationalist quarters to acknowledge the Catholic role in the war. For example, Cardinal Patrick O'Donnell, Catholic archbishop of Armagh, refused to attend the unveiling of the County Armagh war memorial in 1926.[33] More importantly, many unionists came to see Armistice Day as an occasion for the affirmation of their own sense of Ulster or British identity. As Keith Jeffery has written: 'For them the blood sacrifice of the Somme was equal and opposite to that of Easter 1916.'[34] At the unveiling of Coleraine war memorial in 1922 Sir James Craig declared that 'those who passed away have left behind a great message to all of them to stand firm, and to give away none of Ulster's soil'.[35] Only Protestant clergy attended the unveiling of the cenotaph at the Belfast City Hall in 1929 and there were no official representatives from the 16th (Irish) Division in which Belfast Catholics had tended to serve.[36]

The Northern Ireland government played no direct role in organising events on Armistice Day and speeches were rarely made on the occasion. Nonetheless, the large parades and well-attended services on the day with army and police involved were seen by many not only as an expression of grief but also as a mark of the British link among the unionist community. It would be wrong, however, to write off entirely Catholic and nationalist participation in the Armistice Day commemorations. Catholic ex-servicemen continued to mark the occasion in some places. In Newry in the 1930s on Armistice Day ex-servicemen held a parade before making their way to their respective Catholic and Protestant churches for memorial services.[37] During the 1930s Armistice Day wreaths were laid in Belfast for the men of the 16th (Irish) Division and in Derry for the 'Irish Catholic officers and men who fell in the great war', while at Portadown a wreath was laid for the soldiers of the Connaught Rangers, in which Portadown Catholics had served.[38]

After the Second World War, names of many of those who had served or died in the war were added to existing memorials. Parades and services continued as they had done on Armistice Day, and they remained largely the concern of the Protestant and unionist community. While the government had no formal involvement in these events it was quite common for the prime minister or a cabinet minister to take the salute of ex-servicemen on these occasions. There is little evidence of participation by Catholic clergy in public ceremonies at cenotaphs or at council services. At the same time we should note that in some places, such as Dungannon, Newry and Sion Mills, parades of Catholic and Protestant ex-servicemen continued to take place as they had done in the 1930s.[39] The degree of polarisation between the two communities over this commemoration is revealed starkly in a comparison of coverage of these events in Belfast nationalist and unionist papers in the mid-1950s. In 1955 and 1956 the unionist papers, the *Belfast News Letter* and the *Northern Whig*, gave extensive coverage to Remembrance Day in various places in Northern Ireland as well as in London, while the nationalist paper, the *Irish News*, ignored the occasion and carried not a single report on any event connected with the commemoration.[40]

On the first Armistice Day on 11 November 1919, in line with a papal decree, mass was held at all Catholic churches in Ireland to mark the occasion.[41] A two-minute silence at 11 o'clock was observed widely in the south. The *Irish Times*, 12 November 1919, described how: 'The two minutes silence in recognition of the first anniversary of Armistice Day proved a markedly impressive event in Dublin yesterday. When the eleventh hour of the eleventh day of the eleventh month was chimed, a calm and stillness pervaded the entire city that was manifestation of the feelings of the people in regard to the solemnity of the occasion'. Subsequently, with the war of independence and the setting up of the new Irish Free State, commemoration of this event became very controversial. As Jane Leonard has commented: 'division rather than dignity surrounded the commemoration of the war in Ireland'.[42] The civil unrest of the early 1920s restricted public expressions of commemoration. From 1923 onwards, however, Armistice Day was marked not just by a two-minute silence but also by parades and assemblies of ex-servicemen and their friends and families, which were held in Dublin and in other parts of Ireland. Such events were organised by several ex-servicemen's organisations until they were eventually brought together under the British Legion in 1925. War memorials were erected in many places and the poppy was sold widely.[43]

Official attitudes were ambivalent but generally tolerant in the 1920s. Conscious of nationalist and republican susceptibilities, members of the Irish Free State government looked askance at ideas to build a large war memorial in central Dublin, and insisted that it be erected at the outskirts at Islandbridge.[44] At the same time, conscious of the many Irish people who had died during the war, including members of their own families, the government sent representatives to the wreath-laying ceremonies in Dublin and London. The message on the wreath laid by Colonel Maurice Moore, the Irish government representative, at the temporary cenotaph cross in College Green in Dublin on 11 November 1924 read: 'This wreath is placed here by the Free State government to commemorate all the brave men who fell on the field of battle.'[45] In 1923 W.T. Cosgrave and some cabinet colleagues attended an Armistice Day mass in Cork.[46]

Early Armistice Day commemorations in Dublin met with a certain amount of opposition, expressed in actions such as the snatching of poppies. From the mid-1920s, however, the intensity of this opposition grew, with various republican groups organising anti-Armistice Day rallies to protest against 'the flagrant display of British imperialism disguised as Armistice celebrations' and with physical attacks being made on some of the parades.[47] In 1926 this led to the main ceremony being moved from the centre of Dublin to Phoenix Park. De Valera spoke at one of the anti-Armistice Day rallies in 1930 and the formation of a Fianna Fáil government in 1932 led to a further downgrading of the commemorations. Official representatives were withdrawn from the principal wreath-laying ceremony in Dublin from November 1932, although the Irish government continued to be represented at the cenotaph in London until 1936. Permits for the sale of poppies, previously allowed for several days in the week before 11 November, were now reduced to one day only.[48] Those taking part in the annual parade to Phoenix Park in Dublin were prohibited from carrying Union Jacks or British Legion flags featuring a Union Jack. Work on the national war memorial park at Islandbridge was completed and handed over to the government in early 1937, but the official opening was put off a number of times by de Valera, until the outbreak of the Second World War led to its indefinite postponement.[49] The official opening of the magnificent memorial occurred only in 1988 and without the direct involvement of the Fianna Fáil government, although at a later ceremony in 1994, Bertie Ahern, then minister of finance, declared the work on the memorial to be finished.

Armistice ceremonies were held at Phoenix Park in 1939 and at Islandbridge in 1940, although without parades.[50] Thereafter, public demonstrations in Dublin relating to this event were banned until after the war. Indeed the government maintained its ban in November 1945, after the end of the war, because it did not want to see any public demonstration of Irish involvement in the allied war effort. Of course, many thousands of men and women went from the 26 counties of Ireland, along with many other Irish people already living in Great Britain, to serve in British armed forces during the war.[51] The Irish government, however, continued to ignore this matter. As elsewhere, Armistice Day was replaced by Remembrance Sunday, on the Sunday closest to 11 November, and the event was marked by a parade of ex-servicemen in Dublin from Smithfield Market along North Quays to Islandbridge and by discreet wreath-laying ceremonies in other centres.[52] These parades and other commemorative events continued during the 1950s, but for many of those involved, as declining numbers attending Remembrance Day and veterans' memories showed, there was a clear sense that they had become marginalised and excluded from the new Irish identity and sense of history that had now become dominant.[53]

Easter commemorations of 1916 Rising

Annual commemoration of the Dublin Rising of Easter 1916 proved a very contentious issue in the new Irish state, reflecting some of the political divisions that had emerged over the Anglo-Irish Treaty and also personal concerns about any such commemorative event.[54] During the commemorations at Easter 1922, prominent politicians from both the pro-treaty and anti-treaty sides addressed large crowds in various places, but, owing to the civil war, the event was not marked publicly the following year. On Easter Monday 1924 the government organised a ceremony at Arbour Hill (burial place of the executed rebels) for a specially invited list of guests, including politicians, soldiers and relatives of the deceased.[55] Few relatives of the deceased turned up, however, and in this and following years the event was marred by disputes about who should be invited. Also in 1924 republicans organised a march through Dublin to Glasnevin cemetery for the laying of wreaths on a republican plot. Subsequently, large parades to Glasnevin were organised and attended each Easter by republican groups, including Sinn Féin and (after 1927) Fianna Fáil. The Cumann na nGaedheal government did not participate in these marches, although there was some official remembrance of the Easter Rising in 1926 and after, in the form of broadcasts on the subject on the new Radio Eireann.

When de Valera came to power in 1932, the situation did not change greatly. In Dublin there were two parades, the first organised by the semi-official National Commemoration Committee and attended by de Valera and members of Fianna Fáil, which marched to Arbour Hill, and the second by other republican groups, including the IRA, which marched to Glasnevin.[56] The Fianna Fáil government changed the guest list to the Arbour Hill ceremony but also ran into difficulties with relatives of the deceased about who should be present.[57] In 1935 there was a large Irish army parade on Easter Sunday to the General Post Office where a statue of Cuchulainn was unveiled and speeches were made by government ministers. This statue, chosen as symbolic of the 1916 Rising, had in fact been sculpted between 1910 and 1911 and purchased much later for this purpose.[58] The twentieth anniversary of the Dublin Rising saw some additional measures of commemoration, in particular, radio programmes during Easter week on Radio Eireann. The event continued to be commemorated in Dublin principally by the two rival marches to Arbour Hill and Glasnevin. Outside Dublin the 1916 Rising was commemorated at Eastertime by competing republican groups. For example, in Cork the Old IRA Men's Association marched each Easter to several monuments and graves of their dead comrades.[59]

On the twentieth-fifth anniversary of the Easter Rising in 1941, major celebrations were held in Dublin. On Easter Sunday a military parade, described as 'the largest and most spectacular military parade the city has seen', with 10,000 from other groups, took place in Dublin. A report in the *Irish Independent* noted: 'the gay clatter of regimental bands playing unceasingly, armoured cars nozzling by to a marching version of the Londonderry air [sic]: Ireland 1941 – soldiers in field green, regiments of nurses in black stockings and white gloves – an entire nation prepared'.[60] There were speeches at the General Post Office (GPO) from President

Douglas Hyde and members of the government. De Valera also made a broadcast from the GPO urging improvements in the armed forces and vigilance in preserving Ireland's independence. For the remainder of the war public celebrations were severely limited. After 1945 rival parades recommenced in Dublin, with no special government involvement, apart from the appearance of Fianna Fáil ministers at Arbour Hill. In 1949, no doubt for symbolic reasons, the official inauguration of the Irish Republic occurred at one minute past midnight on Easter Monday. Only from 1954 did a military parade at the GPO in Dublin at Easter become an annual event. It was part of the An Tóstal celebrations of that year but was continued in following years.[61] The fortieth anniversary of the rising was celebrated extensively in 1956. The president, Sean T. O'Kelly, the taoiseach, John A. Costello and other government ministers were on the saluting platform at the GPO, there were many radio programmes on the Easter Rising and various groups in different parts of the country held parades.[62] After this the commemorations returned to the practice of a military parade in Dublin and other marches in Dublin and elsewhere organised by various groups.

In Northern Ireland, commemoration at Eastertime of the 1916 Rising was discreet and without much public notice until 1928 when well-publicised ceremonies were held at republican plots in Milltown cemetery in Belfast and in the city cemetery in Derry. In the following year and throughout the 1930s, the government, using the Special Powers Act, prohibited these commemorations. In support of the ban, the minister of home affairs, Sir Dawson Bates, with certain hyperbole, stated that those involved were 'celebrating one of the most treacherous and bloody rebellions that ever took place in the history of the world' and claimed that there was IRA involvement in the commemorations.[63] The nationalist leader, Joseph Devlin, challenged this view in parliament in 1932 and argued that the ban on the commemorations was a denial of people's right to free speech and referred to one such event in Newry as simply 'an annual commemoration for all those who died for Ireland'.[64]

Every Easter during the 1930s commemorative meetings were announced and then declared illegal by the government, but there were often attempts to get round the ban.[65] In 1935, for example, about 500 people gathered on Easter Monday some 50 yards beyond the cemetery gates at Milltown graveyard where they recited a decade of the rosary, while in Derry republicans held their commemorations a week before Easter to get round the ban at Eastertime.[66] On a number of occasions wreath-laying ceremonies at Derry and Armagh were performed on Saturday night, hours before the ban came into operation on Easter

Sunday.[67] Tension arose frequently over the flying of the Irish tricolour and the wearing of the Easter lily, a symbol of the Dublin Easter Rising. The most serious confrontation between the police and republican organisers came in 1942 when active IRA units became involved in the commemorations, leading to shooting in both Dungannon and Belfast, and the murder of a Catholic police constable in Belfast.[68]

By 1948 the Northern Ireland government had decided not to impose a general ban on Easter commemorations of 1916. From this time on commemorative events were held in a number of centres by a range of organisations. In 1950, for example, the main event at Milltown cemetery in Belfast was organised by the National Graves Association.[69] This was followed by a separate service organised under the auspices of the republican labour party, addressed by Harry Diamond MP who referred to 'the shadow of a foreign occupation of a portion of their country'. Finally, there was another ceremony held by the 'Old Pre-Truce IRA'. In Newry a commemorative service was followed by a large parade, led by members of Newry urban council, and including members of the Catholic Boy Scouts, the Foresters and the Hibernians. There were also Easter commemorative events in Counties Armagh and Tyrone and Derry city. Similar events occurred during the 1950s with few problems, although sometimes there was conflict between organisers and police over the flying of the tricolour, as for example in Lurgan in 1952 and 1953 when the RUC confiscated flags and made arrests. In Newry in 1957 arrests were also made over the flying of the tricolour at the Easter commemorations, and in the following year a parade to commemorate 1916 was prohibited in the town, although the ban was ignored.[70]

Twelfth of July anniversary of the Battle of the Boyne (1690)

In the new Northern Ireland of the early 1920s celebrations by Orangemen on the Twelfth of July to mark the anniversary of the Battle of the Boyne were already an important annual event. Since the 1880s the Orange movement had enjoyed widespread support from members of the Protestant community, especially but not only in the nine counties of Ulster, and the July parades were well attended. The Grand Lodge of Ireland, the governing body of the Orange Order, was responsible for most of these parades but the much smaller Independent Orange Order also held an annual parade. The Orange Order headquarters were originally in Dublin, but in consequence of the occupation of the building by republicans in 1922, new headquarters were established in Belfast.

In the early 1920s, however, the exact significance of this date in the calendar of the new state had not yet been established. There is evidence that Sir James Craig and the government sought to place some distance between themselves and the Orange movement. In July 1922 Craig was asked in the Northern Ireland parliament to use his influence to have 12 July made a general holiday. He rejected this call and stated: 'In view of the large number of existing statutory holidays, and the fact that the Twelfth of July has for many years been observed as such, there does not appear to be any necessity to take the action suggested.' Three years later when the matter was raised again in parliament, the minister of home affairs, Dawson Bates, agreed that the date should become a special holiday.[71] In October 1924 the cabinet decided that there was no objection to the proposal but any such measure was postponed until the following year. In August 1925 the cabinet discussed whether the Westminster parliament should be asked to make 12 July a permanent bank holiday or whether this should be done annually by proclamation, and decided to opt for the latter course.[72] By the late 1920s 12 July had become a statutory as well as a general holiday.

There is other evidence that Craig and his fellow ministers tried to downgrade links between themselves and the Orange Order in this early period. Craig and most of his cabinet were Orangemen but at this time they took a minor role in these annual July proceedings. On 12 July 1922 Craig spoke at the Belfast demonstration and described enthusiastically how he and his wife had attended the July celebrations every year since their marriage.[73] In the following year, there was no report of Craig attending the July celebrations and few other ministers spoke from Orange platforms. In July 1923, however, Craig issued a message intended especially for Orange 'brethren' in the USA and Canada, but which was also read at local parades: 'It is our earnest desire to live in peace and amity with the Free State, and to encourage in every way a better understanding between all classes and creeds.'[74] In 1924 there was again no report of Craig's appearance at the Twelfth of July celebrations. In 1925 he sent apologies from England for his non-attendance and explained his absence was due to the recent death of his brother, although, in fact, his brother had died nearly two weeks before the 12 July anniversary.[75] In 1926 the press noted Craig's apologies for his non-attendance but gave no explanation.[76] During these years few of his prominent colleagues spoke on 12 July platforms. Finally, however, in 1927 Craig made a major speech on 12 July at the demonstration in Belfast and from this time on he and other leading ministers attended and spoke regularly on these occasions.[77]

This picture of limited involvement by the unionist leadership in Twelfth of July proceedings in the early 1920s matches other evidence that the government was trying to avoid becoming completely identified with only the Protestant section of the population. Among examples of this are the attempt by Lord Londonderry to establish non-denominational school education and the appointment of Catholic Sir Denis Henry to the post of lord chief justice of Northern Ireland.[78] These gestures of moderation, however, did not continue, partly because of concern about unionist unity in the face of political threats from independent unionists, labour and other groups, and partly because of changes in the south, after 1932. When Craig returned to an Orange platform in 1927 it was to take the opportunity to warn against the danger of division in unionist ranks and to justify the government's plan to abolish proportional representation in elections to the Northern Ireland parliament: it is generally accepted that this move was not designed as an attack on nationalists but was an attempt to curtail unionist splinter groups.[79] From 1927 onwards members of the government used these Twelfth of July parades to espouse their political stance and promote unionist unity. By 1930 Craig made a point of attending the Twelfth of July proceedings every year in a different county of Northern Ireland. Developments in the south, in particular the rise of de Valera and also public declarations of religious/political identity in the early 1930s, helped to lead to a strengthening of unionist/Orange links.[80] These links clearly benefited the government and unionist party, in the face of continuing social and political unrest, but matters were not always under their control. Because of the fear of sectarian violence the authorities tried to stop the Twelfth of July demonstrations in Belfast in 1935 but had to back down owing to strong Orange opposition. The celebrations that year were followed by nine days of serious rioting in Belfast.[81]

At the July parades during the 1930s speeches by politicians, clergymen, other ministers of religion and members ranged over various religious and political subjects. Loyalty to the crown and empire was reaffirmed regularly. In 1933 Craig declared: 'British we are and British we remain'.[82] Protestant principles were upheld and Catholicism was denounced. In 1932 Craig stated: 'Ours is a Protestant government and I am an Orangeman'.[83] Political affairs in the south were often mentioned and the fate of southern Protestants was frequently referred to. Links with the empire were stressed. In 1939 Craig declared that 'the British empire, and all it stands for, is the sun and air of our existence'.[84] The importance of the Twelfth of July commemorations and the Orange Order for unionists was stressed in a report in the *Northern Whig on*

13 July 1933: 'Throughout people recognised the need for keeping at full pitch the unity and strength of the order. It has proved in the past the nucleus around which unionism of the province gathered when danger of submission in a nationalist and Roman Catholic dominated Ireland threatened'. The outbreak of war resulted in the curtailment of parades, 1940–42. These restrictions, voluntary in 1940 and mandatory in 1941 and 1942, covered not only the main Twelfth of July processions but also parades before 12 July, including the annual march to a church service at Drumcree, County Armagh, on the Sunday before 12 July.[85] Thereafter the annual Twelfth of July parades resumed, although in a limited form, for the rest of the war.

During the 1940s and 1950s the government and the unionist party remained strongly identified with the Twelfth of July proceedings and the Orange movement. Speeches by Lord Brookeborough during the 1950s referred to IRA attacks and also the greater economic benefits the north enjoyed compared with the south.[86] Not until the late 1950s and early 1960s did questions begin to emerge from both Orange and unionist circles to challenge the link between the two organisations. On 13 July 1960 an editorial in the *Belfast News Letter* referred to the new thinking on these matters and put it down to a more stable political climate in Northern Ireland and better north–south relations. In Brookeborough's last years as prime minister some Orange leaders urged that the religious aspects of the Twelfth should be increased at the expense of the political and by the early 1960s fewer prominent politicians were involved in the Twelfth of July proceedings.[87] At the same time some politicians urged that unionism should not be restricted to Protestants. In July 1960 R.S. Nixon, MP, declared that 'civil and religious liberty must be for all sections of the community', while in July 1961 W.M. May, MP, stated that 'we must do our best to impress on our Roman Catholic citizens that this order stands for toleration'.[88] Historical ghosts resonated at the Orange demonstration at Bangor, County Down in 1960. A report in the press recounted: 'One of the most unexpected people to turn up at the Bangor demonstration was Michael Collins. When his name was announced over the loudspeakers there was consternation on the faces of the platform party and gathering. But smiles were soon in evidence when it was explained that Michael was a little boy who had got lost'.[89]

Before 1921 Orange parades had occurred regularly in the three Ulster counties of Donegal, Cavan and Monaghan, which became part of the new Irish Free State. These parades were restricted in the early 1920s because of disturbances and violence during the civil war but recommenced in 1923. At the main Orange parade at Clones in County Monaghan in 1923 an Orange spokesman declared that: 'they did not desire to be placed under their present regime, but they paid tribute to whom tribute was due. They were not going to rebel, because it would be useless and would not be right. In face of great difficulties and trials the Free State government had done a great deal, but they had a great deal more to do'.[90] In 1925 it was reckoned that 10,000 people attended an Orange demonstration in July at Newbliss in Co. Monaghan.[91] At a large Twelfth of July demonstration at Rockcorry, Co. Monaghan in 1930 resolutions were passed which declared allegiance to King George V as head of the Commonwealth, support for Orange principles, rejoicing in the good relations in County Monaghan and protest against compulsory use of the Irish language.[92] In the 1920s Orange parades were not so common in Donegal, because members from the county, especially the eastern part, often attended Twelfth of July parades just across the border at Derry and other places in Northern Ireland. South Donegal Orangemen held July demonstrations at Rossnowlagh and Darney.[93] Despite incidents at Orange events in Cavan town in 1930 and in Newtowngore in Co. Leitrim in1931, Twelfth of July Orange demonstrations passed off reasonably peacefully in 1931 in Cootehill, County Cavan, and in Monaghan town.[94] The year 1931, however, proved to be the last time that Orange parades took place in Counties Cavan and Monaghan.

A month after these Twelfth of July celebrations in 1931 a large body of republicans, including IRA units, occupied Cootehill on the eve of a planned demonstration on 12 August by members of the Royal Black Institution from Counties Cavan and Monaghan.[95] The railway line through the town was blown up and there were reports of armed men on the streets. The authorities reacted strongly and troops and extra police were dispatched to Cootehill to restore law and order. Although the Black demonstration did not take place the government gave assurances to local Orange and Black leaders that their parades would be protected.[96] In 1932, however, the Grand County Lodges of Cavan, Donegal and Monaghan cancelled all demonstrations in their counties. The minutes of the Co. Monaghan Grand Lodge show that in June 1932 members received information that 'arms were being distributed by the same party who had caused all the trouble at Cootehill with the object of interfering with our July demonstration'.[97] With a new Fianna Fáil government in place, there was no longer any official assurance of their right to march. The Grand Lodge decided to cancel both this demonstration and also all parades to church services.

In future years Monaghan lodges did have limited marches to church services, but, in spite of the wishes of members throughout the 1930s to resume their Twelfth of July demonstrations, this never happened because of fear of the consequences.[98] Orange activities in Counties Cavan and Monaghan were now restricted to church services and private meetings, and lodges attended the Twelfth of July parades in Northern Ireland. In Co. Donegal, however, July Orange parades resumed in the 1930s at the remote coastal area of Rossnowlagh in the south of the county.[99] After the Second World War some lodges from Cavan and Monaghan attended the Rossnowlagh demonstration, along with Donegal brethren. By the 1950s this parade was sometimes held on the Saturday before 12 July, so allowing Orange members to attend the event and then to take part in Twelfth of July parades across the border.

Final observations

These four decades saw the founding and consolidation of two new political states in Ireland. While both Northern Ireland and the Irish Free State, later Eire and then the Irish Republic, marked all four of the national holidays or days of commemoration examined here, the difference in the manner and extent of the celebrations tell us much about how each state and its citizens viewed its own identity and sense of history. Undoubtedly for many involved the subject of commemoration or celebration, such as Armistice Day or St Patrick's Day, had a personal and heartfelt meaning. At the same time these occasions often took on a special significance, and were related to issues of identity and politics as they affected the broader community. Important changes occurred in how such special days were marked. Sometimes these changes were influenced by the desire of leaders to respond to pressures and divisions within their own group, while other times they were a response by a leader and a group to the actions and statements of their opponents. De Valera's opposition to Armistice Day may have been caused partly by a concern to keep republicans on his side and partly as a reaction to attempts by some in the 1920s to turn 'the 11th November into the 12th July'.[100] Craig's new links with Orangeism and a Protestant identity may have been the result partly of a concern to keep unionist unity and partly as a response by southern politicians who 'boasted of a Catholic state'.[101]

Before 1920 St Patrick's Day and Armistice Day enjoyed widespread support. Between 1920 and 1960, however, these occasions were increasingly dominated and endorsed by one section of the community and rejected by the other. St Patrick's Day was used by nationalists/republicans to help to boost an exclusive nationalist and Catholic view of Irish identity. Partly because of this, and partly because of a concern by some unionists to emphasise British links, many Protestants came to disregard St Patrick's Day. Armistice Day was used by unionists to strengthen an exclusive unionist and Protestant view of British identity. As a result, and thanks also to an effort by some nationalists to ignore or reject this part of their recent history, Catholics and nationalists came to ignore Armistice Day. In Northern Ireland the anniversary of the Battle of the Boyne became institutionalised as an important historical event. In the Irish Free State the anniversary of the Easter Rising was a special historical commemorative date, although different groups sought to claim it. In the case of Boyne commemorations in the south and Easter commemorations in the north, both majority communities showed little tolerance for the historical views and identities of their minorities.

During this period of the early years of both states, political relations between north and south and between the different communities were dominated by religious divisions and conflict over constitutional issues. Some of the developments we have seen here, however, helped to polarise these relations even further. Both St Patrick's Day and Armistice Day had the potential to remind people of a shared history, of common interests and suffering. Instead they were used to emphasise differences and to develop more exclusive versions of identity and history. The Twelfth of July and Easter Sunday represented events special to the histories of Northern Ireland and the Irish Free State, respectively, but neither society showed any understanding of the history of the other nor allowed much opportunity for minorities to mark these events. It has been argued that the passion and confrontation aroused by the large number of commemorations in the 1960s was one of the factors that served to destabilise political society in Northern Ireland and to lead to the outbreak of the troubles.[102] The widely held conflicting views of identity and history, fostered in part by these commemorations of the previous 40 years, helped to create the atmosphere of distrust and misunderstanding that made these 1960s commemorations so divisive and harmful for politics.

Part II

4
Conflict and conciliation: identities and change, 1960–2011

The 1960s witnessed the promise of great improvement in political relations in Ireland, north and south. In the first half of the decade, the new Northern Ireland prime minister, Captain Terence O'Neill, urged tolerance of different religious and political views within Northern Ireland, and encouraged better north–south relations. Sean Lemass, the new Irish taoiseach, welcomed north–south links and a Dáil Éireann committee in December 1967 recommended significant changes to the Irish constitution. Such promise, however, did not materialise. By the end of the decade there had been extensive rioting in Northern Ireland and some loss of life in consequence of which British troops were on northern streets while Irish troops had been moved up to the border. The confrontation and violence continued for another three decades leading to a loss of over 3000 lives. Many attempts were to be made to create 'peace and stability', but all failed until, finally, the Belfast Agreement was signed on Good Friday, 10 April 1998. Nonetheless, it took another decade before these arrangements would operate fully. How do we account for the failure of the early efforts to improve relations? Why did subsequent attempts fail? How do we explain the eventual success of the new arrangements?

At the core of the problem lay a conflict over identity. Because identities were not only prescriptive and exclusive but also inherently confrontational, the mindsets of most people were unable to accept the changes necessary in the 1960s and 1970s to create a meaningful accommodation. Violence ensued. This clash relating to identity arose primarily because of divisions/cleavages over nationality. It was also linked to divisions over other matters, in particular, religion. This chapter looks at developments in Northern Ireland, and considers the identities of both unionists and nationalists. Also, attention is paid to identity

107

and changes in identity in the Republic of Ireland. As Don Akenson has observed, 'What virtually no one recognized, even in the late 1960s, was that these two sets of frozen politics, north and south, were inter-related and that anything which upset the equilibrium in Northern Ireland would cause disequilibrium in the republic as well. If politics in the Six Counties went wild, so would those of the Twenty-Six'.[1] Besides relations within both Northern Ireland and the Republic of Ireland, and between north and south, relations of all sections to Britain were sig-nificant as well. The violent conflict which emerged from the late 1960s onwards was heavily influenced by the particular forms of identity that had developed in both parts of Ireland since 1920. In time these identi-ties underwent significant change, which helped to make possible the new accommodation of 1998 and subsequently.

A good way to make sense of this conflict is to view the situation in the context of political developments in twentieth and twentieth-first century Europe. The major divisions/cleavages and politics in Ireland, north and south, in the 1960s still reflected the shape of society and politics established in the early 1920s, as was the case in many other West European countries. All such political systems, 'frozen' over these four decades, now witnessed significant change in the 1960s and early 1970s with the arrival of new issues and parties, as would prove the situ-ation in Ireland.[2] The importance of religion and nationalism in Ireland, north and south, in the early 1960s was abnormal in comparison with England or America, but was common compared with other places in mainland Europe. A survey of a large range of modern democratic countries in the late 1960s by Richard Rose and Derek Urwin found that 'religion, not class, is the main social basis in the west today', a fact little appreciated in American/British academic circles at the time.[3] In some countries, such as Holland, there were Protestant and Catholic parties while in others, such as Italy and Germany, there were Christian Democratic Parties, based on earlier Catholic movements, which faced secular liberal, socialist or communist parties. In neither part of Ireland were there specifically named religious parties, but in the north the unionist and nationalist parties were firmly rooted in the Protestant/ Catholic divide, while in the south, where anti-clericalism was virtually non-existent or secretive, the main parties were heavily influenced by the strong Catholic character of society.[4]

While religion was a factor of importance in many European countries in the 1960s its effect on politics was often mitigated by the effects of other divisions, such as that caused by class, or by the influence of special consociational-type structures. In the case of Ireland, however, we must note the presence of that other significant source of division absent very largely from other West European countries at this time. All these other countries enjoyed a common nationality which meant each did not face the issue of a national minority, which Gordon Smith has aptly described as 'one of the most fertile sources of political stress'.[5] In Ireland, however, divisions over nationality remained critical, not only between north and south but also within both Northern Ireland and the Irish Republic. In the case of the latter, there was still a Protestant and former unionist minority, but also the main political parties continued to be based on the divisions that had arisen over national issues in the early 1920s. This seemed to set Ireland apart from elsewhere. In the 1920s there had been other countries, like Poland and Czechoslovakia, where matters of nationality and divisions between majorities and national minorities had been important, but this was no longer the case. In 1976 one scholarly commentator on Northern Ireland, Hugh Thomas, could confidently declare that 'most of the old minority problems of Europe have actually been resolved'.[6]

This view, of course, was completely wrong. Such problems had only been hidden, thanks to the intervention of Joseph Stalin, the Red Army and communism in 1945. In some places the matter had been resolved by the mass removal of populations, such as the expulsion of the German minorities from Poland and Czechoslovakia. When the 'iron curtain' fell in the late 1980s, conflict over nationality, sometimes associated with religion or religious division, became very apparent again in many parts of Central and Eastern Europe, including the countries of the former USSR.[7] In addition, in parts of West Europe, the national certainties of the 1960s have been undermined by new or revived national demands, such as in Scotland, Catalonia and the Basque Country. Therefore, these divisions in Ireland, north and south, over nationality and religion, are not unusual in a broad European context. Failure to understand this, and a determination to view matters in a narrow twentieth-century Anglo-American context, where divisions over religion and nationality have been less influential until recent times than elsewhere, has often led to misunderstanding of the situation in Ireland, especially in Northern Ireland. Indeed, one might even suggest, the position here was prescient, given the importance of religion and national conflict in the world today.[8]

Background

In Northern Ireland in the 1960s, as Thomas Hennessey has described well, there were 'two completely different worldviews contained within unionism and nationalism ...'. He observed: 'Unionists tended to be

Protestants: nationalists tended to be Catholics. Unionists described themselves as 'British'; nationalists described themselves as 'Irish' ... These were more than just words. They denoted completely different perceptions of the political, social and cultural world that constituted Northern Ireland in the 1960s ...'.[9] For unionists, British identity was crucial. This involved loyalty to the crown and the British link. For many it also meant an Ulster dimension. This British/Ulster identity, however, related very largely to the Protestant section of the population. There were strong public links between the Ulster Unionist Party (UUP) and the government and the Orange Order. The Protestant churches and the Orange Order had an influential position in society. To many unionists the members of the nationalist and Catholic population seemed to be 'disloyal'. Frequently northern unionist politicians expressed hostility towards the south and towards the Catholic church.

Nationalists, including republicans, within Northern Ireland retained a strong Irish identity and the ideal of a united Ireland. Among northern nationalists, Catholicism and nationalism were often closely intertwined. Besides this conflict over nationality and their role in the state, nationalists suffered a range of inequalities and discrimination. Importantly, nationalists were excluded from meaningful political power because, as former BBC journalist, John Cole, has pointed out: 'the national question dominated politics, and because unionists were in a permanent majority in the population, the unionist party was permanently in power'.[10] At the same time, while divisions in Northern Ireland were sharply demarcated between unionists and nationalists, and between Irish and British, it would be wrong to see their identities as completely exclusive. Richard Rose, in the late 1960s, conducted a survey of people's identities. He found that among Protestants, 39 per cent identified themselves as British, 32 per cent as Ulster and 20 per cent as Irish. He found that among Catholics, 76 per cent saw themselves as Irish, 5 per cent as Ulster and 15 per cent as British.[11] Of course, most Protestants who viewed themselves as Irish would have considered themselves British as well, while most Catholics who described themselves as British would also have regarded themselves as Irish.

While identities in Ireland, north and south, remained largely exclusive and polarised in the 1960s, we can now see the beginning of change. In March 1963 Captain Terence O'Neill became prime minister of Northern Ireland. Shortly after his appointment, he declared to the Ulster Unionist Council: 'Our task will be literally to transform Ulster. To achieve it will demand bold and imaginative measures'. It soon became clear that he intended not only to seek effective social and economic change, but also to 'build bridges between the two traditions within our community' and to 'convince more and more people that the government is working for the good of all in Northern Ireland – not just those who vote unionist'.[12] He met the taoiseach, Sean Lemass, in 1965. Considerable north–south co-operation occurred in the mid-1960s in areas such as electricity supply and trade.[13] There were signs of change in other quarters. In 1962 the new Catholic bishop of Down and Connor, Dr William Philbin, paid a courtesy call on the unionist lord mayor of Belfast, the first such visit by a Catholic bishop since partition. The following year the union flag was flown at half-mast over Belfast city hall on the death of Pope John Paul XXIII. Improved ecumenical relations, arising in part from Vatican II, led some people to question the strong links between politics and religion. The play 'Over the bridge', by Sam Thompson, which opened in January 1960, challenged sectarianism in the Belfast shipyards and served to start important new debate. In 1965 the Presbyterian general assembly passed a resolution asking Catholics to forgive Presbyterians for 'attitudes and actions ... unworthy of our calling as followers of Jesus Christ' and established an investigation into discrimination within the province.[14]

By 1968, however, it was evident that few concrete reforms had actually been achieved. All efforts at reconciliation had been bitterly attacked by some unionists, in particular Rev. Ian Paisley (not a member of the Ulster Unionist Party). A preacher, Paisley had founded his own church called the Free Presbyterian church, which was completely separate from the Presbyterian church, to which a majority of Protestants in Northern Ireland belonged. In 1966 he declared: 'The term of the current prime minister, Capt. Terence O'Neill, has been one sad story of appeasement with the enemies of Northern Ireland ... By his words and actions he has shown himself more interested in his political dictatorship than in keeping Northern Ireland truly Protestant'.[15] At a more extreme level, a paramilitary organisation, the Ulster Volunteer Force (UVF) was formed in 1966 to oppose any change and its members were responsible for violence, including murder. Such extreme response, however, only explains partly the slow progress of change under O'Neill. More important was strong opposition from within the Ulster Unionist Party itself. In a radio broadcast in March 1964, Jack Sayers, editor of the *Belfast Telegraph* noted: 'The unionist party does not strike one as being enthusiastic in helping him to wield a new broom: the threat of a rebellion is always there if he should move too far or too fast'.[16] In the *Belfast Telegraph* in March 1966 Sayers denounced the violent protests of Ian Paisley and his followers: 'not even terrorism is likely to produce a throw-back in Ulster as the rise of the malignant anti-Catholic forces exploiting the psychology of the mob'.[17] At the same time, in his November 1966 report for *The Round Table*, Sayers recognised the depth of opposition to O'Neill: 'the dangers of Paisleyism are not only that it provokes communal strife, but that the belief in its leader's "fundamentalism" in politics as well as religion, colours as much as half of the working-class backbone of unionism'.[18] Even one of his liberal supporters, Brian Magennis, expressed concerns in 1963 of co-operation with the south as the forerunner of a 'take-over bid'.[19] Such attitudes greatly hindered the efforts of O'Neill who remained vigilant of the need to preserve unionist unity, especially in face of a new labour threat.

These developments posed a considerable challenge also to the nationalist party. Immediately after the first O'Neill/Lemass meeting in 1965, Eddie McAteer, a member of the Northern Ireland parliament and leader of the nationalist party there, visited Sean Lemass in Dublin. He was not impressed with his reception, as he later recalled: 'I got neither the encouragement nor understanding of our position ... Lemass said that it appeared to him that Catholics in the north were just as intractable as Protestants'. He continued: 'It was hardly the reaction I expected from a taoiseach with his republican background to the representative of the oppressed minority in the six counties'.[20] Nonetheless, on 2 February 1965, the party announced its decision to become the official opposition. After the failure of its 1956–62 armed campaign, the Irish Republican Army (IRA) was not a major force at this time. Its Dublin leadership concentrated on social and political activism, and in the north republican activists formed republican clubs which sought to promote a republican agenda. Republican candidates continued to contest Westminster parliamentary elections, but with only moderate success. In 1966 the fiftieth anniversary of the Easter Rising was marked in the north by considerable numbers which indicated continued republican support, and which alarmed unionists. In fact, this support may well have arisen in response to official southern efforts to understate the question of Irish unity in their commemorations.[21] This worried northern nationalists and republicans. In November 1966 Eddie McAteer called at the department for external affairs in Dublin to complain that the southern government was 'growing closer to the unionists than to the nationalists' and they felt that they 'were being forgotten about and begin to despair'. He was told that 'he must have regard to the delicate position of Capt. O'Neill *vis-a-vis* his extremists' and Dublin could not be seen to be 'conspiring with the nationalists against him'.[22]

Nonetheless, in this period the grievances of the minority in Northern Ireland attracted new attention that ignored the border issue. In 1962, under the auspices of the Irish Association, two Quakers, Denis Barritt and Charles Carter, published *The Northern Ireland Problem: A Study in Group Relations*, a book that highlighted discrimination against Catholics in a dispassionate manner.[23] In January 1964 in Dungannon, Co. Tyrone, Conn and Patricia McCloskey founded the Campaign for Social Justice (CSJ), which sought to expose what they considered to be injustices against Catholics but within the existing constitutional framework of Northern Ireland. Writing to McAteer, Conn McCloskey argued that the time had come to 'concentrate on getting our rights and trying to overcome gerrymandering ... to mention the border just puts the unionists' backs up and some other poor devils lose their chance of a house or a job'.[24] In 1966 Gerry Fitt was elected as a republican labour member for West Belfast. He sought to raise at Westminster the question of discrimination in Northern Ireland, as did the Campaign for Democracy in Ulster, a group formed in London by members of the British Labour Party. Early in 1967 the Northern Ireland Civil Rights Association was established in Belfast. Its original committee included some republicans who had adopted constitutional politics as part of a new strategy after republican failures of the 1950s, but a majority belonged to reformist groups such as the CSJ, the NILP and the Ulster Liberal Party.[25] From 1965 onwards in Derry, the main challenge to the *status quo* came not from nationalists or republicans, but from liberals (Claud Wilton), Londonderry Labour Party (*sic*) members (Dermot McClenaghan and Eamon McCann), housing groups (John Hume) and even former unionists (Ivan Cooper).[26] These developments gave a new perspective to politics in Northern Ireland.

At the beginning of this period in the south, the main political parties were still those that had arisen out of the national/constitutional split of the early 1920s, although there was also a labour party founded earlier. All these parties shared a strong nationalist viewpoint. Des O'Malley, who became a TD in1968, has recalled how until the early 1960s southern nationalism was 'essentially an aggressive and negative nationalism. It was almost as if the terms 'Irish' and 'anti-British were synonymous or interchangeable'. He continued: 'Effectively, we defined ourselves in terms of our historic conflict with Britain; and that conflict was seen to endure in the struggle to end partition ... There was virtually no acceptance that the northern majority had any right to determine their own constitutional position'.[27] At the same time, we may note the comment by Patrick Keatinge and Brigid Laffan that this view on the north was usually accompanied by nothing more than 'occasional rhetorical posturing and neglect'.[28] Regarding the importance of religion, Basil Chubb in 1970 described how 'to a large extent Catholicism is identified with nationalism in the public mind' and 'the political effects of the dominant position of the Catholic church are immense'.[29]

The election of Sean Lemass as taoiseach in 1959 brought important changes in the economy and society. His first priority was to remove existing economic protectionist policies. At the same time, he started to move Irish identity from the narrow, isolationist position which it had assumed by the 1950s. Changes in the cultural area included the removal of most book censorship in the 1960s. Important improvements in provision of secondary school education were introduced in the mid-1960s. Part of the new approach of Lemass was to take a less confrontational and more conciliatory position on the north. In his first news conference as taoiseach, he announced 'an end to the term 'anti-partition' in official documents about Northern Ireland'.[30] He called for practical co-operation and in April 1964 he declared: 'our hands will always be outstretched in friendship'. At the same time he stated that 'our hope is to bring about Irish reunification by agreement'.[31] Under his influence, there were efforts to make the official 1966 Easter Rising commemorations look to the future rather than the past and not to dwell on partition.[32] Lemass, and his successor as taoiseach, Jack Lynch, held meetings with the northern prime minister, Terence O'Neill, and encouraged north–south co-operation.

Lemass was both pragmatic and generous in his approach to northern unionists, but there were limits to this, because of existing attitudes. He had constantly to declare his desire for a united Ireland to reassure his own followers (which alarmed unionists). While he was restrained in his language, his efforts were undermined by others, in particular, Eamon de Valera. In 1962 de Valera, now president, in an interview with the *New York Times*, returned to his idea of expulsion of northern unionists, while at the 1966 Easter Rising commemorations he called for the British government to bring forward Irish unity over unionist heads.[33] In August 1966 a Dáil Éireann all party committee was initiated by Lemass to review the Irish constitution. After his resignation as taoiseach in late 1966 Lemass chose to serve as a member of the committee. Its report, published in December 1967, recommended significant changes to the Irish constitution. Unanimously it was proposed that article 3 be replaced with a conciliatory statement that 'the Irish nation hereby proclaims its firm will that its territory be reunited in harmony and brotherly affection between all Irishmen'.[34] It also recommended changes to the articles that prohibited divorce and recognised the 'special position' of the Catholic church. The new taoiseach, Jack Lynch, supported co-operation but also a 'more traditionalist policy' towards the north.[35] Some cabinet members were alarmed by the publication of this report, which was seen, in the words of one Fianna Fáil politician, Kevin Boland, as a 'departure from republican principles'.[36] In the event, essentially because of an unwillingness to challenge these key assumptions of nationalist identity, the report was shelved with one exception.[37] The government decided to proceed only on the issue of electoral reform, which, however, had not received unanimous backing and which subsequently the electorate rejected.

By the 1960s the Protestants in the south were just under 5 per cent of the population. By then, for most of them, there was no residual sense of British identity. This was not so, however, in the border counties of Donegal, Cavan and Monaghan, especially among Orangemen, who since the early 1930s had not been able to hold demonstrations in their own areas, apart from a small annual parade at Rossnowlagh, Co. Donegal, and who therefore attended Twelfth of July parades across the border in Northern Ireland.[38] This decade witnessed a strong effort on the part of the minority to play a full part in Irish society. During these years we can observe the fall of many barriers over employment, social activities and educational and cultural matters. Figures such as Dr G.O. Simms, the Church of Ireland archbishop of Dublin, did much to improve religious and community relations in the new atmosphere encouraged by Vatican II. The *Irish Times* changed its policies radically from being identified very largely with the Protestant community to reflecting a general liberal position within Irish society. In 1966 senior religious and lay figures from the Protestant community were involved in the fiftieth anniversary commemorations of the 1916 rising, and there was a united Protestant service in St Patrick's Cathedral, Dublin, to mark the event.[39]

Both O'Neill and Lemass sought to bring significant change to relations within and between the two parts of Ireland. They failed in the end, however, partly because of internal party tensions, more importantly because of the influence of existing, exclusivist identities, which to some degree they shared. In 1963 Sir Robert Gransden, former Northern Ireland cabinet secretary, explained to Hugh McCann, the Irish ambassador in London, that the Northern Ireland government 'cannot get out of step with the thinking of its own supporters and we should recognise that, if the prime minister there attempted to do certain things, he might be 'shot out on his ear'.[40] Faced with the strength of existing attitudes, O'Neill failed to introduce reforms sufficient to satisfy the Catholic community, instead hoping that with general economic progress their position would improve.[41] Lemass sought to be conciliatory to northern unionists but, in order to placate his supporters' traditional views on the north, he often repeated his belief in a united Ireland, which alarmed unionists, as did statements by de Valera. Lemass also hoped that increased economic co-operation would bring reconciliation: at the very end of his career he did try to change some central nationalist ideas, through the constitutional review, but was unsuccessful.[42]

Both Lemass and O'Neill believed that economic progress would improve matters. At the same time, both were unable or unwilling to challenge successfully some of the basic assumptions behind unionism and nationalism. In 1966 Lemass rejected a suggestion that a bridge, part of the original plan for the National War Memorial Park, be finally built to connect Phoenix Park with the war memorial on the grounds that 'it was too late to do anything in recognition of the British soldiers' part of the historical tradition of the Irish nation'.[43] Between August 1963 and March 1964 two prominent northern Catholics, J.J. Campbell and Brian McGuigan, wrote three letters to Terence O'Neill urging that he appoint more Catholics to public boards; but he failed to reply to them and only finally responded when their correspondence was printed in the press. In the event, no such appointments followed.[44] Had either agreed to these suggestions, this would have had great symbolic significance, perhaps of more value than long-term economic improvements, but neither was willing or able to do so.

Challenge and conflict, 1968–74

The late 1960s witnessed the rise of a strong new challenge to the existing political system in Northern Ireland. In some respects this was part of a movement found elsewhere in Europe against systems of politics that had been 'frozen' since the early 1920s and was due to the rise of new issues and organisations.[45] In the case of Northern Ireland it was the outcome of the growth in concern over inequalities and discrimination against Catholics that sought to deal with these matters in a new way, outside traditional unionist–nationalist rivalries and without the usual concerns about the border. This led to the rise of a civil rights movement, influenced no doubt by developments in the USA. The main concerns of this movement were 'one man, one vote', fair public housing allocation, council boundary changes and the Special Powers

Act. During 1968, a number of civil rights marches were held in several locations, most notably in Derry on 5 October when police sought to stop forcefully such a march, leading to wide publicity about civil rights issues and the response of the state. The unionist party was sharply divided in its response to demands over civil rights, and reforms were introduced belatedly. O'Neill's conciliatory position won significant popular support in late 1968 and early 1969, but he was unable to control sufficiently unionist party ranks, and his position was damaged fatally. Hopes for peaceful protest were undermined by unionist/loyalist opponents, as in the attacks on civil rights marchers in Armagh in November 1968 and at Burntollet Bridge in January 1969. In the end, the civil rights movement failed to restrain its own supporters, as in the outbreak of violence in Derry on 12 August 1969 and in Belfast the next day.[46] The ensuing so-called Battle of the Bogside in Derry and the consequent violence in Belfast, including deaths and the burning of homes, mostly Catholic, brought a new level of conflict into the situation. An army unit arrived in Derry on 14 August 1969 to reinforce police. Other units followed in Belfast. Peace was restored, temporarily.

We now witness the impact of paramilitaries (members of illegal and semi-legal armies). Late 1969 saw the re-emergence of the IRA which split into so-called 'official' and 'provisional' wings. Republican violence was matched by new loyalist paramilitary organisations, particularly the Ulster Defence Association (UDA), founded in 1972. The early 1970s saw a rapid escalation in the conflict with shootings, bombs and many people forced from their homes, particularly in Belfast and Derry. Violence spread to the south and to England. The police were reformed, the 'B' Specials were disbanded and a new force, the Ulster Defence Regiment, was formed; but these efforts failed to win wide support for the security forces. By 1973 all the main civil rights demands, in relation to the police, public housing and electoral practices, had been granted but this did not stop the violence. By this stage politics were again clearly divided on religious and national lines.

In 1970, in place of the nationalist party, led by McAteer, the Social Democratic and Labour Party (SDLP) was formed to remedy Catholic grievances and to bring about union with the south by general consent. The year 1970 also saw the formation of the moderate Alliance Party, which drew supporters from both sides of the denominational divide. In 1971 the Democratic Unionist Party (DUP) was established in opposition to the UUP. A rise in violence, and withdrawal of the SDLP from the northern parliament in opposition to government policies, led to increasing pressure on the Northern Ireland government. On 24 March

1972 both the government and parliament were suspended and a secretary of state, a member of the British cabinet, was appointed for Northern Ireland. A government paper of 30 October 1972 asserted the constitutional position of Northern Ireland within the UK; it also laid down principles of the two communities sharing power and of a so-called 'Irish dimension' for the future. After elections to a new assembly in June 1973 extensive discussions led at the end of the year to agreement for an executive composed of the UUP, the SDLP and the Alliance Party, and, after a conference at Sunningdale, Berkshire, for a north–south council. On 1 January 1974 a Northern Ireland power-sharing executive was formed. Within a short time, however, it collapsed.

How do we explain these developments? Why was it not possible to accept promptly the demands of the civil rights movement over issues such as 'one man, one vote' and fair allocation of public housing? Protestants as well as Catholics stood to benefit by such reforms. The household franchise, which applied only to local government elections and not parliamentary elections, actually disqualified more Protestants than Catholics.[47] Control of housing allocation by local councillors who acted in a partisan manner could also disadvantage Protestants. In the notorious case of Caledon, Co. Tyrone in 1968, where the local unionist councillor who ran the village shop allocated a house to a single Protestant rather than a more deserving Catholic family, he refused also to award housing to local members of the RUC who might not have used his shop.[48] In part, the unionist opposition arose because they feared these changes would lead to loss of control of some councils.

More importantly, however, to the minds of many unionists the civil rights movement seemed a real danger. William Craig, minister of home affairs in O'Neill's cabinet, viewed the civil rights march at Derry on 5 October 1968 simply as a 'Nationalist–Republican parade'.[49] In the aftermath of the march and the controversy it caused, on 28 November Craig stated that Ulster faced a very difficult time, with 'all this nonsense centred around civil rights, and behind it all there is our old traditional enemy exploiting the situation'.[50] O'Neill had strong supporters, such as Jack Sayers, editor of the *Belfast Telegraph*, who in *The Round Table*, November 1968, acknowledged that the civil rights movement may have been 'a coat of many colours', but also that its protest against 'outrageous' discrimination in Derry was 'authentic enough'. In his newspaper leader on 5 November 1968 he warned that the threat to Northern Ireland's future came, not from nationalism or the IRA, but from 'Protestant Ulstermen who will not allow themselves to be liberated from the delusion that every Roman Catholic is their enemy'.[51]

Change was opposed by those who were unable to alter long-standing assumptions about their own political position and their opponents.

How do we account for the outbreak of serious violence in August 1969? The report of the Scarman Tribunal, published in April 1972, investigated rival claims that the riots of August 1969 had been planned for the purpose of overthrowing the government or for state or Protestant forces to attack the Catholic community. As the result of its findings the report attributed the violent confrontation in Derry and Belfast in August to the rise of communal tensions over the previous nine months. The outcome was that, 'on the one side people saw themselves, never "the others", charged by a police force which they regarded as partisan: on the other side, police and people saw a violent challenge to the authority of the state'. The report found: 'neither the IRA nor any Protestant organisation nor anybody else planned a campaign of riots'.[52] Nonetheless, it was significant that people viewed matters in these terms and that it was necessary to deal with these charges of conspiracy and ill intent. What this revealed was that in mid-1969 there were two very different interpretations of the whole situation, which reflected a clash of identities. Whatever Scarman's later findings on the matter, the events and violence of summer 1969 served to confirm the view for many that the police and the state were inherently hostile to them, and for others that they faced an attempt to undermine the constitutional position of Northern Ireland. This meant that not only was there now a straightforward confrontation over the position and role of the state, but a significant level of violence had entered the situation. Cahal Daly, later archbishop of Armagh and Cardinal, commented: 'The tragedy is that the incipient growth of understanding and mutual understanding which marked the ten years up to August 1969 has now been blighted by the frost of violence'.[53]

This period, the years 1969–74, witnessed the rise of paramilitary groups on both republican and loyalist sides. To some extent these organisations developed in response to the deteriorating situation of communal violence and a breakdown in law and order. The actions of such groups, however, went far beyond self-defence, and must be seen as arising from the world-view of their members, based on particular identities that justified their actions. In the nationalist camp the IRA had not been a significant force in events before August 1969 but increasingly it became important. For some nationalists the ongoing conflict now revived ideas of total republican opposition to Britain and the Northern Ireland state. The republican movement would suffer an ideological split at the end of 1969 and at the beginning of 1970 over the form of this opposition, with the so-called 'official' wing backing political action and eventually calling a ceasefire while the so-called 'provisional' wing would oppose political action and continue to back violence. The first public statement of the Provisional IRA (as it came to be called) announced: 'We declare our allegiance to the thirty-two-county Irish republic, proclaimed at Easter 1916, established by Dáil Éireann in 1919, overthrown by force of arms in 1922 and suppressed to this day by the existing British-imposed six-county and twenty-six-county partition states'.[54] Violence against security personnel and civilians was justified to make the state ungovernable and to force a 'British withdrawal'.[55] Supporters of the UVF or UDA justified their position by arguing that these organisations defended Northern Ireland and were prepared to use violence to destroy its enemies and their perceived supporters. Some violent events stand out from this period, 1970–74, such as Bloody Friday in Belfast, Bloody Sunday in Derry, the Aldershot bomb, the McGurk's Bar bomb (Belfast) and the Dublin bombing. Equally disturbing was the fact that in this short period over 1200 lost their lives and many thousands were wounded by gunfire or explosives.[56]

After August 1969 matters of reform and security issues dominated the political scene in Northern Ireland, and significant new divisions emerged not only between but also within existing unionist and nationalist blocks, which often related to different identities. The leadership of the Ulster Unionist Party, under James Chichester Clarke and later Brian Faulkner, showed an increased acceptance of the idea of accommodation with the Catholic and nationalist community. This change was partly due to pressure from London but also because some unionists began to develop a new approach. In 1971 Brian Faulkner declared: 'I look forward to the day when my unionist colleagues on this Front Bench will be Protestant and Catholic and no one will even think it worthy of comment. Neither Unionist nor Ulster will survive in the long run if we take any other course'.[57] Finally, in October 1971 he appointed as a minister of state in the prime minister's office a Catholic, G.B. Newe, who had made a much discussed speech at Garron Tower in 1958. This move, however, came too late to make a positive impact. Local politics had now become polarised over the rise in violence and also the introduction of internment, which was handled badly and served to enflame matters further.

The outbreak of violence in August 1969 had eventually brought about the collapse of the nationalist party in Northern Ireland. In August 1970 there emerged a new political opposition, called the Social Democratic and Labour Party (SDLP), which contained former members of the nationalist party, such as Austin Currie, former labour supporters, such as republican labour Gerry Fitt and NILP member Paddy Devlin, and members of the civil rights movement, such as John Hume. Hume originally believed that some sort of party concerned only with civil rights and social reform could be established, but these events of August made it inevitable that the national question should assume a role in the objectives of this new party. The emphasis in its original policy statement was on the promotion of social and civil rights reform within Northern Ireland. At the same time, it sought to promote understanding between north and south 'with a view to the eventual reunification of Ireland through the consent of the majority of the people in the north and in the south'.[58] For a time the party, led by Gerry Fitt, co-operated with the unionist government. The introduction of internment, however, led to its withdrawal from Stormont in July 1971. In April 1970 another new party was formed, the Alliance Party, the stated aim of which was to provide an organisation of 'moderate people, which is firm on the constitutional issue ... and combines Catholics and Protestants together in a partnership which is the essential prerequisite for a new deal in Northern Ireland'.[59] In early October 1971 the Democratic Unionist Party (DUP) was established, under the leadership of Ian Paisley, to 'provide security for persons and property and to maintain the Constitution, two fields in which the official Unionist Party had failed'.[60]

Events of August 1969 would have important consequences in the Irish Republic as well as in Northern Ireland. The scenes of violence led to the Irish government not only making a humanitarian response but also taking a strong political position which reflected nationalist opinion in the south. In a television broadcast on 13 August, Irish Taoiseach Jack Lynch, announced that the south could 'no longer stand by and see innocent people injured and perhaps worse', and that emergency facilities would be offered by the Irish army at certain positions on the border. He then declared: 'recognising ... that the reunification of the national territory can provide the only permanent solution for the problem', his government intended to enter into early negotiations with the British government to 'review the present constitutional position of the Six Counties of Northern Ireland'.[61] On 20 August 1969 Irish minister for external affairs, Patrick Hillery, spoke at the UN Security Council in New York to urge that a UN peacekeeping force be sent to Northern Ireland. He denounced partition as 'a concession to an intransigent minority', refused to accept that Britain had any right to jurisdiction over what he kept calling the 'Six Counties', and stated that the government's policy was 'reunification by peaceful means'.[62] On 28 August Lynch sought to clarify the government's position on the use of force: 'The government agree that the border cannot be changed by force; it is, and has been, their policy to seek the reunification of the country by peaceful means'.[63]

These actions and statements by the Irish government were seen by unionists as 'hostile propaganda' and very threatening towards them.[64] While the civil rights movement had tried to avoid linking the situation to the partition issue, Lynch and Hillery had done exactly that. In fact, the statements reflected a compromise position in the Irish cabinet, which was sharply divided over the subject of partition and the principle of consent. An influential section of the cabinet, in particular Neil Blaney and Kevin Boland, wanted a strongly aggressive response by the Irish state to the situation. As John Walsh has written, they were not seeking simply to protect beleaguered Catholics: 'both men saw the outbreak of violence as an opportunity to undermine partition and force Britain to concede a united Ireland. Their extreme position invoked the traditional certainties of rhetorical nationalism and had a powerful appeal in the volatile conditions of August 1969'.[65] Patrick Hillery later recalled cabinet meetings in summer 1969; 'When it blew up, a meeting was like a ballad session. They were all warriors. I remember government meetings and you would be a traitor, not to be looking for war. They were caught, they were republicans, and now there was an opportunity to become active republicans'.[66]

These divisions within the Irish government were temporarily controlled, but in the closing months of 1969 and early months of 1970, two cabinet ministers, Charles Haughey and Neil Blaney, not only sent money to republican groups in Northern Ireland but also tried to arrange the secret supply of guns from Belgium to such groups.[67] Lynch and other members of the cabinet, however, were strongly opposed to this and moved to stop the guns and arrest those responsible. The outcome was the removal of the two ministers from office and the resignation of a third, and a major political upset in the south. Over the next three years Lynch maintained control not only of the government but also of official policy in relation to Northern Ireland. In a major speech on 10 July 1971 he stated: 'Let us today rededicate ourselves to reconciliation among Irishmen, north and south'. He urged a broader sense of being Irish to accommodate different groups. At the same time, however, he linked firmly such developments to Irish unity.[68] In an earlier interview on the BBC programme, *Panorama*, on 1 March 1971, Lynch declared that the constitutional claim over the six counties was fundamental.[69]

As a gesture towards a more inclusive society in the south, however, on 7 December 1972 the government successfully held a referendum to remove reference to the 'special position' of the Catholic church from the constitution, as recommended by the constitutional review of 1967, although its other recommendations were ignored.[70]

The 1973 general election saw the fall of the Fianna Fáil government and the formation of a Fine Gael and Labour coalition. The members of the new government reflected a range of views on identity. They included Garret FitzGerald, who, in his 1972 book *Towards a New Ireland*, outlined changes he believed would 'have to be made in order to achieve a society which is acceptable to all Irishmen', and also Conor Cruise O'Brien, who, in his 1972 book *States of Ireland*, tried 'to understand some of the feelings shared by most Ulster Protestants and to communicate some notion of these feelings to Catholics in the Republic'.[71] The new government stated its desire for better north–south relations and improved contacts over security matters, but its approach was constrained by legal and political considerations. In the communiqué to the Sunningdale Agreement the Irish government declared its acceptance of the current status of Northern Ireland but avoided describing Northern Ireland as a part of the UK. When challenged in the Dublin courts in early 1974 by Kevin Boland that the Sunningdale Agreement was contrary to the Irish constitution, the Irish attorney general, Declan Costello, argued that it could 'not be construed as meaning that we did not lay claim over the Six Counties'.[72] Only on 14 March 1974 was Cosgrave able to announce formally that 'the factual position of Northern Ireland within the United Kingdom cannot be changed except by a decision of a majority of the people of Northern Ireland'.[73] Suggestions by Conor Cruise O'Brien and others that articles 2 and 3 of the constitution should be adapted or dropped were not pursued, because it was believed that in a referendum, which would be necessary, such changes would be rejected.

This period, 1969–73, saw important contacts between the Irish and British governments, which led, eventually, to a new understanding of the role of the former in Northern Ireland. When the Irish minister for external affairs, Patrick Hillery, met the British foreign secretary, Michael Stewart, in London in early August 1969 to discuss concerns about the forthcoming Apprentice Boys' parade in Derry, he was told that the Irish government had no right to influence British policy on Northern Ireland: 'I must say to you that there is a limit to the extent to which we can discuss with outsiders – even our nearest neighbours, this internal matter'.[74] Later developments, in Northern Ireland and subsequently in the United Nations, would lead to friction between the two governments. In February 1972 Patrick Hillery declared: 'From now on my aim is to get Britain out of Ireland'.[75] Nonetheless, we now see the development of new relations between the British and Irish governments and a series of meetings of the heads of the two governments were held. On 17 September 1973 the British prime minister, Edward Heath, and the taoiseach, Liam Cosgrave, met at Baldonnel airfield outside Dublin, the first such meeting in the south since the foundation of the Irish state. By this stage the British government had come to accept that the Irish government should be consulted on Northern Ireland.

On 24 March 1972, with the continued rise of violence and the withdrawal of the SDLP from Stormont, the Northern Ireland parliament was suspended and direct rule was introduced from London. Almost exactly a year later, the British government published a white paper on the way forward for Northern Ireland. These included the principles of an Irish dimension and executive power sharing. This latter idea of power sharing had first been put forward by the NILP in the 1960s and promoted by journalist John Cole in the *Guardian* newspaper from August 1969 onwards.[76] Despite internal opposition, Brian Faulkner was able to gain the support of his party for a new settlement, although arrangements for north–south relations with a proposed council of Ireland caused considerable concern. On 22 November 1973 the leaders of the UUP, Alliance and SDLP parties agreed to form a power-sharing executive for Northern Ireland. At the end of the month a tripartite conference, involving also the British and Irish governments, was held at Sunningdale, Berkshire, to explore the Irish dimension, which led to agreement over the formation of a council of Ireland. The new Northern Ireland executive took office on 1 January 1974. In his first speech as chief executive, Brian Faulkner declared: 'We stand here of our own free will in a partnership which seeks to face the realities of life in Northern Ireland today. Can anyone doubt that if this province is to have good government, we must turn aside from our old divisions? I believe not only that what we are engaged upon is right, but there is no alternative to it'.[77] At the same time, Gerry Fitt, deputy chief executive, stated: 'I believe we are entering a new era ... neither I nor my colleagues are going to be intimidated by men of violence from whichever side they emerge'.[78]

Within six months these arrangements had collapsed. How do we explain this failure? Crucial was the general strike of May 1974 organised by the Ulster Workers' Council, which had been set up to 'obtain a secure future for Ulster', and to oppose power sharing and a council of Ireland.[79] Including loyalist paramilitaries, anti-Sunningdale politicians and major sections of loyalist workers, and involving widespread intimidation, the strike brought Northern Ireland to a standstill and forced the resignation of the executive at the end of May. The authorities failed to maintain law and order. Loyalist violence included bombs in Dublin, after which the UDA spokesman, Samuel Smyth declared: 'I am very happy about the bombings. There is a war with the Free State and now we are laughing at them'.[80] Critical also to the collapse of the new arrangements was the opposition from the IRA. Their violence intensified during this period, serving to undermine the new structures in unionist eyes.[81] Power sharing was denounced in the *Republican News* on 15 December 1973: 'In the past few weeks Gerry Fitt and Co. have sold us all out. For a few paltry pounds a year they have sold out the people of Ireland'.[82] In a 1974 New Year message, the Provisional IRA declared: 'We look forward with confidence to 1974 as a year in which the British rule in Ireland shall be destroyed and the curse of alien power banished from our land for all time'.[83]

While violent opposition from the extremes played an essential part in destroying the power-sharing executive, so also did failures on the part of many in mainstream unionist and nationalist communities to accept the compromises necessary to allow this new accommodation to work. William Craig, who had formed the Ulster Vanguard Party, criticised these moves by both the British and Northern Ireland governments, and even showed a willingness to promote some sort of Ulster independence.[84] The DUP was also strongly opposed to such accommodation with nationalists which it saw as leading to the destruction of Northern Ireland. For Faulkner, the main problem was to keep members of his own unionist party behind these changes. When ideas of power sharing and a north–south dimension were first presented in the government proposals, Faulkner was able to bring a majority of his party with him, but subsequently he and his supporters lost control of the party. On 4 January 1974 a majority of the Ulster Unionist Council opposed him. The Westminster general election which followed shortly afterwards saw all the unionist seats taken by Faulkner's opponents, who organised under an umbrella organisation of the United Ulster Unionist Council (UUUC). Subsequently at a rally at parliament buildings at Stormont on 9 March 1974, William Craig told the crowd that they would get the keys of Stormont and would eject the 'power-sharing pirates', while Ian Paisley declared that the Sunningdale Agreement was dead: 'Ashes to ashes, dust to dust and no resurrection'.[85]

This unwillingness among many unionists to accept compromise was replicated in a failure among many in nationalist ranks, north and south, to moderate their demands in order to establish a widely acceptable compromise. As Alvin Jackson has pointed out, 'influential elements within the SDLP, and thus within the Irish government, seem to have been concerned more with quickly securing the mechanisms for national reunification than with a workable internal settlement in the North'.[86] The powers of the north–south council were pushed strongly before and during the Sunningdale conference by John Hume and Garret FitzGerald, despite efforts by Paddy Devlin and Conor Cruise O'Brien to moderate demands.[87] FitzGerald would later acknowledge that 'O'Brien was more nearly right than I and the rest of us were in the run-up to Sunningdale and in his judgement of the conference itself'.[88] Reports of statements by the Irish attorney general, Declan Costello, defending the south's 'claim over the six counties' and by SDLP MP Hugh Logue that the council of Ireland could 'trundle' unionists into a united Ireland, had served greatly to alarm unionists.[89] In his memoirs, published in 1978, Brian Faulkner criticised the southern government for its delay in its acceptance of the status of Northern Ireland and for its failure to amend the Irish constitution, all of which had weakened his position, but he accepted that Cosgrave had wanted to make these changes. 'He and I were both struggling with deeply rooted traditions which made it difficult for us to work together as we wished, but I never doubted his goodwill, and I believed that in time we could have overcome these obstacles'.[90]

Stalemate, 1974–1990

During the years following the fall of the power-sharing executive attempts were made to create widely acceptable political institutions and to bring peace and stability to Northern Ireland. These failed. At the same time this period witnessed the beginning of important change, although its full effects were not to be realised until the late 1990s. In mid-1975 the British government called a constitutional convention with elections to provide a forum for the parties to consider the form of a future government, but one which had to include provisions for power sharing and an Irish dimension.[91] The convention was wound up in early 1976 after failing to reach an agreement with cross-party support. Attempts by Secretaries of State for Northern Ireland, Humphrey Atkins, in 1979 and 1980, and James Prior, in 1982 and 1983, failed in consequence of a boycott of Atkins by the Ulster Unionist Party and of Prior by the SDLP. Hunger strikes by republican prisoners in the early 1980s were to present a challenge not only to the British government but also to the SDLP and the Irish government. Writing in 1978 Denis

Donoghue remarked: 'Politics in regard to Northern Ireland is drifting back into the old story, after a few years in which ostensibly new forms of narrative were tried'.[92]

In the Irish Republic, especially among members of Fianna Fáil, aspects of identity reverted also to earlier positions in relation to Northern Ireland. With the arrival of a new coalition led by Garret FitzGerald, an attempt to take a new approach was made by the establishment of the New Ireland Forum in Dublin. This forum served to examine critically some aspects of southern identity but failed to gain northern unionist support or appreciation. In 1985 an important new departure was the Anglo-Irish Agreement, signed by FitzGerald and the British prime minister Margaret Thatcher. This provided for the first time a consultative role for the Irish government in northern affairs and established close links between the British and Irish governments. This Agreement was welcomed by the SDLP but denounced by both the UUP and the DUP who mounted a campaign against it. Throughout all this time violence continued to take many lives and to cause enormous destruction, not only in Northern Ireland but also in Britain and the Irish Republic.

At a constitutional convention of 1975/6, it seemed for a time that an important breakthrough in relations between the parties might occur, owing to an initiative by William Craig of the Vanguard Party. Originally Craig shared the complete opposition of the UUUC to power sharing or co-operation with nationalists. Nonetheless, in February 1975 he told a unionist rally: 'It is only when Ulster men and women share the same allegiance that the conflict can end. We would like to see the minority give its allegiance to the country they live in and we are willing to consider ways and means of encouraging it'.[93] In August 1975 he proposed that, in light of the great crisis facing Northern Ireland, a voluntary unionist/SDLP coalition, similar to that in Britain during the Second World War, for a temporary period, should be considered. This was a highly innovative way of getting round unionist objections to power sharing which they characterised as un-British. On 8 September 1975, however, by 37 votes to Craig's one, the UUUC convention members, decided that they 'could not agree to republicans taking part in any future cabinet of Northern Ireland', which in their view excluded the SDLP.[94] The UUUC backed the return to a majority type government. In the end, Craig was able to rely on the support of only three other Vanguard Party assembly colleagues (including David Trimble and loyalist leader Glenn Barr).

This rejection of Craig's new approach can be viewed as partly the outcome of political calculations by the other UUUC leaders, Ian

Paisley and Harry West, to undermine his position. More importantly, it reflected 'how deeply embedded exclusivist forms of unionist ideology' were in Northern Ireland, which allowed for no meaningful compromise.[95] Gerry Fitt, leader of the SDLP, was indeed a republican, but he was a constitutional republican who had lost a brother in the Irish Guards at Normandy in 1944 and who had served in the merchant navy on the convoys to Russia during the Second World War. Later in his political career he strongly denounced republican violence, which caused him to lose his home and to be forced into exile in London where he became a member of the House of Lords. In 1975, however, unionists deemed him unsuitable to serve in a Northern Ireland government. Political initiatives within the unionist parties now shifted to other ideas about integration or independence, and any form of shared government continued to be rejected.

Within the ranks of the SDLP important changes of approach also occurred in the late 1970s. These developments can be seen as both a response to the unionist rejection of power sharing and also the outcome of a 'greening' of the party. After the collapse of the convention, the SDLP leadership under Fitt continued to place a priority on establishing some form of 'partnership' government in Northern Ireland. By 1978, however, a much stronger emphasis was put on the so-called Irish dimension, which included advocacy of British withdrawal and Irish unity. At the 1978 party conference a motion supporting 'British disengagement' from Ireland was passed by all but two of the 500 delegates. Speakers declared that their objective was 'to promote the cause of Irish unity' and that 'the six-county statelet had failed'. A rare discordant note was struck by Paddy O'Hanlon who described the debate as 'a drift towards the right, towards nationalism as it was originally conceived ... a charge towards unity, a rush back into the cultural ghetto, and the cultural womb where everyone could feel comfortable'.[96] This trend led to the resignation of Paddy Devlin that same year and Gerry Fitt in 1979. Later Fitt recorded how party meetings became 'greener and greener', while Devlin wrote that 'the party was now populated with straightforward nationalists who were Catholic by religion and conservative in economic and social policies'.[97] In spite of initial objections, the SDLP under its new leader, John Hume, would partake in the Atkins talks but would boycott the Prior talks, because of the lack of an Irish dimension.

After the fall of the power-sharing executive, Cosgrave's administration was reluctant to get actively involved in northern affairs, partly because of the fear of the spread of violence to the south. A Fianna Fáil government came to power again at the end of 1977. On 8 January 1978 Lynch called for a British government declaration of intent to withdraw from Northern Ireland, but subsequently sought to contain the situation rather than to promote new initiatives. As a result, however, he faced internal party criticism for security co-operation with the northern authorities and not sufficiently opposing partition, reasons which led to his replacement by Charles Haughey at the end of 1979.[98] At the Fianna Fáil ard fheis on 16 February 1980, Haughey declared that Northern Ireland had failed as a political entity and that his government's 'first political priority' was to end partition.[99] He also made it clear that his plan was to work with the British government over the heads of the northern unionists. At a Dublin summit meeting in December 1980 Haughey and Prime Minister Margaret Thatcher, agreed to promote the relationship between the two countries, although clearly they had different views on what this meant. In November 1981, during Garret FitzGerald's brief tenure as taoiseach, an Anglo-Irish Intergovernmental Council was established. Such tentative steps towards some sort of Anglo-Irish process, however, had ceased by mid-1982, because of southern objections to British government initiatives in the north and British resentment at Haughey's pro-Argentine stance during the Falkland's War.

The return to office in late 1982 of Garret FitzGerald as leader of a Fine Gael/Labour coalition government led to several important new initiatives in response to Northern Ireland. In 1981 FitzGerald had proposed a 'crusade' to change the southern constitution, laws and attitudes which reflected 'a majority ethos': 'If I were a northern Protestant today, I cannot see how I could be attracted to getting involved with a state that is itself sectarian'.[100] In keeping with this idea, and in response to urging from the SDLP for Irish government action, he initiated in early 1983 the establishment of a New Ireland Forum to bring together all constitutional parties to deliberate on the shape of a new Ireland. Dermot Keogh has described the forum as 'the most comprehensive review of Irish identity conducted since the drafting of the 1937 constitution'.[101] Sittings of the Forum began in May 1983 and involved all constitutional nationalist parties, but no unionist party attended. Its report appeared a year later.

Significantly, in a new language for Irish nationalists, the report proposed that 'The validity of both the nationalist and unionist identities in Ireland and the democratic rights of every citizen on this island must be accepted'. It continued: 'both of these identities must have equally satisfactory, secure and durable, political, administrative and symbolic expression and protection'. Although the final report promised recognition of 'the unionist identity and ethos', its main proposal was a 32-county unitary state, while joint authority and a federal system were also presented as possible options.[102] The report represented an effort by constitutional nationalists to promote a broader and more plural-ist sense of identity in Ireland, but FitzGerald later acknowledged 'the nationalist bias of the historical section and the ritual obeisance to the concept of a unitary state'.[103] The findings of the report were rejected outright by the unionist parties. Fine Gael TD John Kelly warned that for unionists the three options offered were 'like trying to supply liquor to a teetotal house'.[104] The British prime minister, Margaret Thatcher, also rejected these proposals.

Nonetheless, because of the lack of progress and the threat posed to the SDLP by a rise in backing for Sinn Féin as a consequence of hunger strikes by republican prisoners in support of political status, as well as American pressure, negotiations between the British and Irish govern-ments resulted in the Anglo-Irish Agreement of 15 November. 1985. This agreement acknowledged formally a consultative role for the Irish government in northern affairs, on behalf of northern nationalists. The two governments affirmed that 'any change in the status of Northern Ireland would only come about with the consent of a majority of the people of Northern Ireland'. It was stated also that if a majority wanted a united Ireland, the British government would accept this. It established an inter-governmental conference and secretariat, to deal with political and other matters, including 'measures to 'recognise and accommodate the rights and identities of the two traditions in Northern Ireland'.[105] The agreement was registered in the United Nations and won strong international support. Over the next few years new levels of co-operation between the British and Irish government were achieved, which was significant.

At the same time, however, the agreement met strong opposition within Ireland, and it failed to produce either 'peace or stability', as intended. Many unionists saw this new role for the Irish government as a betrayal of their unionism and British identity, and conducted a strong political campaign, including civil disobedience, against the agreement. The agreement satisfied many SDLP supporters but did not win over republicans. The Sinn Féin president, Gerry Adams, denounced the agreement, because he said it represented 'the formal recognition of the partition of Ireland'.[106] Unionists remained suspicious of the motives of the southern government, in spite of their claims that articles 2 and 3 of the Irish constitution were just aspirational. Ironically, it was two north-ern unionist brothers, Michael and Christopher McGimpsey, who raised the matter in the Dublin Supreme Court, which reaffirmed the objective of a united Ireland as a 'constitutional imperative'.[107] The agreement brought about considerable inter-governmental co-operation, but did not achieve peace, owing to restrictive and confrontational identities, north and south.

This inherent conflict was understood most clearly at the time by Mary Robinson, a labour member of the Irish senate who resigned from her party over the agreement (four years later she would be elected as president of Ireland). She criticised unionists for failing to create 'the conditions for bringing the two communities into a framework of common allegiance. They have never had sufficient regard for the needs of the nationalist culture and identity'.[108] At the same time, however, she argued that the Irish government had agreed this 'deal' with the British government over the heads of unionists, without any consultation, despite its emphasis on 'consent'. Also there had not been any effort to change the 'existing constitutional claim' contained in articles 2 and 3 of the Irish constitution.[109] FitzGerald regretted that both articles were in the constitution, but he refused to initiate a debate on their change, no doubt conscious of the strident Fianna Fáil position on the matter.[110] In the Dáil debate on the agreement, Charles Haughey, the Fianna Fáil leader, cited these articles to declare that only Irish unity would 'provide peace and stability for Ireland', that the Fianna Fáil party refused to accept 'the legitimacy of Northern Ireland' and that they would continue to work for 'the reunification of Ireland and the withdrawal of the British presence'.[111] Later, in government, Haughey worked pragmatically with London under the agreement, but he did not change this viewpoint in any significant way. These diametrically opposed mindsets meant that such an agreement could not work effectively, whatever the ambitions of the British and Irish governments, or international concerns.

In the two decades between the beginning of 1969 and the end of 1989 a total of 3088 persons were killed as a result of political violence.[112] Most deaths occurred in Northern Ireland, but some also took place in Britain, the Irish Republic and continental Europe. Of these, a majority, 1649, were civilians, 475 were members of the army, 379 members of local security forces (such as the police and the Ulster Defence Regiment), 343 from republican paramilitary organisations and 114 from loyalist paramilitary organisations. The local security forces were responsible for 1.7 per cent of deaths, the army for 9.1 per cent, loyalist paramilitaries for 26.6 per cent and republican paramilitaries for 59.9 per cent (others or unidentified 2.5 per cent).

Of the local civilian dead, 978 were Catholics and 584 were Protestant. This simple comparison, however, understates the number of victims in the Protestant community because it leaves out members of the local security forces who were recruited primarily from Protestant civilians.[113] Of Catholic civilian deaths, a majority were the responsibility of loyalists, but nearly 1 in 5 was caused by republican paramilitaries, which was higher than Catholic civilian deaths due to the army and local security forces. Of Protestant civilian deaths, a majority were the responsiblity of republicans, but nearly 1 in 5 was also the work of loyalist paramilitaries.[114] In this conflict the paramilitaries sustained fewer deaths than either category of civilian or the army and local security forces. Of paramilitary deaths, a sizeable number were the result of 'accidents' or 'executions' by members of their own or breakaway groups. John Hume has noted that in these two decades: 'More than one out of two nationalist paramilitaries who lost their lives did so at their own hands'.[115] Significant numbers of loyalists also met their deaths in similar circumstances.

Among paramilitaries, claims that their actions were 'defensive' or 'reactive' were made sometimes, but more important were ideological claims to justify their violence. On the loyalist side the main paramilitary organisations were the UDA with its political wing, the Ulster Democratic Party (UDP), and the UVF with its political wing, the Progressive Unionist Party (PUP). Under the leadership of Andy Tyrie and John McMichael, a section of the UDA in the 1980s made efforts to develop a 'politically constructive way forward'.[116] At the same time, loyalist paramilitaries continued their violence. Gusty Spence, a veteran loyalist, described their approach: 'If it wasn't possible to get at the IRA then some thought, "We'll get those who are harbouring them, comforting them and supporting them"'.[117] In 1970 the IRA had split into two main wings, 'Official' and 'Provisional', over political aims and the role of violence. The 'Official' wing adopted a ceasefire in 1972, which they maintained largely thereafter, while putting their efforts into a political, left-wing struggle for 'democratic rights and social advance'.[118] They criticised the violence of the Provisional IRA as encouraging sectarianism. Both republican wings had political counterparts in the so-called Official Sinn Féin and Provisional Sinn Féin. The 'Officials' renamed themselves the Workers' Party in 1982; some broke away in 1992 to form a new party, Democratic Left. Both parties won seats in the south, but would be less successful in the north.

For the 'Provisional' wing of the republican movement, the primary aim remained a united Ireland. The Provisional IRA, after some temporary truces in the early 1970s, returned to the use of violence. After a rise in public support for republicans following the death of hunger strike prisoners in 1981–82, however, their political wing, 'Provisional' Sinn Féin, started to contest elections, north and south, and to adopt a broader political platform. In November 1985 the Sinn Féin ard fheis voted to end their abstentionist policy from the Dáil and so recognised the southern state and government. Nonetheless, the Sinn Féin leadership continued to justify violence. In 1986 Gerry Adams declared: 'armed struggle is a necessary form of resistance ... armed struggle becomes unnecessary only when the British presence has been removed ... if at any time Sinn Féin decide to disown the armed struggle, they won't have me as a member'.[119]

Despite the obvious political stalemate during these years, it is possible to detect some changes in aspects of identity. Southern accession in 1973 to the EEC (later the EU) was important. It served to further undermine much of the economic, social and moral isolation under which the country had suffered previously, and which had been linked to restrictive identities. It questioned narrow ideas of sovereignty, normalised cross-border co-operation and placed greater emphasis on conciliation rather than confrontation.[120] European law challenged some of the restrictive links between church and state in areas such as divorce, contraception and homosexuality. FitzGerald's 'crusade' for a more pluralist society gained considerable support, even though efforts to change the country's ban on divorce by a referendum in 1987 were unsuccessful and the government was persuaded to add legislation on abortion into the constitution in 1983, amid great controversy. FitzGerald's efforts at social reform were opposed not only by conservative Catholic forces but also by Charles Haughey and Fianna Fáil for short-term gain.[121] These decades also saw a retreat from compulsory Irish. In the 1970s a pass in Irish was made no longer essential for the leaving certificate in education and Irish was dropped as a mandatory requirement for the civil service. Strong support survived for the Irish language but these elements of compulsion were seen as neither effective nor pluralist, and a bar to any possible future connections with the north.[122]

During these decades the Protestant community in the south enjoyed mixed fortunes. A referendum in 1972 removed the 'special position' of the Catholic church from the constitution. In 1973 the Protestant TD Erskine Childers was elected as Irish president. By 1991 nearly one-quarter of all married persons from the religious minority were in mixed marriages.[123] With the outbreak of conflict in Northern Ireland, southern Protestants, through letters to the press and at the Church of

Ireland synod, expressed support for civil rights, while Protestant pupils joined the protest march to the British embassy after Bloody Sunday in 1972.[124] All this showed an attempt by society to be more pluralist and by Protestants to play a full role, but there was also evidence that they remained a marginalised minority. In 1970, the only southern Orange July demonstration at Rossnowlagh, Co. Donegal, was cancelled owing to threats, and did not resume until 1978. At the 1977 general election just one Protestant TD, James White of Fine Gael in Donegal, was elected compared with three in 1969. Of the three Protestant TDs from 1969, Erskine Childers, Fianna Fáil, Monaghan, became president; Henry Dockrell, Fine Gael, Dun Laoghaire, lost his seat; and Billy Fox, Fine Gael, Monaghan, and a senator from 1973, was murdered by republicans. There was only one Protestant TD in the Dáil until the early 1990s.[125]

In 1973, after becoming Irish minister for external affairs, Garret FitzGerald raised with the Vatican the subject of the damaging consequences for the southern Protestant population of the Catholic church laws on mixed marriages. He was informed that this matter was the responsibility of the Irish bishops. When questioned on the issue at the New Ireland Forum, the bishops' spokesman claimed this was the responsibility of Rome.[126] Changes to such laws in these years were minimal in Ireland. The 1966 Vatican document on intermarriage dropped the requirement from canon law that the Catholic partner had to 'work prudently for the conversion of the non-Catholic spouse'.[127] Another Vatican document in 1970 allowed local bishops to relax the rules on mixed marriages. This change had important effects in some countries with mixed populations, such as Switzerland and Germany, where Catholic bishops allowed the parents to decide on the religious upbringing of children.[128] 'In Ireland', however, as Declan Deane, a Jesuit priest commented in 1974, 'where the need for visible inter-church fellowship is most acute, we have seen perhaps the least liberal implementation of the papal instruction'.[129] The Catholic bishops in Ireland strongly opposed such liberalisation until the 1980s.[130] The Protestant community continued to decrease; it was 107,000 and just 3 per cent of the population in 1991.[131] This decline in southern Protestant numbers was important not only for the south, but also for the north. In 1995 John Dunlop, a former moderator of the Presbyterian church in Ireland, recorded his opinion that 'more than any other single factor, the observed decline in the Protestant population in the republic has confirmed northern Protestants in their prejudices and fears'.[132]

Despite the political stalemate, important changes occurred in Northern Ireland. Membership of the EEC from 1973 was significant. This was especially so for the SDLP, whose leader, John Hume, viewed the European ideal as a lesson for people in Ireland, north and south, in how to reconcile old differences and to emphasise people over territory. Both the two unionist parties and Sinn Féin expressed scepticism towards Europe, the former because it weakened British sovereignty and the latter because it weakened Irish sovereignty. Nonetheless, for many people the EU did eventually introduce the ideals and practice of national co-operation.[133] These decades saw new levels of church co-operation. Efforts were made to encourage better relations among clergy and congregations and to challenge links between religion and politics. In 1985, for example, Cahal Daly, Catholic bishop of Down and Connor, stated that it was good neither for religion nor for politics that to be born a Protestant should mean being born a unionist, and that to be born a Catholic should mean being born a nationalist.[134] Various religious and non-religious groups, such as Protestant and Catholic Encounter and Corrymeela, sought to promote reconciliation.

A Central Community Relations Unit was established in 1987 by the government in Northern Ireland to coordinate efforts to improve relations between communities, and in January 1990 the Community Relations Council was formed. The Cultural Traditions Group was established in 1988 to promote public awareness of cultural diversity involving different identities and traditions.[135] From early 1989, it ran conferences on cultural traditions looking at 'varieties' of Britishness and Irishness, and supported publications exploring different cultural traditions. A survey in 1989 revealed interesting changes in identities, compared with the late 1960s.[136] Among Protestants only 3 per cent now viewed themselves as Irish, compared with 68 per cent who regarded themselves as British and 10 per cent as Ulster. This decline in Irish identity among Protestants can be attributed very largely to republican violence. Among Catholics, those who saw themselves as British had fallen to 12 per cent, compared with 61 per cent who regarded themselves as Irish and 1 per cent as Ulster. This fall in British identity was due mainly to loyalist violence. At the same time 16 per cent of Protestants and 25 per cent of Catholics now saw themselves as Northern Irish, a new category of identity. As Karen Trew has pointed out, this new identity does not have the status of a national identity and is somewhat ambiguous, but it expresses a concern for a shared identity and involves 'identification with both the Irish and British strands of life in the region'.[137]

Change and agreement, 1990–98

This period witnessed the rise of a peace process that brought about not only important agreements and structures but also significant changes in identities. Negotiations took place between governments, political parties and paramilitaries (through their political wings). On 15 December 1993 the British and Irish heads of government signed the Downing Street Declaration, by which the two governments promised to work towards a new political framework within Northern Ireland, between north and south and between Britain and Ireland. The British government accepted the right of self-determination for the people of Ireland as a whole, while the Irish government acknowledged that any such self-determination was subject to the consent of the majority of the people of Northern Ireland. The declaration talked of 'the rights and identities of both traditions in Ireland'.[138] On 31 August 1994 the IRA called a ceasefire, to be followed on 13 October 1994 by a ceasefire by loyalist paramilitaries. February 1995 saw the publication of the document, *Frameworks for the Future*, which proposed arrangements for government in Northern Ireland, and co-operation between north and south, which would fully respect 'the identity, sense of allegiance, aspiration and ethos of both the unionist and nationalist communities there'.[139]

Difficulties were to ensue subsequently over various issues, but on 15 September 1997 formal talks started at Stormont, involving all parties and the two governments. On 10 April 1998 there emerged an agreement, known as the Belfast Agreement, or the Good Friday Agreement as it is sometimes called. Referenda on 22 May in both parts of Ireland recorded sizeable majorities in favour of the new agreement. In Northern Ireland this involved a vote on the agreement, while in the Irish Republic it involved a vote in favour of changes to the Irish Constitution, arising out of the agreement. These developments were followed by a major reduction in political violence after 1998. At the same time, we should note that, during this period of negotiations from 1990 to March 1998 over 500 people lost their lives owing to political violence.[140]

A number of factors were important for bringing about these new arrangements. Undoubtedly, after several decades of violence, many were keen for peace. By the late 1980s both British government and republican sources conceded that there was a military stalemate between the security forces and the IRA.[141] The security forces had largely contained the violence but they were unable to end it, partly due to the constraints of a liberal democracy and political considerations. There emerged opinion in both government circles and the leadership of the paramilitaries that some political way forward provided a better solution rather than a purely military one. Outside influences, especially from America, backed an agreement. Considerable British government investment helped to provide employment in the north which assisted in ameliorating any economic sources of conflict. The EU from 1995 contributed large sums to assist peace and reconciliation, as did the International Fund for Ireland.[142] In addition, as Cathal McCall has argued, EU national co-operation led to 'transterritorialism' and a new sense of space which has helped to promote 'inclusion and identity realignment'.[143]

Reforms within Northern Ireland had removed injustices and discrimination which had been causes of resentment in the 1960s and 1970s. Strong efforts were made to promote full equality in employment. Capital funding for Catholic schools was increased to 100 per cent by 1992. Catholics now participated fully in public life in Northern Ireland. By 1981 Catholics were 38 per cent of the Northern Ireland population and by 2001 this figure stood at 44 per cent. Catholics in Northern Ireland in 2001 numbered 737,412 compared with 430,161 in the same six counties in 1911: this contrasted with the situation in the Irish Republic where Protestant numbers stood at 146,226 in 2002 compared with 327,179 in 1911. On the religious front, efforts continued to advance reconciliation and co-operation.[144] Within civil society a wide range of organisations, such as Co-operation Ireland, promoted better relations between different parts and sections of Ireland. In the schools the programme of Education for Mutual Understanding helped to increase respect for diversity and mutual understanding.[145]

Important changes occurred in the south. The election of Mary Robinson as president in 1990 was significant. In her presidential inaugural speech, she began by declaring her intention to represent a 'new Ireland, open, tolerant, inclusive'. In the final part of the speech, she turned to 'another place close to my heart, Northern Ireland'. She stated: 'as the elected choice of the people of this part of our island I want to extend the hand of friendship and of love to both communities in the other part. And I want to do this with no string attached, no hidden agenda ... I will seek to encourage mutual understanding and tolerance between all the different communities sharing this island'.[146] Besides showing support for a more conciliatory approach towards Northern Ireland, her election reflected the rise of a strong women's movement which challenged male dominance not only in the work place and society but also in politics and the prevailing national identity. She was succeeded as president in 1997 by Mary McAleese (born, brought up and educated in Northern Ireland), again symbolising the new role of women in modern Ireland. In her inaugural speech President McAleese described herself as the 'first president from Ulster' and declared that the theme of her presidency would be 'Building bridges'.[147]

This decade witnessed strong efforts to promote pluralism in Irish society. There was increased questioning of links of church and state. A referendum in 1995 permitted the removal of the ban on divorce in the Irish constitution. A number of scandals and court cases involving some members of the Catholic clergy and church-run institutions served to undermine not only clericalism in society but also the relationship between Catholicism and Irish nationalist identity.[148] The Forum for Peace and Reconciliation was established in Dublin in 1995 to examine 'the steps required to remove barriers of distrust on the basis of promoting respect for the equal rights and validity of both traditions and identities'.[149] In an important speech on 2 February 1995, to the joint houses of the Irish parliament, President Robinson declared: 'Irishness as a concept seems to me to be at its strongest when it reaches out to everyone on this island and shows itself capable of honouring and listening to those whose sense of identity, and whose cultural values, may be more British than Irish'.[150] Changes in other aspects of the 'national identity code' of the 1950s also affected social and economic life in the south. By the 1990s the efforts of Lemass and others to do away with protectionism and isolationism had brought new prosperity to the Irish Republic. The improvements in education begun in the mid-1960s and efforts to attract international investment and employment to Ireland resulted in a substantial improvement in southern economic performance and eventually an equalling and then out-performance of economic activity in the north, which suffered as a result of the 'troubles'. Economic success continued into the twenty-first century until the consequences of a property boom and unregulated financial markets created dire economic conditions, post-2007.

This new pluralism had an important bearing on the position of Protestants in southern society. Ecumenical relations, among both clergy and laity, improved greatly. In 1997 the Catholic bishop of Killaloe, Dr Willie Walsh, described the *Ne Temere* ruling as 'contrary to the spirit of Christian generosity and love' and apologised 'for the hurt and pain inflicted'.[151] These years witnessed a liberalisation of intermarriage arrangements. Catholic church rules were relaxed to some degree. At the same time, Garret FitzGerald noted in 1996, young Irish

Catholics began to ignore what they saw as 'their church's unreasonable demands'.[152] The 1992 general election saw a rise in the number of Protestant deputies from one to four, with the return of Ivan Yates and Seymour Crawford (both Fine Gael), Johnny Fox (Independent) and Trevor Sargent (Green Party). For the first time since the founding of the state the 2002 census showed an increase in Protestant numbers to 146,226 or 3.7 per cent of the total population.[153] In 2005 Michael Webb, a member of the Dublin Diocesan Synod, rejected strongly the view that the south was any longer a 'cold place for the vast majority of Protestants'. He wrote: 'The Church of Ireland in recent years has gained considerable self-confidence. It looks to express its opinions not as a beleaguered minority but as of right as a community that is contributing positively to society'.[154] At the same time, we should note the concern expressed in 2010 of the Church of Ireland archbishop of Dublin, Dr John Neill, that despite new respect for diversity, 'the presence of the majority church is still all pervasive', citing the example of schools under the management of vocational education committees.[155]

Undoubtedly, these factors were supportive of change, but they can only provide part of the explanation for what happened. We must also acknowledge the importance of directly political factors. Outside influences, particularly from the United States, helped to promote this peace process. Yet, as one American diplomat, G.T. Dempsey, has pointed out: 'any American involvement can only be supportive. It is up to the parties at the table to make the necessary judgements concerning trust and forgiveness'.[156] The consociational-type structure developed for Northern Ireland, and the determination of the British and Irish governments to strongly pursue an agreement, were also helpful, but these factors had not delivered peace in the 1970s.[157] The role of American Senator George Mitchell as chairman of the talks leading up to the 1998 agreement was important, as was the determination and patience of other people who assisted in the very lengthy negotiations. At the same time, however, critical for the success of this peace process was the change in identities that occurred at this time among most of the parties involved. Such change within each player in this political drama was influenced heavily by change among the other players. These negotiations and discussions were tortuous and lengthy, and the negotiators faced a vast series of hurdles and problems, but it is possible to draw out some of the new perspectives developed by the different parties and to highlight the significant outcomes which emerged.

In the 1990s, as Christopher Farrington has pointed out, 'new political ideas were important in providing an impetus for political change within unionism'.[158] This applied in particular to members and supporters of the Ulster Unionist Party. To some degree, these new ideas arose from the late 1980s onwards and were due to the experience of power sharing or 'responsibility sharing' in some local councils, supported by unionist politicians such as Ken Maginnis, which introduced novel co-operation for unionists with nationalists. During the early 1990s unionist spokesmen showed a liberalisation in their response towards ideas of power sharing and an Irish dimension.[159] At another level, this period saw some unionists question the close links between religion and politics and call for a 'civic unionism'. Links between the UUP and the Orange Order were questioned, although they were not to be broken until 2005. Concerns about the south had been alleviated somewhat by the evidence of the new pluralism, as seen in the election and example of Mary Robinson, and the efforts in the southern press and elsewhere to understand the unionist position. Partly in response to these new ideas, and partly because of changes in the Irish Republic, unionists now felt more willing to engage in negotiations with nationalists and the southern government.

In his first address in 1995 as the new leader of the UUP David Trimble declared his support for a pluralist British identity: 'The United Kingdom is a genuinely plural state in which it is possible to be Welsh, or Scottish and British. Similarly one can be Irish or Ulster and British as well'.[160] At the same time, concerns about decommissioning and the powers of north–south bodies would be sources of serious contention for unionists. Nonetheless, by the time of the final talks in 1998, important changes had occurred within the UUP, as described by Thomas Hennessey, an Ulster Unionist Party aide at the talks: 'Unionism was no longer arguing for majority rule, nor for total integration within the United Kingdom. Unionists were not opposing a recognition of the validity of the Irish identity of nationalists, or their sense of belonging to the Irish nation, or asking them simply to accept that they were British'.[161] In these negotiations, unionists accepted power sharing and north–south bodies. At the same time the unionists under Trimble were able to achieve the commitment of all to the principles of consent and the rejection of violence, to secure the constitutional recognition of Northern Ireland by the south and to agree to east-west bodies. Showing clearly the important change in the identity of many unionists, Trimble, at the opening of the new assembly, pledged to provide 'a pluralist parliament for a pluralist people', a direct contradiction of Craig's statement of 'a Protestant parliament and a Protestant state'.[162] We must note, however, that members of the DUP did not accept this approach and would leave the talks and oppose the agreement in the referendum.

The SDLP leader, John Hume, headed his party's involvement in this peace process. He continued to emphasise the north–south and Irish–British dimensions as well as relations within Northern Ireland. He played an important role in helping to move the republican movement away from support for violence and in changing nationalist and republican perspectives. In 1988 he declared: 'If I were to lead a civil-rights campaign in Northern Ireland today the major target of that campaign would be the IRA. It is they who carry out the gravest infringements of human and civil rights. The most fundamental right is the right to life'.[163] That same year he entered into private negotiations with Gerry Adams, leader of Sinn Féin, on the role of the IRA and the political future. He argued against violence on the grounds of both morality and efficacy. Two other key issues in these discussions that continued into the 1990s were Irish self-determination, a subject rooted in arguments about the 1918 general election and subsequent partition, and the role of the British government. Hume proposed an 'agreed self-determination', which would involve the right of the people of Ireland, in separate referenda, to determine their future, so satisfying nationalist/republican concerns for self-determination, but also allowing for unionist concerns about consent.[164] As well, he argued that the British government was neutral on the question of unity and that political progress was possible for republicans.

These arguments, along with the responses from the two governments, eventually helped to convince Sinn Féin and the IRA to reject violence and to opt for a purely political programme in order to best promote their republican aims. Another essential part played by Hume was to revise important elements in the core ideology of both Irish nationalism and republicanism in relation to partition and the unionist community.[165] He argued that the root cause of the present conflict lay in divisions in Ireland, rather than in London or in colonialism/imperialism. He emphasised the importance of people over territory and stressed the European context. Hume helped to convince republicans and nationalists, north and south, of the need to accept the legitimacy in Ireland of both main identities (or traditions, as he often called them) and to support arrangements to accommodate unionists with their British identity. The consent principle was extended from accepting the right of unionists to a particular form of a united Ireland to acknowledging their right to reject any such united Ireland. At the same time as he backed the right of consent for unionists, he asserted the right of consent for northern nationalists in the effective recognition of their Irish identity, power-sharing arrangements within Northern Ireland, north–south bodies and the role of the Irish government. Later, when, with David Trimble, he was awarded the Nobel prize for peace, Hume in his acceptance speech declared his belief that the agreement had created 'institutions which respect diversity but ensure that we work together in our common interest'.[166]

A significant part was played in this evolving peace process by the Alliance Party and the Northern Ireland Women's Coalition, even if both groups had relatively small numbers of supporters. The Alliance Party continued to espouse the value of a shared community and to challenge links between confessional groups and political positions. In 1994, after the IRA ceasefire, the Alliance Party leadership were the first non-nationalists to enter discussions with Sinn Féin, and an Alliance delegation attended the Dublin Forum for Peace and Reconciliation, where they emphasised the importance of the consent principle. In the inter-party talks at Stormont, Alliance representatives urged the importance of compromise and achieving new arrangements with broad community support. When the new power-sharing assembly was established the Alliance leader, John Alderdice, was appointed as speaker or chairman, a reflection of the role of Alliance to provide a non-aligned centre position. In April 1996 the Northern Ireland Women's Coalition (NIWC) was formed by a number of women's groups which believed that women had been effectively sidelined from the political process.[167] Representatives from the NIWC participated in the negotiations leading up to the 1998 agreement and were particularly concerned to promote an equality agenda and social inclusiveness. They provided an important voice which emphasised aspects outside 'traditional demands' of many of the other participants.[168]

In this whole process important changes occurred in the approach of the Irish government. In 1991 the first debate occurred in the Dáil, at the instigation of a member of the Workers' Party, on the question of articles 2 and 3 of the Irish constitution. Any suggestion of alteration to these articles was opposed by the Fianna Fáil government. In 1992 Albert Reynolds succeeded Charles Haughey as taoiseach and at first reiterated this fundamentalist position. By 1993, however, after discussions with some northern unionists, in particular Robin Eames, Church of Ireland archbishop of Armagh, he came to a better understanding of how unionists felt about the matter.[169] The outcome was that in the Downing Street Declaration, for the first time, a Fianna Fáil leader agreed publicly that in a future settlement there could be changes to these constitutional clauses. At the same time Reynolds opened up private negotiations with Sinn Féin through his assistant, Martin Mansergh. They sought to deal with some of the concerns of Sinn Féin regarding a future settlement and an IRA ceasefire. In his memoirs Reynolds remarked how in these debates with Sinn Féin, over matters such as consent and self-determination, 'archaic language was the problem, the expression of ideologies buried in history'.[170]

The Irish government worked closely with the British government in the unfolding peace process to keep all the parties involved, especially the SDLP and Sinn Féin. At the same time that Fianna Fáil leaders, both Reynolds and later Bertie Ahern, gave special support to northern nationalists, other leading southern political figures, in particular Mary Robinson as president,1990–97, and John Bruton as taoiseach, 1995–97, continued to express their support for a pluralist Irish identity and the rights of unionists. In the final negotiations, the taoiseach Bertie Ahern concerned himself not only with nationalist interests but also with listening to what the UUP leader, David Trimble, had to say. Ahern has described how 'we probably built up a common ground. I thought irredentism was dead. I was saying things that differed from what was expected of a nationalist leader'.[171] The Irish government agreed to remove the territorial claim over Northern Ireland by introducing important changes to articles 2 and 3 of the Irish constitution. At a late stage Ahern intervened to curb enthusiasm on the Irish side for more extensive powers for north–south bodies, which alarmed unionists and which had damaged the Sunningdale Agreement.[172] On the final day of the two years of negotiations, on Good Friday, 10 April 1998, Ahern declared: 'This is a day we should treasure – a day when agreement and accommodation have replaced days of differences and division'.[173]

For the British government this period also involved change and efforts to make political progress. In a speech on 26 March 1991, Peter Brooke, secretary of state for Northern Ireland, declared that future discussions would focus on three main stands or relationships: 'we are setting out to achieve a new beginning for relationships within Northern Ireland, within the island of Ireland and between the peoples of these islands'.[174] Although the government's official position was that it would not deal with the IRA as long as violence continued, secret contacts were made with the republican movement to encourage it along a purely political path. In November 1990 Peter Brooke declared that the British government had no 'selfish, strategic or economic interest in Northern Ireland'.[175] On 16 December 1992 Brooke's successor,

Sir Patrick Mayhew, stated that if the IRA ended its campaign, soldiers could be withdrawn from the streets and Sinn Féin could be included in political talks.[176] The government also continued to encourage inter-party talks and to seek a closer relationship with the Irish government over the way forward, leading to the 1993 Downing Street Declaration and the 1995 Framework documents. These moves achieved some success in helping to lead to the ceasefires of 1994, but failed to win much support from unionists, who remained suspicious of the British government's intentions.

The election of a new British labour government with Tony Blair as prime minister changed matters and gave unionists more confidence in the British government. Unionists had been worried about the labour party policy of support for 'Irish unity by consent', but under Blair this changed to a neutral support for consent.[177] David Trimble and his negotiating team accepted Blair's genuine attachment to the consent principle, and this influenced their willingness to be involved in negotiations.[178] At the same time Blair was able to persuade the SDLP and republicans of his willingness to take their concerns seriously. During this period, the actions of the British government showed evidence of significant change in attitude, as can be seen in its new relationship with the Irish government, the Northern Ireland parties and the paramilitaries, all of which helped to bring about the 1998 settlement. During the subsequent referendum, Blair described what he saw as the achievement of the agreement: 'From now on the future of Northern Ireland rests with the principle of consent. At the same time we are offering new ways for the nationalist community to find and express their identity, and to ensure fairness and equality to all'.[179]

During the 1990s significant change occurred in the ideology of republican leaders. This related not only to the subject of violence and the primacy of politics, but also to northern unionists. To some extent these changes were affected by the military stalemate, but just as important was the influence of new thinking about republican perspectives and aims. In the early 1990s debate emerged on the utility of violence. At the annual Sinn Féin commemoration of Wolfe Tone at Bodenstown in June 1992, a leading Sinn Féin spokesman, Jim Gibney, raised questions of whether or not republicans were 'deafened by the deadly sound of their own gunfire' or 'trapped inside a complex web of struggle from which they can't or won't emerge'.[180] Within republicanism also there was an attempt among some 'to empathise with, and explore the identity and real fears of the unionist population'.[181] In 1995, for example, Gibney acknowledged: 'the traditional position that a resolution to the problems with the unionists would have to await the removal of the British government's involvement in Ireland was wrong'. He then argued: 'We must now accept that there are divided political allegiances within the nation and that unionists have a dual identity that must be accommodated'.[182] Secret republican negotiations with Hume and Irish and British government representatives revolved around questions of self-determination, consent and the role of so-called armed struggle. Republicans were now persuaded of the possibility of pursuing their republican goals without the use of violence.

Renunciation of 'armed struggle' and recognition of the unionists' right to consent, which altered republican perspectives, took effect only inter-mittently over this decade, with setbacks along the way. Nonetheless, new acceptance by the Irish government and influential friends in America encouraged the republican movement to become actively involved in the political negotiations between parties and governments. At the same time such acceptance obliged republicans to establish a ceasefire and to accept the terms of the final outcome of these negotiations, even though originally many had expected a more radical settlement. The new agreement included the republican goal of national self-determination, but also, on account of the consent principle, the right of the majority unionist community in Northern Ireland to remain within the United Kingdom. The identity and rights of Irish republicans/nationalists were guaranteed in the new arrangements for Northern Ireland, and a united Ireland remained an acceptable future option, even if only with consent of a majority of northern and southern citizens. At the same time other gains for republicans included early release of paramilitary prisoners and reform of the police. Acceptance of such a settlement, and the abandonment of 'armed struggle' by republicans, reflected how much changed perspectives and goals now influenced republican identity.

Among loyalist paramilitaries and their supporters important changes also occurred. During the late 1980s and early 1990s a number of prominent loyalist spokesmen urged the need for a political solution and began to challenge the use of violence. In April 1991 the Combined Loyalist Military Command (CLMC) was established as an umbrella body for loyalist paramilitary organisations. Violence continued, but political considerations now became more important, particularly because of the influence of the former UVF prisoner and leader Gusty Spence.[183] Secret contacts were established with the Irish and British governments. In 1994, in response to the Downing Street Declaration and the IRA ceasefire announcement, they sought assurances from both governments that no secret deal had been done with the IRA. The result was that on 13 October

1994 the CLMC declared a ceasefire, stating that the union was safe and offering 'abject and true remorse' to 'innocent victims'.[184] Reflecting the change within loyalism, David Ervine, a leading member of the loyalist organisation, the Progressive Unionist Party, declared in early October 1994: 'The politics of division see thousands of people dead, most of them working class, and headstones on the graves of young men. We have been fools: let's not be fools any longer. All elements must be comfortable within Northern Ireland. We have got to extend the hand of friendship ...'.[185]

The loyalist leadership now supported efforts at negotiation over the following years leading up to the 1998 agreement. They were influenced both by what they saw as important developments among republicans and by concern to construct a more inclusive and peaceful society.[186] A new willingness to accept change, reflecting a significant shift in loyalist attitudes, would lead to loyalists acting as 'an enabling influence in very tangible and practical ways through the talks process leading to the Good Friday Agreement', especially in relation to unionism.[187] Their approval for the agreement was critical because lack of such loyalist support had undermined the power-sharing arrangements in 1974 and their backing in 1998 was necessary to establish a unionist majority for the new arrangements. For loyalists the principal gain of the Belfast Agreement was the guarantee that Northern Ireland would remain part of the UK, as long as that was the wish of the majority of the people of Northern Ireland.

Belfast Agreement and aftermath

In its opening declaration the Belfast Agreement, sometimes called the Good Friday Agreement, stated a commitment to 'partnership, equality and mutual respect' as the basis of relationships 'within Northern Ireland, between north and south, and between these islands' and reaffirmed a commitment to 'exclusively democratic and peaceful means of resolving differences'.[188] The principle of consent was firmly established, as was the right of self-determination. The agreement guaranteed the status of Northern Ireland as part of the United Kingdom, as reflecting the wishes of the majority, but also accepted the right of a majority to change this status in the future. The agreement sought to acknowledge and respect different national aspirations and identities. It referred to all the people of Northern Ireland 'in the diversity of their identities and traditions' and promised parity of esteem and equal treatment 'for the identity, ethos, and aspirations of both communities'. The agreement recognised the 'birthright of all the people of Northern Ireland to identify themselves and be accepted as Irish or British, or both, as they may so choose'. The right of everyone to hold British or Irish citizenship was confirmed. The two governments agreed to support changes in, respectively, the Irish constitution and British legislation relating to the constitutional position of Northern Ireland.

The agreement set out proposals for new structures and institutions, constitutional and legal change, and various reforms and issues. Democratic structures of an assembly and a government for Northern Ireland, with inbuilt cross-community mechanisms, were to be established. North–south bodies were created alongside an east–west council. Other matters included changes to policing, early prisoner release and decommissioning of paramilitary organisations. At referenda on 22 May 1998 the new arrangements were accepted by 71 per cent in the north and, in effect, by 94 per cent in the south. The claim in the Irish constitution to jurisdiction over Northern Ireland was replaced with an aspiration to unity. Article 3 now declared 'the firm will of the Irish nation, in harmony and friendship, to unite all the people who share the territory of Ireland, in all the diversity of their identities and traditions', and recognised that 'a united Ireland shall be brought about only by peaceful means with the consent of a majority of the people, democratically expressed in both jurisdictions'.[189] The Government of Ireland Act of 1920 and the Anglo-Irish Agreement of 1985 were repealed.

What was achieved with this agreement was significant. Of course, it represented an accommodation rather than a removal of differences. The agreement acknowledged 'the substantial differences between our continuing, and equally legitimate, political aspirations' and pledged to strive towards 'reconciliation and rapprochement', by means of these new arrangements. Unionists remained unionist, nationalists remained nationalist and there were still differences between north and south and between Britain and Ireland. Some aspects of the agreement were ambiguous and some problems were left to the future. Nonetheless, the agreement was a major achievement. It established innovative ways for people and communities to co-exist and to create broadly acceptable accommodation of different views. This new approach reflected significant changes in the identities of most of those involved, without which an end to violence and agreed structures of government in Northern Ireland could not have been achieved. A power-sharing executive was formed in 1998 with David Trimble of the UUP as first minister and Seamus Mallon of the SDLP as deputy first minister, respectively. At the end of 2001 Mark Durkan became head of the SDLP and deputy first minister.

These changes must not be exaggerated. Over the next decade, severe difficulties emerged between the parties in operating the new arrangements, and the assembly and government faced a number of serious crises. To some extent, these problems existed because of specific concerns over issues such as early release of prisoners, reform of the police and decommissioning. More importantly, many on each side had only partially embraced these changes and there remained a lack of trust. A small group of dissident republicans rejected the agreement as a betrayal of the republican cause and carried out a number of shootings and bombings. In particular the bombing of a busy street at Omagh cost 29 lives. Intra-loyalist violence persisted. Between April 1998 and 2006 another 128 people died, bringing the total lives lost due to the 'troubles', from 1969 to 2006, to 3717: security forces had caused 367 deaths, loyalists 1109, republicans 2152 and others 89.[190] The DUP opposed the agreement, principally on matters of sharing power with republicans and north–south bodies, and also over decommissioning. They did, however, take up positions in the new executive. Sinn Féin was cautious at first and then came to accept the agreement and seats on the executive, but rejected calls for the IRA to put all its arms out of use or to disband.

Concerns about the working of the agreement were to result in the DUP and Sinn Féin at the assembly elections of 2003 becoming the largest parties in their respective camps. Nonetheless, there was still widespread support for these arrangements to survive and the main parties responded positively to this. Subsequent negotiations were to lead to final IRA decommissioning and in July 2005 the IRA formally declared an end to its campaign. Talks between the parties in Scotland in late 2006 resulted in the St Andrews Agreement, which made some changes to the 1998 agreement. The outcome was that Sinn Féin declared its support for policing and the DUP stated its willingness to go into government with Sinn Féin. Following an assembly election in March 2007, when Sinn Féin and the DUP again emerged as the two largest parties, a new power-sharing executive was formed with the DUP leader, Ian Paisley, as first minister, and a Sinn Féin leader, Martin McGuinness as deputy first minister. In 2008 Peter Robinson became leader of the DUP and took over from Ian Paisley as first minister.

This result, whereby the DUP accepted power sharing with Sinn Féin and north–south bodies and Sinn Féin delivered full IRA decommissioning and disbanding and also support for the police, marked an important stage in the outworking of the Belfast Agreement. No doubt this happened partly because these two parties saw such a move as politically advantageous. At the same time it can be argued that this development involved an important change in attitudes. Inaugural speeches on 8 May 2007 by both Paisley and McGuinness on taking office in the new executive revealed these changed perspectives. Paisley declared that he had not changed his unionism, but went on to say how 'we are all aiming to build a Northern Ireland in which all can live together in peace, being equal under the law and equally subject to the law ... I believe that Northern Ireland has come to a time of peace, a time when hate will no longer rule. How good it will be to be part of a wonderful healing in our province'. McGuinness stated his pride in being a republican, but proceeded to talk of striving 'towards a society moving from division and disharmony to one which celebrates our diversity and is determined to provide a better future for all our people'.[191]

Four days later, as Northern Ireland's first minister, Ian Paisley met the Irish taoiseach, Bertie Ahern, at the deeply symbolic site of the Battle of the Boyne in Co. Meath. Paisley declared that by their meeting they were 'cementing a better relationship between Northern Ireland and the Republic, one based on mutual respect and good neighbourliness', while Ahern stated how 'we can now celebrate our diversity, as well as what we have in common'.[192] Since this time there have been problems in relations between the main parties in Northern Ireland over various issues such as education and policing and justice, but all have continued to work through the power-sharing arrangements and institutions established under the recent agreements. A settlement of the justice issue was followed by the appointment in 2011 of Alliance Party member, David Forde, as agreed justice minister. The strength of these revised identities was shown in March 2009 when republican dissidents killed two off-duty British soldiers at Antrim. Sinn Féin Deputy First Minister Martin McGuinness was unequivocal in his condemnation: 'these people are traitors to the island of Ireland'.[193] Such comments from McGuinness, and his new working relationship with Paisley, caused the latter in May 2009 to describe political developments in the north in recent years as a 'modern miracle'.[194] There was strong, united condemnation of the murder by dissident republicans of two members of the new Police Service of Northern Ireland. In spite of internal tensions, the power-sharing executive successfully completed its first full term of office in March 2011, and the following month a new government and assembly were elected.

Final observations

By the first decade of the twenty-first century, a number of important agreements are in place between the British and Irish governments, between north and south and between the main parties in Northern

Ireland. New institutions, with popular support, have been established to provide the structures to promote these relationships. Central to this improved situation has been significant change in the political identity of both individuals and national communities. Hitherto difficult problems over matters such as self-determination, sovereignty, nationality and consent have been tackled successfully, thanks in considerable part to this change. Whereas identities in the past were prescriptive, exclusive and confrontational, which helped to cause conflict and violence, the emergence of revised identities, which are more inclusive, pluralist and reconciliatory, assisted in bringing peace and stability. This has meant far-reaching changes in the essential character of unionism and nationalism and of people's senses of Irishness and Britishness. Substantial differences remain between unionists and nationalists, between north and south and between Britain and Ireland, but changes in identity have allowed for significant accommodation between the main sections.

Religion is still important in Ireland but links between religious allegiance and political identity have been challenged in an influential way. On 17 March 1962, speaking in a broadcast from Rome, President Eamon de Valera declared that 'loyalty to the See of Rome has been an outstanding characteristic of the Irish people's faith'.[195] Again in Rome, nearly 50 years later in the Irish Pontifical College, on 4 June 2011, President Mary McAleese gave another view of Ireland. She said that despite 'past political and religious conflicts' modern Ireland has emerged as 'a country, a family, which is at once Catholic, Protestant, agnostic, atheist, Islamic, Jewish'. She stated that all were to be 'cherished equally', referring to 'the powerful words of the Proclamation of 1916'.[196] In late 1959 Ian Paisley and other protestors demanded that the Northern Ireland prime minister, Lord Brookeborough, expel from the UUP Sir Clarence Graham and Brian Magennis, who had proposed that Catholics should be admitted to membership of the party and that 'greater toleration and co-operation between all sections of the community – whether of politics, class or creed – was desirable'.[197] Brookeborough refused their demand but he also rejected the proposals of Graham and Magennis. Fifty years later, in June 2011, Paisley's successor as head of the DUP and Northern Ireland's first minister, Peter Robinson, wrote that he and his party 'respect difference and cherish the freedom of individuals to follow their own faith'. He declared that his task was 'to make voting DUP as comfortable a choice for a Catholic as for anyone else' and that he welcomed how 'people are not prepared to be pigeonholed based on their religious belief' He stated that it was his job 'as first minister to work for everyone'.[198] Six weeks earlier, in an unprecedented step for a DUP politician, Robinson had attended a funeral mass conducted by Cardinal Brady for murdered police officer Ronan Kerr.

We can see these political changes well in the approach and comments of prominent spokespersons and politicians over this period. In the middle of 1971 the British prime minister, Ted Heath, informed the Irish taoiseach, Jack Lynch, that he could not accept that 'anyone from outside the United Kingdom can participate in meetings to promote the political development of any part of the United Kingdom', while early in 1972 Irish minister for external affairs, Patrick Hillery, declared that 'my aim is to get Britain out of Ireland'.[199] Relations between the British and Irish governments now reflect radically changed attitudes. On 12 April 2008, the outgoing taoiseach Bertie Ahern commented: 'The relationship between Britain and Ireland has been transformed. Last year I was honoured to address the houses of parliament at Westminster. We now have a shared agenda based on our strong economic and cultural links and our vision for a peaceful, stable future for Northern Ireland'.[200] On that occasion, Prime Minister Tony Blair remarked: 'Suddenly in a few short years, our countries have shuffled off all the old disagreeable sentiment and replaced them with affection founded on a modern vision of these islands – one of peace and progress'.[201]

Ideas of nationalism and Irishness remain important for political identity in the Irish Republic but in new ways. In April 2008 Ahern spoke of how he and others in Fianna Fáil hoped to see eventually a united Ireland: 'It's our view that would best be achieved on the basis of consent, and by working together to build up an island economy, and working on our north–south relationships, and somewhere in the future I hope that we can achieve that'.[202] Again in April 2008 he remarked on the subject of unity: 'If it doesn't prove possible, then it stays the way it is under the Good Friday Agreement, and people will just have to be tolerant of that if it's not possible to bring it any further'.[203] On the same subject in April 2010 Ahern's successor as taoiseach, Brian Cowen, spoke of the importance through the various agreements of 'recognising the legitimacy of our respective traditions – one loyal to Britain, the other looking to Irish unity as a legitimate objective, but one that will only be pursued peacefully by common consent. Therefore there would be no threatening, exclusivist political philosophy which would make people defensive or insular or non co-operative'. He declared: 'The genius of all these agreements is that we are all on a common journey together where we have not decided on the destination ... Let's go on a journey and forget about the destination – the destination isn't really important in that respect. We can all work for what it is we would like ideally to see, but this is not something that can be forced or imposed upon people on either side of the island'.[204] The subject of Irishness was addressed in a new manner by President Mary McAleese in November 2008, during a visit to Brakey Orange Hall, Bailieborough, Co. Cavan. She declared: 'It is possible to be both Irish and British, possible to be both Orange and Irish'.[205]

Within Northern Ireland, there is clear evidence of how identities have changed. Unionism and Britishness are still important for unionists but in different ways from before. In 2004, at a UUP party conference, the party leader, David Trimble declared: 'We are pluralist in our culture ... For us, unionism is not the same thing as Protestantism. We know the union is in the best interests of all. But we accept difference. We accept other points of view. We want a Northern Ireland where everyone, irrespective of religion, gender, race or lifestyle, can be comfortable and proud to call home'. He also argued for an inclusive sense of Britishness: 'Emerson Tennant, one of the MPs for Belfast in the mid-19th century, put it as follows; "We wish to add to the glory of being British the distinction of being Irish"'.[206] At his meeting with Ahern in Dublin in April 2007 the DUP leader, Paisley, spoke of how mutual respect is 'key to cementing good and civilised relationships on this island' and of how he trusted that 'old suspicions and discord can be buried forever under the prospect of mutual and respectful co-operation'. He also remarked: 'I am proud to be an Ulsterman, but I am also proud of my Irish roots'.[207] Following a reference to 'our people' in a speech in November 2004 to his constituency association, DUP deputy leader, and later Paisley's successor as leader, Peter Robinson explained: 'When I speak of "our people", I speak of those who share my unionist philosophy and those who do not. I speak of both the Planter and the Gael'.[208] In May 2009, as Northern Ireland's first minister, Robinson declared: 'It is vital that we get everybody in our community to recognise the benefits of making progress and going forward together as a shared society'.[209]

Nationalism/republicanism and Irishness are still central for the nationalist/republican population in Northern Ireland, but these ideas are now understood differently from previously. Shortly before becoming deputy first minister in 2001, the SDLP leader, Mark Durkan, remarked that, while the SDLP would work for unity: 'We can see beyond majorities and minorities – we recognise that we will always require agreed structures of government involving the two great traditions of this island'.[210] In a speech at her first party conference after being elected the leader of the SDLP in 2010, Margaret Ritchie stated that her party was 'not afraid to say Northern Ireland' and then declared: 'We will not deny our goal of Irish unity but we can honestly say that we want this place to be a social and economic success here and now'.[211] In May 2003 Sinn Féin president, Gerry Adams, stated: 'Nationalists and unionists, republicans and loyalists have to come to terms with and recognise each other's integrity. We recognise that for many people who live in the north of Ireland their sense of Britishness, however that is defined, is as important to them as being Irish is to us'.[212] In April 2010 Adams wrote: 'Since the Good Friday Agreement in 1998, we have a means of recognising our constitutional differences and maintaining our respective positions on the issue of partition and Irish unity, while working for the common good'. He continued: 'Sinn Féin is proud to be an Irish republican party and we want to see the people of Ireland united, a goal we pursue by peaceful and democratic means'.[213]

Other comments on these political changes can be noted. On 13 June 2011 newly-elected Taoiseach Enda Kenny addressed the British Irish parliamentary assembly in Cork. He acknowledged how 'the transformation of society in this state was a key enabler in building the rapprochement with those from the other tradition on this island'. He spoke of the impact on Irish–British relations of the visit of Queen Elizabeth to Ireland the previous month. He stated: 'The question of identity has been central. Coming to terms with the issue of identity has played a large part of the progress that has been made between our two countries. Equal respect for Irish and British identity also lies at the very heart of the Good Friday Agreement – the bedrock of our new relationship. It has underpinned all of the significant progress that has been made in Northern Ireland since 1998'. Kenny then remarked: 'That respect was captured perfectly by the presence, the words and the gestures of President McAleese and Queen Elizabeth – at Dublin Castle, at the Garden of Remembrance and at the National War Memorial'.[214] At the same time, we must note some concerns about aspects of the new accommodation in Northern Ireland. David Forde, leader of the Alliance Party, which has always supported the idea of shared government, has criticised the power-sharing executive for failing to promote sufficiently a shared society.[215] British Prime Minister David Cameron in June 2011 at the Northern Ireland Assembly warned that 'Northern Ireland needs a genuinely shared future; not a shared-out future'.[216] Others have expressed worries that identities might become locked in the past and not be sufficiently forward looking and tolerant of others. Nonetheless, the widespread desire to make the new arrangements work gives good reason to believe such concerns can be dealt with.

These comments by leading politicians are evidence of radically altered identities in the two Irelands, compared with 40 years ago.

They illustrate the very significant changes that have occurred among individuals and communities since the late 1980s in how people view themselves and how they view others. Often, changes on one side encouraged changes on the other. Such developments have affected relations within north and south, between north and south and between Britain and Ireland. In the Republic of Ireland political parties are still rooted in the national/political divisions of the 1920s, and some church–state issues remain unresolved. Nonetheless, there has been a very significant growth in pluralism in ideas of identity that has dramatically altered southern society and has also changed its approach to the people of Northern Ireland, nationalist and unionist. In Northern Ireland, national and other divisions, particularly over religion, remain important, and the violence and suffering have left a painful legacy. There continues to be strong party rivalry within the main northern political groups, and not everyone has accepted the new arrangements. There are still sectarian difficulties as seen in recent riots in some areas. At the same time, the major changes in identity among all the main sections in Northern Ireland have helped to alter fundamentally the political picture there to allow for accomodation and conciliation. For both unionists and nationalists in the north, the transformed relationship with the south is an important part of this new scene. These changes allow for the peaceful and positive handling of such divisions and difficulties.

5
Remembering and reclaiming: commemorations and identity, 1960–2011

Since the 1960s commemorations and anniversaries have continued to be an important feature of the annual public calendar in both Northern Ireland and the Republic of Ireland. In 1995, in an address to both houses of the Irish parliament, President Mary Robinson stated that 'commemoration is a moral act'. In the same year, in her Christmas message, Queen Elizabeth declared: 'commemoration and anniversaries are very important elements in our national life'.[1] These acts of commemoration serve to remind people and communities of important moments or individuals in their history. By such means, the achievements, bravery, endurance and suffering of past individuals and generations are honoured and remembered. This chapter will look principally at four such dates of commemoration that are celebrated annually in the two parts of Ireland. These are 17 March and St Patrick, Easter and the Dublin Rising of 1916, 12 July and the Battle of the Boyne in 1690, and Remembrance Sunday on the Sunday nearest 11 November.

While commemoration often has this moral aspect about the past, at the same time it can perform a particular purpose in our modern world. The way these events are marked can not only reflect important parts of the history of a community, but can also serve to help define its contemporary identity. Edna Longley has remarked: 'commemoration is a means whereby communities renew their own *religio*: literally, what ties them together, the rope around the individual sticks'.[2] Commemoration of such important events helps to shape and bolster community and national identities. It serves, in the words of Rebecca Graff-McRae, 'to unify groups by providing a basis for a shared identity and a practice to re-inscribe a common history'.[3] At the same time, however, as Edna Longley has also pointed out, 'commemorations are as selective as sympathies. They honour our dead, not your dead'.[4] In Ireland, north and south, different communities have placed different emphases on the four major commemorative acts examined here, which is not surprising given the varied historical and contemporary experiences of these communities. What comes as a real surprise is how the ways in which people have marked these events have changed in just half a century. To some extent these changes merely reflect developments in contemporary identities, but it is clear also that such changes have had an important influence on society and have helped to alter how people understand and express their identities, with important consequences for current politics. These changes have affected how people see themselves and their own community, and how they see others and other communities.

Referring to the 1960s, Sir Kenneth Bloomfield remarked: 'Anniversaries are the curse of Ireland. Like saints' days, the dates of historically resonant events punctuate the Northern Ireland calendar, calling for an orgy of reminiscence, celebration and demonstration from some section or other of the population'. He continued: 'It does not seem to matter that some of these demonstrations annoy or infuriate other people; this is, indeed, for some at least of the participants, a principal attraction'.[5] By the latter part of this period, however, new ways of viewing and celebrating these commemorations had helped to modify identities significantly. In 1980 the Irish president was forbidden expressly by the Irish government to accept an invitation to attend a Remembrance Sunday service in St Patrick's cathedral in Dublin. In 1993 President Mary Robinson accepted another such invitation, and every year since then the Irish president has attended the service. By the 1960s St Patrick's Day was little celebrated in Northern Ireland. From 1999 an official St Patrick's Day reception has been held annually in the Northern Ireland Assembly Buildings at Stormont. Commemoration of the Battle of the Boyne has been viewed usually as an exclusively Protestant and unionist event. Since 1998 President Mary McAleese has held an official reception, especially, although not only, for southern Orangemen and Protestants, every July at her presidential residence, the Áras an Uachtaráin in Dublin, to mark the Boyne and to recall all the 'Jacobites and Williamites' who were involved. The fiftieth anniversary of the Easter Rising in 1966 was celebrated in Dublin as a purely nationalist event. The ninetieth anniversary in Dublin involved the presence of the British ambassador on the government platform at the General Post Office and included mention of the sacrifice of Irishmen at the Battle of the Somme, also in 1916.

Remembrance Sunday

By the 1960s commemoration of Remembrance Sunday in the Republic of Ireland in honour of those from Ireland who had died during the two world wars was no longer prominent or widespread, compared with Armistice Day commemorations in the 1920s and 1930s. The main commemorative events on that day were held in Dublin. On that morning there were usually two parades of members of the British Legion and the Old Comrades Association, to the Church of Ireland national cathedral, St Patrick's, and to the Catholic pro-cathedral, St Mary's, where services were held. In the afternoon or evening there was a joint parade from the Dublin quays to the Irish National War Memorial at Islandbridge.[6] This latter event was attended by members of the diplomatic corps from many countries who laid wreaths, but there was no Irish government represent-ative. Some Remembrance Sunday ceremonies were held elsewhere. In 1967, for example, there was such an event at the war memorial in Sligo town, presided over by John Fallon, who was secretary of the Sligo branch of the British Legion and chairman of Sligo County Council.[7]

By the 1960s Remembrance Sunday continued to be marked widely in Northern Ireland, but this was an event viewed differently by unionist and nationalist communities. In the early 1960s the Belfast unionist paper, the *Belfast News Letter*, carried prominently reports of commemo-rative services and ceremonies in many centres throughout Northern Ireland.[8] Such services were held most often in Protestant churches, but occasionally in Catholic churches, as in Newry and Strabane; attend-ance, of course, was strongly denominationally based. At parades and other ceremonies there were normally no speeches, although often unionist politicians were reported as present and sometimes govern-ment ministers took the salute at the march past. In sharp contrast the Belfast nationalist paper, the *Irish News*, carried virtually no mention of these events. On 13 November 1962 an editorial in the *Irish News* acknowledged that memorial services had taken place in many places on the previous Sunday for those who died in two world wars, and declared: 'remembrance is something we all owe to the dead'. Despite this, the paper carried only one short report of commemorations. Such polarisation over this event continued during the 1960s but there were occasional instances of change. In 1965 two Catholic members of the Ballymoney council, both ex-servicemen, attended for the first time the Remembrance Sunday Service in Ballymoney First Presbyterian church. In 1967, for the first time, a Catholic priest, a D Day veteran, participated in the ceremony at the cenotaph in Bangor.[9]

The 1970s and 1980s witnessed important developments in how Remembrance Sunday commemorations were held. In 1971 the British Legion in both Northern Ireland and the Republic of Ireland cancelled all public parades and ceremonies on Remembrance Sunday because of the deteriorating situation in Northern Ireland. In the following year such public events resumed in the north but not in the south. At many of the northern services and commemorative ceremonies tribute was paid not only to those who had died in the two world wars but also to members of the security forces killed in the conflict in Northern Ireland. As before, these events involved primarily but not exclusively members of the unionist and Protestant communities. In 1978 considerable controversy arose when DUP members of Ballymena council objected to and prevented a Catholic priest taking part at the annual remembrance service at the town cenotaph, even though the man concerned, Hugh Murphy, was an ex-Royal Navy chaplain and holder of the military cross. Their actions were condemned widely and the British Legion withdrew from the event.[10] We can find still occasions when an effort was made to keep the occasion a broad one. For example, in Irvinestown, Co. Fermanagh, during the 1970s and 1980s, it was customary for the Remembrance Sunday parade to stop to lay wreaths at both the Sacred Heart Church and the Cenotaph, before proceeding to the memorial service in the Church of Ireland church.[11] From the early 1980s Father Hugh Murphy, now Canon, represented the Catholic diocese of Down and Connor in a Remembrance Sunday service in Belfast at St Anne's Church of Ireland cathedral.[12] SDLP councillors, however, did not attend these events.

In 1971 the Remembrance Sunday ceremony at the Irish National War Memorial at Islandbridge in Dublin was cancelled. Subsequently, in face of republican hostility, neither this event nor other public occasions of commemoration of the Irish world war dead were restored in the south. Annual collections for ex-servicemen's charities ceased largely and many British Legion branches closed.[13] The state of the war memorial and gardens at Islandbridge deteriorated until by 1979, as Kevin Myers later recalled, they were 'a vandalised tiphead, covered in weeds and grazing horses, the great stonework festooned with graffiti'.[14] In Dublin in 1971, however, an ecumenical service of remembrance was held on Remembrance Sunday afternoon in the Church of Ireland, St Patrick's cathedral.[15] This became an annual event attended by members of the public and of the diplomatic corps. During the service the congregation remembered not just the Irish dead of the two world wars, but also members of the modern Irish army who had died in the Congo under the United Nations flag. During his time as dean of St Patrick's, from 1969 until 1991, Victor Griffin made a special effort to make sure that this event was 'uncompromisingly Irish'.[16]

In 1980 considerable controversy arose when the Irish president, Patrick Hillery, turned down an invitation to attend the remembrance service in St Patrick's. He acted on the instructions of the taoiseach, who was then Charles Haughey, that it would be inappropriate for the president to attend, what were described as, memorial services for the armed forces of other countries.[17] Embarrassed over this matter, the Fianna Fáil government sent a minister to the service in 1980 and in the following year, but declined to do so in 1982, owing to poor Irish–British government relations.[18] A new coalition government in 1983 agreed to attendance at St Patrick's by government ministers and representatives of the Irish Defence Forces who participated in the service, despite protest from Fianna Fáil spokesmen and others. In 1987, after the return of a Fianna Fáil government in that year, no minister was present at the St Patrick's service. In the mid-1980s, partly in response to criticism over this matter, the Irish government instituted a National Day of Commemoration to be marked at the Garden of Remembrance in Dublin on 11 July, the anniversary of the Truce in 1921, to commemorate the deaths of all Irishmen and women in all wars and conflicts as well as United Nations service.

Over the following decade, however, the nature of these world war commemorations, north and south, changed markedly. An important factor was the reaction to the 11 deaths caused by an IRA bomb in Enniskillen, Co. Fermanagh, on Remembrance Sunday, 8 November 1987. There was immediate widespread condemnation in the south of this bombing. In addition, as Jane Leonard has pointed out, public revulsion over the matter 'fuelled a recent desire in the Republic of Ireland to remember the Irish who served in both world wars'.[19] As a result of this change of opinion, over the following years a number of war memorials were restored and public parades and commemorative events were held once again on Remembrance Sunday, in some places such as Limerick and Drogheda.[20] The sale of poppies increased greatly. A key moment in this change of attitude was Remembrance Sunday 1993 when, for the first time, the Irish president, Mary Robinson, attended the Remembrance Day ceremonies in St Patrick's cathedral, Dublin.[21] The president's husband, Nicholas Robinson, wore a poppy, although the president did not. The following day, an editorial in the *Irish Independent* remarked that President Robinson, as the first president to attend this event, had 'made her own contribution to the on-going process of healing old wounds'.

It concluded: 'There will be real peace on this island when the government officially attends such ceremonies, and it does not make news. We will have turned our backs on old prejudices'.[22] During the rest of her term of office, President Robinson continued to attend the Remembrance Sunday service in St Patrick's cathedral, as did her successor President Mary McAleese.

From 1988 the British Legion and the Irish government worked together to restore the Irish National War Memorial at Islandbridge. The memorial park was opened formally in 1994 by the Fianna Fáil minister for finance, Bertie Ahern. In the following year, a ceremony was held there to mark the end of the Second World War and to honour those Irishmen and Irishwomen who had served in British or Allied forces. Present on this occasion were the taoiseach, John Bruton, and representatives from all southern parties, as well as the Northern Ireland Secretary of State, Sir Patrick Mayhew, representatives from the north of the Ulster Unionist Party, the SDLP and the Alliance Party. For the first time at any such event, Sinn Féin was represented, the party's national chairman and Belfast city councillor, Tom Hartley, attending.[23] The following Monday an editorial in the *Irish Times* talked of the breaking of taboos created by history and described this event as being of 'enormous importance'. The editorial declared: 'The Taoiseach, Mr Bruton, found the words to express what has never been said aloud by any of his predecessors when he told the gathering at Islandbridge that the Second World War had been brought to an end 'by the courage, the struggle, and the sacrifice of Europeans, some of whom were Irish, whose bravery we remember today'.[24]

In Northern Ireland the decade that followed the Enniskillen bomb also witnessed important changes in how Remembrance Sunday was marked. The sense of outrage caused by this event, and admiration for the courage and forbearance of many of the survivors, as well as a growing concern to promote reconciliation led, eventually, to efforts to view Remembrance Sunday in a more inclusive way, once again. In the late 1980s and early 1990s, Dorita Field, a Second World War veteran and SDLP councillor, attended the ceremony in Belfast on behalf of her party. In 1994 all five SDLP councillors in Belfast attended the remembrance ceremony in what their leader, Alex Atwood, termed 'an act of reconciliation'.[25] On 8 November 1992 Paddy McGowan, the SDLP chairman of Omagh District Council, was the first nationalist councillor to lay a wreath at the town's cenotaph.[26] In the early 1990s in Derry some SDLP councillors attended the ceremony at the cenotaph in an individual capacity. For the first time, on 12 November 1995, a Catholic mayor,

John Kerr of the SDLP, laid a wreath at the cenotaph.[27] As a reflection of the considerable changes that took place in this decade we can note that on Remembrance Sunday 1997 wreaths were laid at their local cenotaphs by SDLP mayors or chairmen of councils in Belfast, Derry, Omagh, Armagh and Dungannon, and by an independent nationalist chairman in Enniskillen.[28]

Other events reflected the new-found desire to view these commemorations in a more inclusive way. The Somme Association, founded in 1988 under the chairmanship of unionist councillor, Dr Ian Adamson, established in 1994 at Newtownards, Co. Down, the Somme Heritage Centre, which remembered all soldiers from Ireland (not only members of the 36th Ulster Division), who had died at the Battle of the Somme. Belfast City Council honoured finally the late James Magennis, the Belfast Catholic submariner and the only Northern Ireland holder of a VC, awarded for 'extreme valour', in the Second World War. When he returned to Belfast in 1945 he was at first honoured by the local citizens, but the city council, on which there was an Ulster Unionist majority, declined to give him the freedom of the city. When he visited his old school, the De La Salle brother who introduced him to the pupils said that he was a brave man but he had not been brave for Ireland.[29] In 1995 his portrait was placed in the city hall and in October 1998 a memorial sculpture to honour him was erected in the city hall grounds. An important cross-border initiative to build a peace park at Messines in Belgium, in memory of all the Irish who died in the First World War, involved Paddy Harte, a former Fine Gael deputy for Donegal, and Glenn Barr, a former Derry loyalist leader, as well as many young volunteers from north and south. At the ceremony on 11 November 1998 to inaugurate the park, attended by the British queen, the Irish president, the king of the Belgians, and large numbers of people from all over Ireland, Harte and Barr together recalled the 'solidarity and trust that developed between Protestant and Catholic soldiers when they served together in these trenches'. On that occasion, which was the eightieth anniversary of the 1918 armistice, they declared that a 'fitting tribute to the principles for which men and women from the island of Ireland died in both wars would be permanent peace in Ireland'.[30] The next day an editorial in the *Belfast News Letter* commented: 'Yesterday's poignant events marked a further thawing in the unofficial cold war that has existed between the two countries for most of this century'.[31]

These changes have continued into the present century. In 2002 the *Irish News* reported an account by a County Donegal woman, Nellie O'Donnell, of what happened to her father James Duffy, VC, when he returned to the county after the First World War. Because he had received the award of the Victoria Cross from the British crown, and he attended VC reunion events in England, he was treated as a 'traitor', and he and his family were shunned in their neighbourhood for many years.[32] That same year, 2002, however, reflecting the great change in attitude to this matter, a Fianna Fáil government minister, Noel Dempsey, chaired the launch of a *County Donegal Book of Honour*, a publication organised by Fine Gael's Paddy Harte, to remember all Donegal men and women who were killed in the First World War. In 2006 the Irish government organised a formal event to commemorate the Battle of the Somme. Two years later Brian Lenihan, the Irish minister for finance, commented: 'The impact the ceremony had was on Irish people in the street, Catholic people mainly, who felt that part of that history had been hidden and concealed from them and was now revived by the Irish state'.[33] In February 2008 a delegation from Roscommon County Council, accompanied by four senior officers of the Irish defence forces, laid a wreath of poppies at the Round Tower in the Ireland Peace Park at Messines to honour those from Ireland who died in the First World War, including an estimated 330 from the county itself. A card attached read: 'Thank you for your efforts and sacrifice. You have helped to shape the Ireland, the Europe and the freedom that we enjoy today. From the people of Roscommon'.[34]

On 1 July 2002 the Sinn Féin Lord Mayor of Belfast, Alex Maskey, laid a laurel wreath at the cenotaph outside City Hall, although he did not participate in the official commemoration ceremony.[35] After a brief Sinn Féin ban on party members attending 'British military commemorations', on 1 July 2008 another Sinn Féin Lord Mayor, Tom Hartley, again placed a laurel wreath at the Belfast cenotaph to remember those who fell at the Somme.[36] On 30 April 2003, a special service was held at St Anne's cathedral in Belfast to remember all those from Belfast who died in the First World War. The congregation included the Queen's Lord Lieutenant for Belfast, Lady Carswell, the General Officer in Command, Northern Ireland, General Philip Trousdell, the Sinn Féin Lord Mayor, Alex Maskey, and an ex-IRA member, Martin Meehan, whose grandfather, a soldier in the Inniskilling Fusiliers, died in northern France in April 1916.[37] On 6 November 2005 a ceremony organised by Glenn Barr was held at the Derry cenotaph to honour all those from Ireland who had died at Messines, including 14-year-old John Condon from Waterford (believed to be the youngest Allied soldier to die in the war), whose family attended the event. For the first time the tricolour was flown at the cenotaph alongside the union flag. Afterwards Barr commented: 'It was an excellent service involving people from both sides and from all walks of life ... The whole theme of our work is reconciliation through remembrance for all and that was reflected in the service'. He added: 'It's been a long time in coming to have the British and Irish flags flying together at the cenotaph here in this city, but I always knew this day would come'.[38]

In 2007 the first official meeting of the Irish president and the Northern Ireland first minister (Mary McAleese and Ian Paisley) took place at the Somme Heritage Centre at Newtownards, Co. Down, to open an exhibition on the 36th Ulster Division and the 16th Irish Division. Ian Paisley declared how the purpose of the Somme Centre was 'to remember all the heroes of this entire island who fought so that our freedoms could survive. Mary McAleese and myself have come here to pay tribute in unity to all those who fought and died for us. There may have been division then, but not now'.[39] The first official visit to the Centre for members of Sinn Féin occurred on 26 January 2010 when Belfast Deputy Lord Mayor, Danny Lavery, and Councillor Tom Hartley visited the Centre. In November 2010, Margaret Ritchie, leader of the SDLP, became the first nationalist leader to wear a poppy on Remembrance Sunday in Northern Ireland. She said that it was a signal of a new 'progressive nationalism' and that 'it was about moving the community forward'. She stated that thousands of nationalists died in two world wars and it 'was no longer acceptable for Irish nationalism to airbrush them out of history'. She declared: 'If you want to share the future then you have to be able to share and understand our history and past'.[40]

St Patrick's Day

During the 1960s celebrations of St Patrick's Day continued to reflect highly polarised views on this event, but some small elements of change can be discerned. On St Patrick's Day 1960 Irish President, Eamon de Valera, issued a greeting to the friends of Ireland overseas. He expressed hope that the occasion would strengthen 'your determination to continue your support of the motherland's just claims to the unity of the national territory'. In his 1960 message to Irish men and women abroad Taoiseach Sean Lemass declared that 'politically the aim of national objectives was the unity of Ireland, which would be achieved ultimately', but for the first time he expressed also his support for better understanding with the north.[41] In 1962 de Valera visited the Pope in Rome and, in a Radio Éireann broadcast from there on St Patrick's Day, he stated that 'loyalty to the See of Peter has been an outstanding characteristic of the Irish people's faith, and it is well that in commemorating St Patrick we should give national expression of this great historic fact and pledge continuance'.[42]

Subsequently, St Patrick's Day messages from the taoiseach, Sean Lemass and then Jack Lynch, often contained expressions of hope of co-operation and better understanding between north and south, although these would be qualified usually by the stated belief that good-will arising from this 'would surely hasten the day of reunification'.[43] Other leading politicians, such as Neil Blaney and George Colley, used the occasion in the mid-1960s to call for cross-border co-operation in matters such as tourism.[44] St Patrick's Day was observed widely in the south. It was a public holiday and there were various parades and church services. The Patrician year of 1961 involved large numbers and visiting Catholic church dignitaries. The ban on the sale of alcohol on St Patrick's Day was lifted in 1961. In Dublin throughout this period the main event was a trades and industries parade.

In Northern Ireland celebration of St Patrick's Day in the 1960s was generally restrained compared with the south. It remained a bank holiday, when government and public offices were closed, but the press reported usually that it was a 'working day for most people and shops and other businesses remained open'.[45] Shamrock was distributed specially to British army regiments from Northern Ireland, both at home and abroad, and to the Irish Guards. In Belfast there was no parade but a small number of cultural and sporting events took place normally. St Patrick's Day assumed greater significance among members of the Catholic community. There were services in many Catholic churches to commemorate St Patrick's Day. Usually the Ancient Order of Hibernians (AOH) organised several well-attended demonstrations on the day. On St Patrick's Day in 1960 a statement from northern nationalist MPs and senators that 'towards the ideal of a united Ireland we will strive unceasingly', was published on the front page of the *Irish News*, along-side the St Patrick's Day messages from the taoiseach and president, also calling for reunification.[46] There were a few small scale parades, as in Downpatrick and Armagh, connected with Catholic church services.

During this decade, however, we can see some effort to make the event more important and more widely appreciated. The government did not organise official events or issue statements but the Northern Ireland premier, Capt. Terence O'Neill, took advantage of the day on a number of occasions to make special visits to Canada and America.[47] The pilgrimage and church services at Downpatrick, organised by the Church of Ireland, became more popular and in 1961 both the diocesan synod of Down and Dromore and the annual conference of the Young Unionists, the young people's organisation of the Ulster Unionist Party, urged more support for the day.[48] Some correspondents in the press argued that St Patrick's Day should be ignored in the north because of the way it had become politicised, but influential editorials in the *Belfast Telegraph* backed calls to give more importance to the day.[49]

From the early 1970s celebration of St Patrick's Day changed, especially in the south. The most conspicuous change was in the character of the Dublin parade after its organisation was taken over in 1970 by Dublin Tourism. There were now bands and majorettes as well as many visitors from the USA and Canada in the parade, which took on a new tourist and commercial aspect. Significant changes also occurred in other areas. An editorial in the *Irish Independent*, on 16 March 1974, pointed out that 'since the troubles began in the north' speakers at St Patrick's Day parades have become 'hyper-sensitive about words, concepts, tributes and ideologies which hitherto had been taken for granted' and talked of a new growing acceptance of different traditions and a slow redefinition of Irish patriotism. Speeches by leading politicians no longer contained strong condemnation of partition, and, both in America and at home, Irish government ministers often denounced violence and support for the IRA.[50] On a religious level also, efforts were made to overcome the denominational divisions associated with the saint's day. On St Patrick's Day 1972 a Jesuit priest, Father Michael Hurley, became the first Catholic priest since the Reformation to preach in St Patrick's Church of Ireland cathedral in Dublin. Interdenominational services were now held on the day and an ecumenical blessing of the shamrock became a regular feature of the Dublin parade.[51]

A new organisation was set up in 1995 to run the Dublin parade, which has become part of an all-day cultural and tourist festival. In 1996 the chairman, Michael Colgan, declared: 'The day is long gone when you could have an electrical company with washing machines on a float and a girl in a sash'.[52] Another new feature of St Patrick's Day has been efforts by the Irish government to promote Ireland abroad and to connect with members of the Irish diaspora. Previously some government ministers had attended celebrations of St Patrick's Day in Britain and the USA. By the early 2000s, however, over a dozen government ministers and large numbers of councillors visited such events, all over the globe. From the mid-1990s it became an annual feature for the taoiseach to present shamrock to the American president at the White House. On 17 March 2004 an editorial in the *Irish Times* declared: 'Ireland looks inwards and outwards on St Patrick's Day, celebrating Irish identity and communicating it to other peoples. The holiday ... has a remarkable outreach to the Irish abroad, to their host societies and to the wider world. In recent years these dimensions have been projected even more strongly by a growing internationalisation of Ireland's economic, cultural and political life'. It observed: 'St Patrick remains an appropriate figure to express these changing realities. He has been reimagined to fit them, as is often the case with such national symbols'.

In Northern Ireland changes in the observation of St Patrick's Day were slower to come. During the 1970s and 1980s the occasion continued to be celebrated in an unremarkable way. It remained a bank holiday but there was little special about it apart from some sporting events, several AOH parades and a number of religious services. There were celebrations still in Newry, Armagh and other towns, and occasionally parades on the Falls Road in Belfast and in Derry. There were some new instances of interdenominational co-operation on the day. The first joint Protestant/Catholic service in Down Church of Ireland cathedral was held on 17 March 1985, while on 17 March 1990 in Armagh Catholic cathedral an ecumenical service commemorated the laying of the cathedral foundation.[53] Nonetheless, such events did not arouse widespread support. On 17 March 1992 an editorial in the *Belfast Telegraph* commented: 'A casual visitor to Ulster would need to be very perceptive to realise that this is St Patrick's Day. Our celebrations are so muted as to be invisible. Yet across the border March 17 is an occasion for national rejoicing by people and government'.

From the early 1990s, however, the event began to assume greater importance. Parades in nationalist towns such as Newry and Downpatrick were revitalised. At the same time there was an effort to give these events a cross-community focus, especially in Downpatrick. From 1994, at unionist instigation, the flag of St Patrick was flown at Belfast City Hall. By the late 1990s members of the Apprentice Boys of Derry in the city of Derry and a number of Ulster Scots groups had become involved in celebrations on the day. Efforts to organise a major parade in Belfast were dogged by controversy over flags and emblems. The first such parades in the late 1990s and early 2000s proved controversial but subsequently they achieved wider, if not universal, support. By 2006 the event in Belfast had become a major festival organised by Belfast City Council. From 1994 unionist politicians began to visit Washington on 17 March to attend events at the White House, where SDLP and Sinn Féin leaders had already been guests on St Patrick's Day.

After 1998 the first and deputy first ministers were received at the White House by the president on the day. In 1999 the speaker of the

Northern Ireland Assembly, John Alderdice, organised the first official reception on St Patrick's Day at the assembly buildings at Stormont, and this has continued annually (although cancelled in 2010 so that the speaker could attend the St Patrick's Day celebrations in the White House). Politicians, including Ian Paisley, have urged that St Patrick's Day be made a public holiday in Northern Ireland.[54] This has not happened, but St Patrick's Day now enjoys markedly wider support than before. On St Patrick's Day 2003 a *Belfast News Letter* editorial declared that: 'March 17 is increasingly seen as a day when the peoples of the two main traditions in our province can share the Christian legacy and inheritance of St Patrick. Marking St Patrick's day in an appropriate way should not be seen as a threat to the culture and aspirations of the pro-union population and the events should be celebrated in a manner that offends no one'.

Easter Rising

During the 1960s in the Irish Republic commemoration of the Easter Rising was a regular feature of the state and public calendar, although some IRA veterans expressed concern in 1962 that 'every year these parades are becoming less impressive and have ceased to command the respect to which they are entitled from the public'.[55] On Easter Sunday, 17 April 1960, for example, there was a military parade of some 3000 troops in Dublin which marched past the General Post Office where President Eamon de Valera, took the salute.[56] Later that day, the taoiseach, Sean Lemass, laid a wreath at a Fianna Fáil commemoration at the graves of the executed 1916 leaders at Arbour Hill. There was also a small Sinn Féin parade to Glasnevin cemetery. In various other parts of the country there were some parades to special masses or to cemeteries, involving members of the Irish army, trade unions, Gaelic League and the Old IRA. Normally, these occasions were not marked by speeches, but they involved the reciting of the Rosary and the reading of the 1916 proclamation, often in Irish. In Northern Ireland commemoration of the Rising was very different. On Easter Sunday 1960 in Belfast, a ceremony was organised by the National Graves Association at the republican plot at Milltown Cemetery. Here an estimated crowd of 800 people heard a speech from Leo Martin which declared that 'the British government had placed the present government in existence in the north in order to divide the Irish people', and called for 'a republican form of government'.[57] There were Easter 1916 commemorations in a number of other centres, including Derry and Armagh.

In 1966 the fiftieth anniversary of the Rising attracted greatly increased interest, both south and north. The Irish government organised a two-week long series of commemorative events, starting on Easter Sunday, including television programmes, open air theatrical events and parades. These events were used by the government to laud the achievement of the state over the previous half century. Reunification was sometimes raised, but was not stressed, reflecting new links with the British and Northern Ireland governments.[58] On Easter Sunday a very large crowd in Dublin watched the main parade of soldiers, IRA veterans and members of various organisations, march past the GPO, where President de Valera took the salute. The GPO platform of dignitaries included leading Fianna Fáil figures, but neither northern politicians nor the leaders of either the Fine Gael or Labour parties were present.[59] On Easter Monday a Garden of Remembrance for those republicans who died in the war of independence, 1916–21, was opened at Parnell Square. Outside Dublin many ceremonies took place to mark the Rising. In Northern Ireland, where various local committees organised events, the fiftieth anniversary commemorations resulted in considerable tension, not only between the government and the organisers but also between supporters of these events and unionist protestors, including Ian Paisley. On Easter Sunday there was a parade of some 5000 to the republican plot at Milltown Cemetery in Belfast and other parades in various centres. At Milltown, Niall Fagan, treasurer of Sinn Féin, called for a new constitution for a new all-Ireland state and urged the intervention of the United Nations. Some speakers elsewhere took a more militant line. In Armagh Sean Stephenson (an Englishman, whose original name was John Stephenson and who later called himself Seán Mac Stiofáin) declared that 'the Irish Republican Army had never ceased its physical struggle with Britain and it would continue to seize every opportunity to carry it on', which caused the nationalist senator, James Lennon, to state that 'the methods of the past cannot be those of 1966 and onwards'.[60]

After 1966 commemoration of the Easter Rising, in both north and south, was more constrained again. The outbreak of violence in Northern Ireland had a disquieting effect. In 1972 the military parade in Dublin was cancelled, reportedly because troops were required for border duty and to protect important installations. Instead, there were two brief ceremonies at the GPO and the Garden of Remembrance attended by President De Valera and Taoiseach Jack Lynch.[61] In 1974 even these events were called off by the new coalition government. An editorial appearing in the Fianna Fáil newspaper, the *Irish Press*, on 31 March 1975, complained that 'there has been a deliberate official playing down of the national commemoration'. A new Fianna Fáil government in 1977 made no difference to this policy, which continued in following decades, of not holding such official public commemorations of the 1916 Rising. The government's concern was that such an event might appear to condone contemporary republican violence. There was still a small Fianna Fáil wreath-laying ceremony at Arbour Hill and Sinn Féin commemorations at Glasnevin, although republican splits meant that there were parades to the latter not only by Official and Provisional Sinn Féin but also by other republican parties. Commemoration of the Rising continued elsewhere, often involving various republican bodies, but fewer councillors and civic group members who had participated earlier. On the 75th anniversary of the Rising in 1991 at the GPO, there was what one newspaper called, 'a low-key military ceremony' watched by a few hundred people 'in stark contrast to the celebration of the 50th anniversary in 1966'.[62] President Mary Robinson and Taoiseach Charles Haughey were present, along with various Fianna Fáil ministers, plus the former Fine Gael leader, Liam Cosgrave, and SDLP deputy leader, Seamus Mallon.

Commemoration of the 1916 Rising in Northern Ireland witnessed both increased and strongly divided involvement after 1969. Separate parades were held by the so-called official and provisional wings of Sinn Féin: they drew at first similar numbers but, within a few years, the latter enjoyed greater support. There were also parades organised by the Irish Republican Socialist Party (from 1975) and Republican Sinn Féin (from 1987). Orations and statements on such occasions brought out differences between these groups. On Easter Sunday 1977, at the Belfast parade of Provisional Sinn Féin, James Drumm recalled those who had died over the past seven years 'trying to establish the Republic that the men of 1916 had died for'. An IRA statement attacked the British government and pledged to 'continue the war' to obtain 'British withdrawal'.[63] On Easter Sunday 1978, in Belfast at the parade of Official Sinn Féin (whose military wing was on a ceasefire), Malachy McGurran called for peace and urged working people to unite 'in a struggle for a humane, just and equal society in our country'. He attacked 'purported republicans who daily make a mockery of the republican philosophy by a bloody and savage campaign of sectarian slaughter'.[64] Speeches at subsequent Easter events reflected changes within the republican movement, especially within Provisional Sinn Féin. These would lead to support for political action in the 1980s and for the peace process in the 1990s, which sometimes speakers sought to justify in terms of 1916. For example, on Easter Sunday 1996, at a Provisional Sinn Féin commemoration at Crossmaglen, south Armagh, Pamela Kane stated: 'It is not enough to quote the Proclamation, Easter after Easter. We have the responsibility to translate the language of the Proclamation into the reality of today'.[65]

In the early years of the twenty-first century official commemoration of the 1916 Rising remained subdued, marked usually by a ceremony at Arbour Hill, attended by the Irish president, members of the government and representatives of the armed services. At the event in 2004 the Catholic archbishop of Dublin, Dr Diarmuid Martin, spoke about the many new arrivals in Ireland and urged tolerance, remarking that the 1916 leaders had a 'dream of an Ireland of harmony and of sharing'. He also declared that 'the "historical memory" of the 1916 rising must be lived out today as a rejection of violence. In a new Ireland we must reject violence, anywhere, for whatever reason'.[66] In 2006, however, the ninetieth anniversary of the Rising witnessed a new level of participation in this commemoration. On Easter Sunday 2006 the Irish government organised a well-attended military parade to the GPO in Dublin, the first such parade in over three decades.[67] The decision to stage this event was seen at first by some as an action by the Fianna Fáil-led government to gain an advantage over other parties, and to respond to a perceived threat from Sinn Féin in southern elections. As things turned out, however, the ninetieth anniversary provided an opportunity for the state to reclaim this event, in light of the peace process, and to give it a new image. In contrast to 1966, the distinguished guests at the GPO included not only the president, the taoiseach and cabinet members, but also the British ambassador, leaders of Fine Gael, the Labour Party, the Green Party and the SDLP. Leaders of the northern unionist parties and Sinn Féin were invited but did not attend.

At a wreath-laying ceremony at Kilmainham Gaol on the morning of Easter Sunday, Taoiseach Bertie Ahern declared that 'our generation still cherishes the ideals of the courageous men and women who fought for Ireland in Easter week ... and we remember with gratitude the great sacrifices they made for us', before going on to say that 'as we look to the future, we must be generous and inclusive'.[68] The previous day, the press reported a tribute from President Mary McAleese which recalled not only the leaders of the 1916 Rising but also those who died on the Somme in 1916.[69] Elsewhere in Ireland, north and south, there were many commemorative ceremonies on this ninetieth anniversary. At Sinn Féin events in 2006 speeches called for reunification and also acknowledged the new political changes.[70] Since this time, a small military parade has continued to take place in Dublin and other commemorations are held in various places. At events organised by Sinn Féin there are no longer statements from the IRA.[71] A new feature of republican parades in Belfast has been the appearance of marchers dressed as historical figures, such as Wexford pikemen from 1798 and 1950s campaign 'volunteers'.

The Twelfth of July and the Battle of the Boyne

In Northern Ireland in the 1960s the Twelfth of July parades attracted large numbers of marchers and spectators. On 12 July 1960 there were 20 demonstrations throughout Northern Ireland, including a Belfast parade of some 300 lodges and 20,000 brethren. As usual these events concluded with speeches and prayers. At Ballinamallard, Co. Fermanagh, Prime Minister Lord Brookeborough declared: 'We shall not compromise on the question of our constitutional position. We shall remain on our guard against threats or force, persuasion or entice-ment'.[72] From the early 1960s, however, the message from these pro-ceedings became less strident and more conciliatory. On 12 July 1965, at Ballymena, Co. Antrim, Brookeborough's successor, Capt. Terence O'Neill, expressed the hope that 'the Orange Order will always be used as a force for positive Protestantism which makes sure that a man does his own duty to God and country before he criticises any other'. At the Belfast parade, Sir George Clark, head of the Orange governing body, resolutely faced down hecklers to acknowledge the changes in the Catholic church due to the Ecumenical Council, which he believed 'must lead to a better understanding between the peoples of both reli-gious beliefs'. A resolution that year welcomed the government's efforts for 'a better understanding between the peoples of Ireland, which we trust will lead to an extension of the economy of the two countries, thus leading to more harmonious relationships between all men', while another declared the resolve of the brethren 'to uphold our position under her majesty the Queen, and within the framework of the United Kingdom and British Commonwealth'.[73]

On 12 July 1960, Rossnowlagh, on the south coast of Co. Donegal, was the scene of an Orange parade organised by Co. Donegal Grand Lodge, the only such event in the Irish Republic, as a number of northern papers pointed out.[74] The meeting was addressed by John Taylor, president of the Young Unionist Association, and accepted three resolutions reported as being 'specially framed for a demonstration in Éire, pledging loyalty to the Orange Institution and Protestant faith, and praying for God's blessing on the queen and royal family'.[75] Quite small numbers of Orangemen attended this occasion, but brethren from south of the border marched in parades in Northern Ireland. The Belfast parade that year was led by 'a small but proudly marching group from Dublin and Wicklow'.[76] Larger numbers of members of Orange lodges situated in Counties Cavan and Monaghan, and in Protestant parts of East Donegal, attended demonstrations in neighbouring areas in Northern Ireland. In 1960 some 20 lodges from Cavan and Monaghan joined the parade at Lisbellaw, Co. Fermanagh. By the mid-1960s the emphasis at Rossnowlagh had become largely religious and the meeting was usually addressed solely by a clergyman. On 12 July 1965 the speaker, the Rev. C.A.M. Meldrum, stated: 'Today the main terms of reference for Orangeism in the Republic are religious and our Order would do itself a costly disservice and injustice if it involved itself in any other sphere. I am happy to say that such is the role Orangeism plays in the republic today'. He went on to declare that Orangeism had proved 'a vital incentive to a religious minority needing encouragement, a sense of unity, fellowship and a common aim'.[77]

From 1966, however, the Twelfth of July demonstrations in Northern Ireland revealed strong divisions between the leadership of the Orange Order and a vocal section strongly opposed to the politics of Terence O'Neill. On 12 July 1966 O'Neill warned: 'If there is one way to endanger the constitution of Northern Ireland, it is by violence, by abuse and by the gun'.[78] This was a reference, however, not to the IRA but to violent demonstrations organised by Ian Paisley over the previous year and to the three murders committed by the newly-formed paramilitary Ulster Volunteer Force. He urged the need to 'show mutual respect inside Northern Ireland' and to 'retain the respect of our fellow-citizens in the United Kingdom as a whole', which could be jeopardised by these actions. Other government ministers and leading Orange figures in their speeches supported O'Neill, but they found themselves under attack over the O'Neill/Lemass meeting and the ecumenical movement, from Orangemen, who were supporters of Paisley.[79] At Kilkeel, Co. Down, Roy Bradford, MP, and Senator Nelson Elder had to be given police protection as they left the 'field'. This public conflict was very evident at July parades until the fall of O'Neill. From the early 1970s the character of the Twelfth of July parades changed. After the fall of the Northern Ireland executive there were no longer government ministers at these events, but unionist politicians still addressed the meetings. Resolutions continued to express loyalty to the crown and support for the Protestant faith. We now see strong criticism of the British government on these occasions. For example, on 12 July 1986 John McCrea, the Grand Master of the

Belfast Orange Lodge, stated that loyalty to the Queen could not extend to a conservative government that 'imposed the Anglo-Irish Agreement on Northern Ireland against the will of its majority'.[80]

At first, numbers attending as marchers and spectators at these events remained high. Over the next two decades, however, the total of demonstrations continued the same but the figures for those attending fell, although it is difficult to achieve an accurate picture on this matter. At the same time, these annual parades continued to attract more participants than any other annual commemoration in Northern Ireland. Included in their ranks were Orange brethren from the Irish republic (often given pride of place in parades), Scotland, Canada and New Zealand. By and large, the main parades were able to continue unimpeded. From the mid-1980s, however, conflict arose between nationalists and Orangemen in relation to some 'feeder' parades to the demonstrations, and certain places, such as Portadown, witnessed serious disturbances in the 1990s. The tercentenary of the Battle of the Boyne in 1990 saw not only a large turnout, but other associated events.[81]

In 1970 the parade at Rossnowlagh, Co. Donegal, was cancelled, owing to a threat against the event at a meeting of Donegal County Council by a local senator Bernard McGlinchey. His remarks were condemned by several Republican Clubs in Derry city and Co. Tyrone.[82] The matter was also raised in the Dáil, where Desmond O'Malley, minister for justice, backed strongly the right of the Donegal Orangemen to parade. He declared: 'That these traditions are not those of the great majority in the locality in no way diminishes the right of those who adhere to them to express themselves. Rather does it place on the majority a special obligation to ensure that their right is respected and upheld and to ensure also that it is seen to be a right and not something that is only tolerated'.[83] He then praised the Orange organisers for calling off the parade to avoid the possibility of giving offence. The next parade at Rossnowlagh resumed only in 1978, although a short church parade was held in Donegal town in July 1975.[84] At first this revived parade involved small numbers of marchers but, by 1993, it was attracting up to 10,000 men and women, including supporters from Northern Ireland. At the event in 1987 a speaker declared that patriotism was 'being a good citizen wherever God in his providence has placed us', while the sole resolution was one 'committing the members to the proper practice and defence of Protestantism'.[85]

The last decade has seen important new developments in how the Twelfth of July celebrations are marked. The most surprising changes have occurred in the Irish republic. As part of a bridge-building exercise, on 11 July 1998, President Mary McAleese hosted a reception at her official residence, Áras an Uachtaráin, to honour the Protestant community in the south, particularly the Orangemen, many of whom were invited to the occasion. Since then she has held a July reception every year to mark the Battle of the Boyne anniversary – the only state-sponsored commemoration of the battle anywhere in Ireland. On one of these occasions, 12 July 2003, she remarked: 'We gather here today a new generation of Jacobites and Williamites in a new era seeking to comprehend and befriend each other, so that the generations to come will not know the waste of violence, the hurt of contempt'.[86] At another, on 12 July 2008, she reminded her audience that in the ten years since the first such commemoration 'our context has changed', stated that 'Williamite and Jacobite work together in government in Northern Ireland' and described the relationship between Britain and Ireland as 'the best it has ever been in history and keeps getting better'.[87] On 27 November 2008 President Mary McAleese visited Brakey Orange Hall, Bailieborough, Co. Cavan, the first such visit by an Irish president. She urged that a new sense of culture of acceptance and inclusion be built, following the success of the Belfast Agreement. 'It is possible', she declared, 'to be both Irish and British, possible to be both Orange and Irish. We face into a landscape of new possibilities and understandings'.[88] Orange parades have continued at Rossnowlagh and now attract greater numbers than previously, partly because they are held on the Saturday before the Twelfth, so allowing the attendance of Orangemen from not only the southern border counties but also from Northern Ireland. At the Rossnowlagh parade in 2010, Orange Grand Chaplain, Rev. Stanley Gamble, stated that President McAleese had made Ireland a 'warm house for Protestants'.[89]

During the first decade of the twenty-first century in the north there have been changes too in how the Twelfth of July Boyne anniversary has been celebrated. There are still widespread demonstrations at which resolutions are passed declaring loyalty to the crown and support for the Protestant religion. Divisions among Orangeman, particularly over the Belfast Agreement, led to the end of the links between the Ulster Unionist Party and the order in March 2005. In late 2005 some members of the Belfast Grand Lodge decided to make the 'Twelfth' celebrations more of a festival and they came up with the idea of 'Orangefest'. Since July 2006 demonstrations in a number of areas have included Ulster Scots events and historical enactments, and efforts have been made to make the day more family and tourist friendly.[90] In July 2008 Peter Robinson, DUP leader and first minister, remarked that Orangefest 'not only allows our tradition to be celebrated, but does so in a way that

opens it up to those from outside our own background and tradition'.[91]
Disputes with nationalists continued over some parades. Recently
Orange Order representatives have sought to explain their position
to others. On 5 June 2006, for the first time, representatives of the
'loyal orders', including the Orange Order, held a meeting, at their own
request, with the Catholic archbishop of Armagh, to discuss the parades
issue. Their spokesman described the event as 'a cordial, businesslike
and useful exchange of views'.[92] Archbishop Brady remarked that the
desire of the leadership of the 'loyal orders' to meet him 'represents
their willingness to go beyond the barriers of history [and]... to explain
the customs, principles and values of their organizations to leaders
in the Catholic community. This is to be welcomed'.[93]

Final observations

Over the last half century, there have been major changes in the character and meaning of these four major annual occasions for commemoration in Ireland. Ian McBride has commented: 'What is so striking
about the Irish case is not simply the tendency for present conflicts to
express themselves through the personalities of the past, but the way
in which commemorative rituals have become historical forces in their
own right'.[94] Remembrance Sunday fifty years ago was an event marked
primarily by unionists and ignored very largely by nationalists. Today,
this situation has changed markedly, north and south. In the Irish
republic there is now a wide appreciation of the involvement of Irish
people in British and Allied forces in two world wars. This has meant
that Irish identity for many southerners is now viewed in a less exclusive way. In Northern Ireland, among nationalists there is also a new
sympathy for this part of their history. No doubt, it is true to say that
for many northern unionists Remembrance Sunday remains a special
day for them as part of their British and unionist identity: for many
this occasion serves also to remember security forces' dead due to the
recent 'troubles'. At the same time the willingness to remember explic-
itly all those Irish in British and Commonwealth armed forces killed in
the two world wars, and also in British forces killed in wars since 1945,
represents a more generous form of Ulster/British identity. The manner in which Remembrance Sunday is marked today, and the renewed
common memories about these past sacrifices, have brought a new and
reconciling element to existing identities.

In the case of St Patrick's Day we have seen how this event by the
middle of the last century had become very largely associated with

Catholic and nationalist identities, north and south. Over the next half century, matters changed considerably so that eventually it became a more inclusive celebration. In the south, its religious and political features were affected quite rapidly by the impact of the new challenges to older certainties. In the north, it has not been until recent years that celebration of St Patrick's Day has involved both unionists and nationalists. No doubt it is true to say that for many northern nationalists this event is seen as a special part of their Irish and nationalist identity: efforts to make the day neutral for all sides have sometimes involved preventing the flying of the Irish tricolour, which makes some nationalists unhappy. For some unionists there is concern that the day still has nationalist political connotations. Nonetheless, despite these differences in attitude, efforts by many to make St Patrick's Day meaningful to the whole community has meant a new tolerance between existing identities, around a common symbol.

In the commemoration of both St Patrick's Day and Remembrance Sunday, in recent times, it is possible to see a new sense of shared identity between many people of very different national and political allegiances. In the case of the Twelfth of July celebrations of the Battle of the Boyne and Easter commemorations for the 1916 Dublin Rising it is very unlikely that anything similar can happen. At the same time there have been important developments in how these events have been marked. In both instances there have been efforts to make them less threatening to others and to explain their position to opposing groups. The Easter Rising ninetieth anniversary commemorations in Dublin marked an important event for many Irish nationalists/republicans, but also reflected an awareness of the position of others, as revealed by the presence of the British ambassador and concern for the Somme dead. In the north, Easter commemorations remain important for republicans, partly to justify their current political positions and partly to remember republican dead in the recent conflict, but there have been efforts to make these events less threatening to others. The Twelfth of July celebrations remain important for many unionists, but recent efforts by the Orange Order, such as promoting Orangefest and dialogue with other parties, show a willingness to make the event better understood and not so intimidating to others. The willingness in the last decade of the Irish president, Mary McAleese, to acknowledge southern Orangemen, has impacted positively in the north as well as the south.

The changes in the way in which these key dates are marked reflect significant changes in identity. The events and people remembered on these occasions form important elements in the identities of the main groups in both Northern Ireland and the Republic of Ireland. For all those from a unionist and British background, or a nationalist and Irish background, or some other background, these changes mean modification of existing identities. Such developments in recent decades are a result not only of changes within particular sections, due to the influence of individuals, groups and governments, but are also very often a response to changes within others. Certainly these developments have been helped by various institutional or political changes in contemporary society. At the same time they have played an important role in altering people's attitudes and affecting how they deal with the deep national and political problems at the heart of the conflict. The new, more reconciliatory approach taken by many to these key commemorations has been an important part of the effort to achieve effective accommodation and peace.

6
The past and the present: history, identity and the peace process

A sense of history is often important for the identity of individuals, communities and, particularly, national communities. Ideas of history are communicated in various ways: commemorations, academic histories, popular accounts, myths and songs. These are learned in the home, in the school or in the public arena. They serve to provide an historical narrative at the core of the identity of both individuals and national groups. This historical story helps to provide people with an understanding not only of their past but of where they are today. It can give members of society a collective memory that serves to give unity and sense of purpose for the contemporary world. All this is true for the role of history throughout modern Europe. Ireland, north and south, is no exception. Nor is it unusual in a European context, that in Ireland there are often strongly different and conflicting views of history, arising from important national and religious divisions. What is unusual, in the case of Ireland, is the widespread belief held strongly by many until recently that matters in Ireland are greatly influenced by history and that events of the past determine the present to an exceptional degree.

The importance of the past for the present in Ireland has often been noted by people from outside as well as inside the country. In October 1996 a South African church leader, Michael Cassidy, after a visit to Ireland, remarked: 'One notices how people are gripped by the past, remembering the past, feeding on the past; people are constantly remembering this betrayal or that battle; ... this martyr or this murderer'. He concluded that 'these realities of the past feed into the present in Ireland more than anywhere I have been'.[1] In 1992, indeed, the novelist Dermot Bolger felt compelled to protest that in Ireland 'we must go back three centuries to explain any fight outside a chip shop'.[2] In speeches in the 1990s, the American president, Bill Clinton, made frequent mention of the role of 'ancient enmities' in Northern Ireland.[3] In the comments of Ian Paisley we find many references to unionists' 'traditional enemies'.[4] In 1971 he declared: 'God has been our help in 1641, 1688, 1690, 1798, 1912, 1920, and He will not fail us in the future'.[5] In 1996 Ruari Ó Brádaigh of Republican Sinn Féin was reported to have declared: 'In Ireland we have no need of your Che Guevaras and your Ho Chi Minhs. We have Robert Emmet, O'Donovan Rossa, Cathal Brugha, Dan Breen'.[6] Later commentators have often seen the success of the peace process as evidence of triumph over such historical forces. During a visit to Northern Ireland in 2009 the American secretary of state, Hillary Clinton, remarked on how 'ancient hatreds have yielded to new hopes'.[7]

Can we say that the history of Ireland has special importance for the present and that Ireland has a unique past? The answer to this is that history is as significant for the contemporary world in Ireland as for anywhere else, but no more significant than in other countries. The shape of politics and society in Ireland is influenced by historical developments, but that history is neither unique nor responsible for predetermining political conflict among the inhabitants of Ireland. In seventeenth-century Germany and the Netherlands, as in Ireland, there was also bitter religious and political conflict, but such a history does not *determine* events today in these countries, even though it has had influence on the modern world. What is very important for all these countries is the more modern history of the late nineteenth and twentieth centuries which has affected the shape of their societies and influenced the present. In the case of Ireland, it is not correct to say that historical events here were more dreadful or more deterministic for the future than elsewhere in Europe. In 1942 Nicholas Mansergh wrote that the history of Ireland 'is no more unhappy than that of other small nations in Europe, the Belgians, the Serbs, the Poles or the Greeks'.[8] These comments by Mansergh are fair in relation to the early history of Ireland and the other countries. They are not fair, however, in relation to the more recent past when these countries endured dreadful events which Ireland did not. The Greeks suffered very substantial population expulsions and deaths just over two decades earlier, and all these countries were invaded by the German army, 1939–42, which led to heavy loss of life.

For Ireland, north and south, what has been critically important for the contemporary world has been matters relating to present-day problems, in particular over nationality but also over religion. These problems have affected many other parts of Europe. Such challenges to both politicians and citizens do not relate to a special history that predetermines the present. At the same time, it is clear that many people have believed this to be the case. There has been a strong belief that these historical roots are especially important and lie at the heart of conflict in Ireland. Such a view is challenged here. Nonetheless, it is clear that 'views of the past', 'historical perceptions' or 'historical myths' have been very important. Often such ideas are part of a sense of history, which individuals or communities have created for themselves in response to contemporary challenges or needs. It is argued here that, even though the situation in Ireland is not influenced by special historical circumstances, such strongly and widely held perceptions are of considerable significance and must be taken seriously. These views have served to inform and shape the main political identities in Ireland and have helped in part to cause the conflict and violence that persisted for three decades from the late 1960s. Efforts to challenge these historical perceptions have played an important role in the emergence of reconfigured identities which have allowed significant reconciliation.

Reasons for and consequences of these historical perceptions

Anthony D. Smith observed in his book, *National Identity*, that historical memories have been very important for the creation of national identity in our modern world.[9] It is a common feature of nineteenth- and twentieth-century nationalist movements in Europe that they developed or 'constructed' historical traditions as part of their ideology, and this has been true of both unionism and nationalism in Ireland.[10] It has also been noted that history remains more significant in modern societies divided over national and religious matters than in those where these problems have been resolved or do not matter.[11] This has certainly been the case in Ireland. History can provide the explanation and means of personal and public discourse by which people understand and articulate the debate over the main national/religious problems. Often these accounts of the past are selective or based partly on myths, and are closer to what Walker Connor has called 'sentient or felt history' than to 'chronological or factual history'.[12] Nonetheless, such views have remained important for many. The historical dimension has often seemed plausible, because in our dominant Anglo-American world people until recently have been unable to understand the importance of ethnic/national/religious conflict.[13] For many, both in Ireland and outside, to blame the situation on history has seemed reasonable. In the early twenty-first century, of course, there is a better understanding of such conflict.

Historical narratives, created from verifiable historical phenomena and from myths and selective views that surround them, have served to give the past an important role in the identity of individuals and national communities in Ireland, north and south. A.T.Q. Stewart remarked: 'To the Irish all history is applied history and the past is simply a convenient quarry which provides ammunition to use against enemies in the present'. He continued: 'when we say that the Irish are too much influenced by the past, we really mean that they are too much influenced by Irish history, which is a different matter'.[14] We often find references to historical events in speeches by politicians from Northern Ireland, as, for example, in the debate at Westminster in 1985 on the Anglo-Irish Agreement.[15] John Hume talked of events of 1912, stating that the 'divisions in Ireland go back well beyond partition' and referring to the United Irishmen and C.S. Parnell. In the same debate, Ian Paisley declared: 'Anyone who has read history should understand that this did not start in 1920, but goes far back to the days of the plantation settlement and back into the dim and distant past'. In his presidential address to the Fianna Fáil ard fheis, 26 February 1983, Charles J. Haughey declared that 'the right to territorial integrity is derived from history. From time immemorial the island of Ireland has belonged to the Irish people'.[16]

Members of loyalist and republican bodies have been influenced by a strong historical sense. In his study of their many periodicals and journals over the period 1966–92, Richard Davis has described 'the attitude of republicans and loyalists to a history which both acknowledge as fundamental to their respective positions'.[17] A former IRA volunteer, Shane Paul O'Doherty, has described his reasons for joining the organisation: 'My attraction to the IRA was not initially based on the sight or experience of any particular social injustice, though, when I did join the IRA, injustices were foremost in my motivation. It was the discovery of the tragedies of Irish history which first caused my desire to give myself to the IRA ...'.[18] Others joined because of events that occurred after 1969, but then they would have become very aware of this historical dimension, with its emphasis on matters such as the 1916 Rising and the 1918 general election. A belief in the physical force historical tradition has been integral to the role of the IRA in the late twentieth century. When the first of the loyalist paramilitary groups was founded in 1966 it very consciously called itself the Ulster Volunteer Force after the 1912 unionist organisation of that name. Loyalist paramilitaries, as psychologist Geoffrey Beatty, has pointed out, have used the Battle of the Somme, to 'sanction their own actions in a very different sort of combat'.[19]

Such historical narratives, however, have been not only an important part of people's identity in Ireland: they have also served to impede efforts to achieve political accommodation. They have helped to give selective, incomplete and often inaccurate pictures to communities of their own history, and little or no understanding of the experiences of other communities. In the past in Northern Ireland the school system had little formal or direct part in giving the sense of history held by the public, because there was little Irish history on the curriculum. In a press interview in February 1998 the Northern Ireland Protestant playwright, 34-year-old Gary Mitchell, said: 'We never learned Irish history at school, which was really strange. It was all English history geared towards the exams. We didn't do 1798, even though, woops, Wolfe Tone and Henry McCracken were Protestants'.[20] People picked up knowledge of their history from songs, popular historical accounts or annual commemorations of important events or individuals from the past. For many in the Protestant and unionist community, their sense of history focused on events such as the Siege of Derry and the Battle of the Boyne in the seventeenth century and the Battle of the Somme in the twentieth century, which served to explain themselves as a people who have faced siege and sacrifice from these earlier times to the present. This historical narrative does relate to historical experiences of that community, but is selective and contains myths. It ignores periods when Protestants were not greatly concerned about such events, when they were divided, and when many of them co-operated with Catholics, as in the United Irishmen of the 1790s or in the agrarian agitation of three quarters of a century later.

Among nationalists there was an historical narrative of an heroic Irish people who had suffered invasion and conquest but who always survived. In 1994 Bernadette McAliskey recalled how she learned her history from her father, 'everything from the tales of the Tuatha De Dannan, and Celtic mythology, to Larkin and Connolly'.[21] In a news-paper article in 1994, John Hume wrote of the 'traditional nationalist philosophy with which we all grew up – a philosophy that the essence of patriotism – à la 1916 – was the nobility of dying for Ireland and struggling against the British occupation of Ireland'. He referred not only to northern but also to southern 'traditional nationalist think-ing'. He stated: 'All the major parties in the Dáil were born out of that philosophy and their founders were the progenitors of it'.[22] In the south, nationalist opinion retained a strong historical dimension, sup-ported, unlike in the north, by the educational system and the state. In 1996 a Fianna Fail deputy, Conor Lenihan, recalled his schooling in the 1960s: 'history was a heady and potent thing then. In our school in Athlone there were posters of the seven signatories of the 1916 proclamation hung up all over the place'.[23] This historical narrative of the nationalist and Catholic community does reflect its historical experiences, but is also selective and includes myths. This account leaves out periods when Irish Catholics did not pursue separatist goals, when they were divided among themselves and when many of them were aligned with Protestants, as in the British army in the First World War.

These historical views that inform and influence people's identities have helped to cause distrust between individuals and communities. The Mitchell commission of 1996, which looked into the decommissioning of paramilitary arms in Northern Ireland, emphasised the importance of trust between parties. It noted how because of the historical arguments about why the other side cannot be trusted, 'even well-intentioned acts are often viewed with suspicion and hostility'.[24] It urged that 'what is really needed is the decommissioning of mindsets in Northern Ireland'. Another major problem about these historical views linking the current situation to the remote past is that they help to create what Arthur Aughey has called an 'historic culture of fatalism', that makes it difficult to achieve compromise and peaceful co-existence, both for people and for parties.[25] George Mitchell, formerly a member of the United States senate, who became the president's special envoy to Northern Ireland in 1995, has recorded how when he came first to Northern Ireland in 1995 to take up a mediating role, people welcomed him, but then said: 'You are wasting your time. This conflict cannot be ended. We have been killing each other for centuries and we are doomed to go on killing each other for ever'.[26] Strongly felt ideas of historical struggle or siege can make acceptance of change difficult.

Fascination with a supposedly unique history has led to a failure to learn from elsewhere. Other European countries have faced these vexed matters over nationality and religion and have dealt with them better than has been the case in Ireland. In their modern nineteenth- and twentieth-century histories, countries such as the Netherlands and Switzerland experienced serious religious divisions while others like Norway and Italy had to deal with deep divisions over nationalism, but they have managed to cope successfully with these problems. Finally, these historical views have helped to legitimise the use of violence. In his 1993 book, *The Irish Troubles: A Generation of Violence, 1967–92*, J. Bowyer Bell observed that in other countries people were emboldened to act 'by Lenin's or Mao's example, by Allah's word or the people's need'. In Ireland, however, the enemy was killed to 'history's tune and the blare

of those unseen trumpets, audible always to the faithful'. Bell continued: 'In Ireland legitimacy was won from history, a legacy and clearly
defined responsibility'.[27] This historical dimension to contemporary
identities helps to account for the actions and atrocities of loyalist and
republican paramilitaries that cannot be explained only by social and
political factors.

Changes in public discourse on history, from early
1990s to the Agreement

During the 1990s there were important changes in the ways many people
viewed and expressed their history in Ireland. The Opsahl Commission,
which in 1992 and 1993 considered the future of Northern Ireland,
received submissions from hundreds of individuals and groups. It found
evidence of a widespread desire to question many current assumptions
about community identity, including the historical dimension, and urged
greater emphasis on a common Irish history and culture in the schools.[28]
In schools in Northern Ireland teaching of Irish history had increased
since the 1960s. This was given impetus with the introduction in 1989
of a new common history curriculum, with textbooks looking at Irish
history from a range of perspectives.[29] Other educational initiatives
included an annual series of Irish history lectures, known as the Rockwell
lectures, organised for schoolchildren between 1990 and 2000 at Queen's
University Belfast, and a local history schools' competition, run by an
interdenominational church group. At the Ulster Museum two major
exhibitions, curated by W.A. Maguire, addressed two of the most contentious events in Irish history in a manner that gained cross-community as
well as academic respect. The first was 'Kings in conflict', marking the tercentenary of the Battle of the Boyne (1990); the second was 'Up in arms!',
which marked the bicentenary of the 1798 rebellion (1998).

Organisations such as Protestant and Catholic Encounter and church
groups organised lectures and seminars to explore popular historical
myths. Different historical traditions were explored through the programmes and projects of the Cultural Traditions Group, established in
1989 under the Community Relations Council. The 1990s witnessed the
appearance of new popular histories, such as Jonathan Bardon's *A History
of Ulster*.[30] In her study of identities in Northern Ireland, Máiréad Nic
Craith observed how historians 'have heightened public consciousness regarding the collective history of the region [Northern Ireland]
and contributed to a non-partisan awareness of this past'.[31] During the
period from the late 1980s until the early 2000s, over 200 books on

local history were produced by local publishers, such as Blackstaff Press, Friar's Bush Press and the Institute of Irish Studies. The Federation for Ulster Local Studies witnessed a large growth in the number and activities of local community historical societies.

In the south, new Irish historical writing helped to undermine widely held, over-simplified views of past heroes and events. Books and journal articles explored various historical myths and also sought to provide a scholarly and non-partisan treatment of Irish history. One such major project, which began in the late 1960s, was the multi-volumed, *New History of Ireland*, published under the auspices of the Royal Irish Academy, containing material from leading scholars in Ireland and aimed at a wide public. In the 1970s authors, such as Conor Cruise O'Brien and Ruth Dudley Edwards, sought to challenge influential historical myths.[32] This revision of Irish history, however, had little immediate effect on public opinion. It was not until the late 1980s and early 1990s that new historical ideas started to percolate significantly from academic to both popular and government levels, perhaps because of the publicity caused by some opposition which emerged to revisionism in the late 1980s.[33] At the same time, there was a growing awareness of the harm of some historical myths. A number of best-selling books, including Roy Foster's *Modern Ireland* (1988), Marianne Elliott's *Wolfe Tone* (1989), Tim Pat Coogan's *De Valera* (1993) and Conor Cruise O'Brien's *Ancestral Voices* (1994), challenged widely held historical views.[34] Journalists, such as Kevin Myers, Eoghan Harris and Ruth Dudley Edwards, interrogated historical matters, as did broadcasters, like John Bowman and Myles Dungan.

The change in attitudes to history was reflected in the way in which commemorations were now used by many to recall important events in their history. In her 1996 study of war commemorations, Jane Leonard remarked how 'in Ireland politicians and local communities have endeavoured to replace the partisan character of existing war commemorations with more inclusive, generous forms of acknowledging the Irish past'.[35] From the early 1990s both unionist and nationalist politicians were involved together in Remembrance Day services in many places in Northern Ireland: previously this particular commemoration had largely been dominated by unionists and ignored by nationalists. In the Irish Republic the 1990s saw a new effort to acknowledge the role of Irish servicemen in the two world wars. In 1995 a ceremony in Dublin, led by President Mary Robinson, to mark the end of the Second World War, was attended by representatives of nearly all Irish parties, including Sinn Féin. In memory of the Irish who died in the First World War, a peace park was built by groups from the north and south of Ireland at Messines in Belgium and opened by President Mary McAleese and Queen Elizabeth in 1998. In her speech on this occasion, President McAleese declared: 'Those whom we commemorate here were doubly tragic. They fell victim to a war against oppression in Europe. Their memory, too, fell victim to a war for independence at home in Ireland'. She continued: 'Respect for the memory of one set of heroes was often at the expense of respect for the memory of the other'.[36]

In the course of commemorations for the Great Irish Famine, the prime minister, Tony Blair apologised on behalf of the British government for not having done more to help during this catastrophe. The bicentenary of the 1798 rebellion in Ireland was commemorated widely, north and south, as a shared historical event. George Boyce has commented how in the bicentenary celebrations of the event in 1998 'memory was directed towards the significance of pluralist thinking in the Irish past, and academics mediated between the state and the citizen, playing a public role'.[37] In the second half of the1990s the Irish government actively supported a number of these commemorations, whereas in previous decades it had shown reserve about historical matters.[38] The education committee of the Orange Order held a commemorative dinner on the eve of the bicentenary of the Battle of Ballynahinch, Co. Down, at Parliament Buildings at Stormont, attended not only by members of the order, but also by the lord mayors of Belfast and Dublin, the heads of most of the universities of Ireland and prominent journalists. The speaker on this occasion recalled all those who died at Ballynahinch in 1798, including 'the brave Catholic soldiers of the Monaghan Militia who fought and died to save Ireland for the crown and those gallant presbyterian United Irishmen who fought and died for a new Ireland'.[39]

From the early 1990s we can see evidence of the beginning of a different attitude to the importance of the past in political speech and approach. These changes can be observed at government, party and popular level. They are apparent not only in the north and the south but also in Britain. Sometimes this new attitude has meant an outright rejection of any role for history or an effort to draw a line under the past. After a particularly gruesome murder by the IRA in south Armagh in 1992, Dundalk priest, John Duffy, declared: 'if that is how you write Irish history then it is not worth giving to anyone'.[40] In 1995 the author Eugene McCabe warned about the impact of myths in Ireland: 'Throughout the country, family mythology, local mythology, historical mythology, should all be tagged with a health warning: myth can induce a form of madness and zealotry that leads to death'.[41] More commonly, it has involved an effort to deal with the past or to draw either a different or more inclusive lesson from history. People have become aware of 'shared history'. At the same time, however, it must be stressed that many people, including some who have at times taken this new approach, have continued to see events within the customary, historical framework discussed earlier.

This new approach was reflected among politicians and others in the development of the peace process from the early 1990s. In an important speech on government policy in Coleraine on 16 December 1992, the secretary of state for Northern Ireland, Sir Patrick Mayhew, declared that there was much 'in the long and often tragic history of Ireland for deep regret' and the British government 'for its part shares in that regret to the full'.[42] After a meeting of a unionist delegation and members of the Irish government in November 1992, unionist MP Ken Maginnis remarked that 'the real disappointment was that the Fianna Fáil party was caught up by a large 1922 warp'.[43] In mid-April 1993, however, in response to questions about changes to articles two and three of the Irish constitution, Albert Reynolds, the Fianna Fáil taoiseach declared: 'We are not tied up in our past. We want to move forward, to look at the changes required to ensure that both communities can live together'.[44] In an address to the annual conference of his Fianna Fáil party in November 1993 Reynolds acknowledged that there was 'a more complex situation than existed during the war of independence struggle from 1916 to 1921'. He stated: 'We must not be prisoners of history' and that 'new patterns must transcend the antagonisms of a century between the two political cultures'.[45]

A number of times in 1993 Dr John Dunlop, moderator of the Presbyterian church, pointed to the danger of an historically based siege mentality for the unionist community.[46] On 7 March 1993 he wrote: 'Protestants talk of siege and survival. For most unionists, the siege of Derry and the Battle of the Boyne only continue as powerful symbols from the past because they speak of the periodic and constantly renewed threats of being overwhelmed by the Irish majority, whether in 1641, 1690, 1798, the home rule crisis of the early 1920s or in the violence of the present.' Dunlop warned that: 'the trouble with the siege mentality is that it leads to defensive thinking, which often does not have the flexibility or generosity of spirit to discern where its own self interest lies, never mind the legitimate interests of other people'. In late 1993, nonetheless, Ian Paisley criticised the existence of talks between John Hume and Gerry Adams, accusing Hume of trying to sell the people of the province 'like cattle on the hoof to their traditional enemies'.[47]

In March 1993 Seamus Mallon, the SDLP MP, criticised the republican movement for being 'weighed down by history', while the following month a South African journalist, Rian Malan, described republicans as being 'so steeped in ancestral memories of martyrdom that they can't see straight any more'.[48] In April 1993 an IRA statement declared that 'the root cause of this conflict is the historic and ongoing violent denial of Irish national rights'.[49] On the BBC television programme *Spotlight* on 21 October 1993, SDLP leader John Hume spoke of the 'distrust of others based on the past', and argued that this was the time to leave the past behind. In an article in the *Irish Times* in April 1994 Hume acknowledged the importance in the recent past of the 'traditional nationalist philosophy' with its strong historical dimension, emphasised the importance of agreement and diversity in modern Ireland and urged the IRA to renounce its campaign of violence, which had been based on 'traditional Irish republican reasons'.[50]

A number of key governmental papers now carried significant references to dealing with the past, in contrast to earlier documents, such as the Anglo-Irish Agreement and the Sunningdale Agreement, which contained no mention of history. The Downing Street Joint Declaration of 15 December 1993, signed by Prime Minister John Major and Taoiseach Albert Reynolds, stated that the most important issue facing the people of Ireland, north and south, and the British and Irish governments together, was to 'remove the causes of conflict, to overcome the legacy of history and to heal the divisions which have resulted'. In paragraph 5, Reynolds, on behalf of the Irish government, stated that 'the lessons of Irish history, and especially of Northern Ireland' show that 'stability and well being' will not be achieved by a political system which 'is refused allegiance or rejected on grounds of identity' by a significant minority. The statement advocated the principles of consent and self determination.[51] The 'Frameworks for the Future' document of 22 February 1995, between the British and Irish governments, contained a foreword by John Major which stated that 'age-old mistrusts need to be consigned to history'. The paper stated that both governments recognised that there was 'deep regret on all sides in the long and often tragic history of Anglo-Irish relations, and of all relations in Ireland. They believe it is now time to lay aside, with dignity and forbearance, the mistakes of the past'.[52]

In October 1993, Gerry Adams, leader of Sinn Féin, declared that his party had now adopted 'a different approach which is more in keeping with the reality of Ireland in 1993 than perhaps harking back to Ireland in 1918'.[53] Again reflecting a change in attitude to the significance of history, the Sinn Féin national chairman, Tom Hartley, in January 1994 wrote of how 'modern republican ideology, while rooted in the past, is above all the result of a 25 year learning process ...'[54] For a time, however, republicans expressed reservations about the Downing Street Declaration, one reason being, in Adams's words, that 'we are dealing with centuries of history'.[55] Eventually, at the end of August 1994, the IRA declared a ceasefire in a statement that did not dwell on the past but referred briefly to all those who had died 'for Irish freedom'. The *Irish News* editorial, 1 September 1994, appearing the day after the ceasefire, saw this announcement in the 'tradition of Patrick Pearse's noble decision to lay down arms after the Easter Rising of 1916. The ceasefire declaration of October 1994 from the loyalist groups carried no reference to the past beyond the recent troubles. Nonetheless, we may note that their statement was read out in North Belfast at Fernhill House, a building with historic links to the original UVF of 1912. The IRA ceasefire collapsed in early 1996 but was renewed in July 1997.

Over the next four years from 1994 we see continuing reference to history in various places. At government level there was often mention of the past and of the need to deal with or leave it behind. On St Patrick's Day 1996, in reference to his recent visit to Northern Ireland, President Bill Clinton spoke of how he had seen optimism 'in the faces of the two communities divided by history' and how 'we must not permit the process of reconciliation in Northern Ireland to be destroyed by those who are blinded by the hatreds of the past'.[56] The secretary of state for Northern Ireland, Sir Patrick Mayhew, spoke in September 1995 of the government's desire for a 'political settlement to the ancient difficulties of Ireland' and, in July 1996, of the difficulties of a process intended 'to overcome divisions which go back centuries'.[57] At the opening of substantive all-party negotiations at Castle Buildings, Belfast, on 12 June 1996, Prime Minister John Major, declared: 'for too long the history of Northern Ireland has poisoned the present and threatened the future. It is time to end all that, however difficult it may be. History has involved too many victims'.[58] In September 1996 Taoiseach John Bruton attacked the use of history to justify the renewal of IRA violence and went on to say: 'we cannot relive our great grandparents' lives ... we are not obliged to take offence on their behalf, any more than we are obliged to atone for their sins'.[59] In June 1996, at Queen's University Belfast, George Mitchell remarked: 'You can't disregard history – that would be a fatal error – but try to break out of the bonds which history sometimes creates and imposes on a society'.[60] When Tony Blair first met Bertie Ahern officially in 1997 he told him that he 'came to the issues with no ideological or historical baggage' while Ahern then said that he 'too came to Northern Ireland with no historical baggage'.[61]

Attitudes to the question of the past among the parties in Northern Ireland during this period have reflected some of these changes. David Ervine, leader of the Progressive Unionist Party, in March 1995 urged unionists to 'break the myths and lay the ghosts', while two months later Gary McMichael of the Ulster Democratic Party warned: 'I think in this society we have developed a very dangerous fashion of looking into history and using history as a weapon and a means of justifying actions that were taken'.[62] In August 1996 Cecil Walker, UUP MP, appealed to his political colleagues to 'scatter the historical cobwebs'.[63] Among members of the SDLP, in particular John Hume, there were various references to leaving the past behind. In December 1995, at the launch of a book on O'Connell, he stated: 'if there is a lesson from Daniel O'Connell it is the aislings [vision poetry] of our ancestors should inspire us, not control us'.[64] On 4 February 1998 he urged: 'In learning the lessons of the past we must not become prisoners of the past, the major obstacle to success is the unwillingness of certain parties to leave the past behind them and their continued use of the language of the past.'[65]

At the same time, ideas of the importance of the past continued to influence people and to hamper efforts to ameliorate the conflict. George Mitchell accompanied President Clinton during his stay in Ireland in 1995 and he later recalled separate meetings the president had with Ian Paisley and Gerry Adams. He described how Paisley launched into a 30-minute account of the history of Northern Ireland from a unionist point of view, while later Adams gave a similar story from a nationalist point of view.[66] The report (published in 1996) of the international body on arms decommissioning, chaired by Mitchell, highlighted the problem of the 'absence of trust' among the various parties. It noted how 'common to many of our meetings were arguments, steeped in history, as to why the other side cannot be trusted', as a consequence of which 'even well-intentioned acts are often viewed with suspicion and hostility'. The report declared that, 'a resolution of the decommissioning issue – or any other issue – will not be found if the parties resort to their vast inventories of historical recrimination. Or, as was put to us several times, what is really needed is the decommissioning of mindsets in Northern Ireland'.[67]

The 1997 report of the independent review of parades and marches, chaired by Peter North, observed that 'remembering in Northern Ireland is complicated by opposing perspectives, by the long, lingering pain of remembered past suffering and conflict'. The report described how: 'We met representatives of the Loyal Orders who have recently suffered at the hands of the Provisional IRA and who recall the deliverance of the Protestant people in a battle which took place more than 300 years ago'. It continued: 'Their Catholic neighbours meantime remember the same battle as a defeat, along with their more recent experience of discrimination at the hands of the unionist administration'.[68] Of great concern to many unionists in these years was the banning of an annual Orange parade at Drumcree, Portadown, which they believed had been held every year since 1807. In fact this parade had been cancelled on a number of occasions over the years but historical myths about uninterrupted traditions were allowed to colour contemporary concerns about parading.[69] Eventually, a South African lawyer, Brian Currin, was brought in to mediate in the conflict over the Drumcree parade. After initial discussions, he spoke in July 2000 of the problems involved and of the need to unpack 'hundreds of years of historical baggage' to come to a better understanding of each other's position.[70] His efforts were not successful.

Such concerns and problems served to hinder progress in the peace process. They made many people reluctant to accept change and caused the parties to be very cautious in their negotiations. Historical perspectives continued to influence republicans in their attitude towards the peace process, in particular to the decommissioning of arms. It was noticeable, however, that at Sinn Féin annual conferences during these years the speeches of Gerry Adams made less mention of history than in the past, apart from general statements such as that 'Anglo-Irish history and the international experience teaches us that the road to peace is often tortuous'.[71] On the unionist side the speeches of Ian Paisley attacking the peace process often contained references to unionists' 'traditional enemies'.[72] On account of David Trimble's part in the dispute over Orangemen parading to Drumcree, the front page of the *Economist*, 13 July 1996, carried a picture of him with the headline 'Wedded to the past'. Later the same year Trimble was prepared to justify negotiations with representatives of the Irish government by referring to James Craig's discussions with southern government representatives in the early 1920s.[73]

Eventually, on 10 April 1998, after extensive and difficult talks between most of the parties and the two governments, the Belfast Agreement was concluded. A month later the document was endorsed by a large majority throughout Ireland, with a vote in Northern Ireland supporting the agreement and a vote in the Republic of Ireland accepting changes to the Irish constitution in accordance with the agreement.[74] The agreement carried virtually no historical references. It acknowledged that 'the tragedies of the past have left a deep and profoundly regrettable legacy of suffering' and remembered those who had died or been injured, and their families. The opening sentence expressed the general belief that it offered 'a truly historic opportunity for a new beginning'. Also, the agreement expressed commitment to 'partnership, equality and mutual respect' as the basis of relationships 'within Northern Ireland, between north and south, and between these islands'. Such relationships were expressed solely in contemporary terms. The agreement laid down important principles and institutions for the future of Northern Ireland, which represented a compromise on the part of the main sections.[75] Its aim was to reconcile opposing unionist/nationalist views on national sovereignty and the method of government and type of society for the conflicting groups. It established the acceptance of the consent of the people of Northern Ireland as to their future relations with the rest of the UK and the rest of Ireland, drew up a structure for a power-sharing government, affirmed various human rights and liberties, and declared an absolute commitment to peaceful means. The agreement created north–south and east–west dimensions and bodies.

While the agreement made only very brief mention of the past, some participants and observers saw it as an important part of an historical process. Shortly before its signing, the British prime minister, Tony Blair, spoke of how he felt the 'hand of history upon our shoulders'.[76] Press coverage showed some confusion on its exact historical impact. An *Irish Times* editorial, 11 April 1998, referred to peacemakers who 'buried the quarrel of 400 years', while a *Belfast Telegraph* editorial, 21 May 1998, talked of a new partnership which will 'replace 800 years of enmity with trust and friendship'. In September 1998 President Bill Clinton praised the progress of Northern Ireland's peace process as helping the whole world to awaken from 'history's nightmares' by showing that 'ancient enmities' could be overcome. He then went on to claim that if the peace process was successfully concluded, then this example could be shown to 'conflict areas in the Middle East, the Aegean, the Indian sub-continent and to the tribal strife of Africa'.[77]

Changes in public discourse on history since the Agreement

Since the Agreement was passed the impact of this historical dimension can be felt in a number of ways. For some there is now a clear understanding that history does not determine the present, that people are not slaves to history. This view was enunciated in a new approach by President Bill Clinton on his last visit to Ireland as president, in December 2000, when he talked of the dangers of 'historical ghosts' and declared that what had happened in Northern Ireland provided proof 'that peace can prevail, that the past is history not destiny'.[78] With others it has involved a belief that the 'positive' or 'shared' aspects of history should be emphasised. Prime Minister Blair, in an address to the joint houses of the Irish parliament, on 22 November 1998, declared: 'No one should ignore the injustices of the past, or the lessons of history. But too often between us one person's history has been another person's myth. We need not be prisoners of our history. My generation in Britain sees Ireland differently today and probably the same generation here feels differently about Britain'.[79] On 14 May 2000 President Mary McAleese spoke at a conference at the Kennedy Centre, Washington, on the subject of 'Ireland: politics, culture and identity'. She remarked how in Ireland 'we have so often raided the past for proof of our difference, for reasons to remain strangers, for memories that prove the iniquity of the other, each piece of evidence shoring up our preconceptions of both self and the other'. She urged: 'As we strive to create a new future together in respectful partnership, might we not look more carefully at our histories and find in shared memories, sources of unity rather than division, sources of enlightenment about one another rather than mutual incomprehension'.[80]

At the popular level in Northern Ireland we can also see evidence of these changing attitudes. An example of shared historical commemorations was cross-party support at Belfast City Hall in 1999 for the erection of a memorial sculpture to James Magennis, the Catholic holder of a Second World War VC. In April 2003 a special service at St Anne's cathedral in Belfast to remember people from Belfast who had died in the First World War involved not only British crown and army representatives but also republicans such as the Sinn Féin lord mayor, Alex Maskey. Most council areas now regularly experience cross-party attendance at Remembrance Day. Recent years have seen unionist backing for the erection of memorials to supporters of the late eighteenth-century United Irish movement. There have also been efforts to make more inclusive the celebrations on 17 March for the historical figure of St Patrick. For many groups there is still a strong belief in the importance of their own history, but we can also see some effort to explain this history to others and to make their commemorations more inclusive. Since 1998 the Apprentice Boys of Derry have held a week-long festival, before their annual August parade, to 'explain their ethos and culture to Derry's wider nationalist community'.[81]

Leading northern politicians have continued to seek to challenge this historical dimension. In his speech accepting the Nobel Peace Prize in 1998 John Hume expressed his hope that with the new institutions in place, 'we will erode the distrust and prejudices of our past'. On the same occasion David Trimble spoke of the 'dark sludge of historical sectarianism' and declared that both communities must leave it behind. In a new approach to unionist history he acknowledged that, 'Ulster unionists, fearful of being isolated on the island, built a solid house, but it was a cold house for Catholics'.[82] At other times Trimble used the example of former unionist leader James Craig to support his actions over controversial matters.[83] On 2 March 2002 John Reid, the Northern Ireland secretary of state, urged people to 'challenge the historical assumptions which drive the conflict in Northern Ireland'.[84] In 2007 Alliance Party leader, David Forde, warned that 'hiding in the seventeenth century isn't an option any more'.[85]

In the south there was also a widespread determination to adopt a more magnanimous and less restrictive view of the past. A leading role in this effort has been played by President Mary McAleese. On 7 May 2003, speaking at a conference on 'Re-imagining Ireland', she declared: 'The old vanities of history are disappearing. Carefully hidden stories like those of the Irish who died in the First World War are coming out of the shoeboxes in the attic and into daylight. We are making new friends, we are influencing new people, we are learning new things about ourselves, we are being changed'.[86] This issue of the Irish in the First World War, which traditional nationalist versions of Irish history had ignored, is one historical theme in particular which President McAleese, Irish politicians and many members of the public have sought to restore to common concern. An even more extraordinary gesture by President McAleese to a broader view of Irish history, as part of a 'bridge-building' policy, has been her annual reception for southern Orangemen and other Protestants around the Twelfth of July at the Áras an Uachtaráin, the residence of the president, to mark the Battle of the Boyne. In 2007 she noted how: 'For 10 years now Áras an Uachtaráin has been the only place on the island of Ireland to offer an official commemoration of that major history-changing episode, the Battle of the Boyne, and to offer it jointly to both Williamite and Jacobite traditions'.[87] At the same time, leading southern figures, such as President McAleese and the Taoiseach Bertie Ahern now felt able to give new attention to commemorating the 1916 Rising, as was seen in the major state commemoration of the event in 2006. Later Ahern wrote that he had been determined 'to take 1916 back from both the IRA and the revisionists for all the people of Ireland'.[88]

Despite all these developments, in special political arrangements and in changes to many people's attitudes, there remained difficulties, which caused the suspension of the assembly and power-sharing executive for a time. The deaths, suffering and bitterness of the last 40 years of conflict have left a legacy that still influences the present.[89] While the Belfast Agreement initially brought wide agreement, it did so partly by a certain ambiguity on important matters such as power-sharing, decommissioning and policing.[90] There was a failure to deal with these problems satisfactorily, mainly because they went to the core of the underlying national political conflict and proved difficult practically to solve to everyone's satisfaction. At the same time there were difficulties due to the survival of what Norman Porter has called 'antagonistic elements of the historical self-understandings of unionism and nationalism'.[91] There were some special efforts after 1998 to develop aspects of a common history, identity and symbols, but more could have been done in this area.[92] For many people historical perceptions continued to exert a powerful influence, which made political accommodation more difficult.

The delay in decommissioning of IRA weapons and in Sinn Féin support for the police can be seen in part as a result of traditional historical attitudes among many republicans. Denis Bradley, a former intermediary between the Irish government and the IRA, commented in 2001 on the problem of decommissioning that 'it takes republicans, like a lot of other organisations that see themselves with long roots into history, quite a considerable time to get round to doing things, a long gestation period'.[93] The same year, at the inter-party and inter-government talks at Weston Park, Shropshire, England, Gerry Adams sought to explain the delays in progress: 'We are dealing with 100 years of conflict, dealing with quite difficult issues'.[94] Among republicans there emerged several small groups of dissenters who were not willing to embrace the peace process which some saw as 'a total and a complete departure from the traditions of the past' and were prepared to resort to violence again.[95]

Among many unionists, in particular members of the DUP, there remained opposition to power sharing and the new 1998 arrangements, which can be viewed as arising in part from their historical sense of siege. In November 2002, at the DUP annual conference, Ian Paisley began his speech with the words 'in every generation, since the plantation settlement in Ulster in the seventeenth century, traditional unionists have been forced to defend to the death their heritage'.[96] Jonathan Powell, chief negotiator for Prime Minister Blair, has written: 'Even after the Good Friday Agreement, the unionists and republicans were still unreconciled people. With all the history that had gone before, they simply could not make the necessary leap of faith in the other side after such a short period of time. It took nine years to build that trust, step by painful step; nine years of allowing the history to work itself out of the system on both sides so that the war could be formally ended and true power-sharing happen'.[97]

Eventually, however, it was possible to reach an agreement over these difficult issues. As the result of a conference at St Andrews in October 2006, the parties were able to deal successfully with outstanding matters to do with power sharing, north–south bodies and support for the police. In 2007 a new Northern Ireland executive was formed with the DUP leader, Ian Paisley, as first minister, and a prominent member of Sinn Féin, Martin McGuinness, as deputy first minister. Various pragmatic factors lay behind this settlement but some of the main figures involved saw matters in a changed historical light which helped to sustain the new arrangements. Such change was most explicit in the cases of Paisley and Ahern, and particularly in the realm of north–south relations. After their first official meeting, in Dublin in April 2007, First Minister Paisley and Taoiseach Ahern declared their intention to have a joint visit to a new heritage centre at the site of the Battle of the Boyne. Paisley stated how 'we both look forward to visiting the battle site at the Boyne, but not to refight it' and expressed his hope that this visit would help to show 'how far we have come when we can celebrate and learn from the past ... and trust that old suspicions and discords may be buried under the prospect of mutual and respectful co-operation'.[98] A month later at the Boyne, Paisley declared: 'I welcome that at last we can embrace this battle site as part of our shared history'.[99] In his speech Ahern remarked: 'In recent years, many of us from the nationalist tradition have come to a greater appreciation of the history, traditions and identity of those of you from the unionist tradition with whom we share this island'. In September 2007 Paisley had his first official meeting with President McAleese. The setting was again symbolic in an historical sense. It was held at the Somme Heritage Centre in Newtownards, Co. Down, on the occasion of their joint opening of an exhibition about the soldiers of the mainly Catholic 16th Irish Division.[100]

The significance of these war commemorations for engendering reconciliation were underlined again in Paisley's words of praise for Bertie Ahern after the announcement of the latter's resignation. He singled out Ahern's willingness to acknowledge the role of Irish soldiers in the two world wars as an important reason for his respect for him.[101] In his memoirs, published in 2009, Ahern stated that 'respect for our shared history was one of the ways that we were trying to build a shared future north and south. It was something that, probably to the surprise of both of us, Ian Paisley and I agreed about. It would turn out to be an important factor in implementing the Good Friday Agreement'.[102] On 30 April 2008 Ahern spoke in Washington at a joint session of the United States Congress and mentioned his forthcoming visit to the site of the Battle of the Boyne to meet Paisley: 'Today, both sides, proud of their history and confident of their identity, can come together in peace and part in harmony'.[103] On 15 May 2008 Ahern addressed both houses of the British parliament. He made a number of historical references about relations between Britain and Ireland and declared: 'Now we look back at history not to justify but to learn, and we look forward to the future in terms not of struggle and victories to be won, but of enduring peace and progress to be achieved together'.[104]

In May 2011 Queen Elizabeth visited Ireland. This visit was seen as very significant in an historical sense, not just as the first trip of a British monarch to the Republic of Ireland since 1921, but also, in the words of the London *Times*, as marking 'the final reconciliation between two peoples after centuries of misunderstanding and resentment'.[105] In the course of this extremely successful four-day visit, there was frequent reference to history, but in a way that included regret for past conflict, an acknowledgement of each other's traditions and history, an appreciation for shared history and a determination to move together to the future. In her speech at Dublin Castle on 18 May the Queen spoke of how so much of the visit reminded people of 'the complexity of our history, its many layers and traditions, but also the importance of forbearance and conciliation; being able to bow to the past but not being bound by it'. She declared: 'With the benefit of hindsight we can all see things we wish had been done differently or not at all'. She also referred to how recent 'events have touched us all, many of us personally, and are a painful legacy. We can never forget those who have died or been injured, or their families'. In her speech President Mary McAleese, commented on 'the difficult centuries which have brought us to this point' and referred to 'the colonisers and the colonised'. She then stated: 'The harsh facts cannot be altered, nor loss nor grief erased, but with time and generosity, interpretations and perspectives can soften and open up space for new accommodation'. President McAleese declared: 'We cannot change the past, we have chosen to change the future'.[106]

A number of events illustrated the 'new accommodation'. On the previous day, the British Queen and the Irish President had visited the Garden of Remembrance where the Queen laid a wreath in honour of all those who died for Irish freedom. The following day she went to the

Irish National War Memorial at Islandbridge where both heads of state laid wreaths in honour of the 50,000 Irishmen who lost their lives in the British forces during the Great War. She also visited Trinity College and Croke Park, the main stadium and headquarters of the GAA. This royal visit, with its frequent historical references, had a great impact on many and in different ways. The ceremony in the Garden of Remembrance was described by Taoiseach Enda Kenny as 'symbolism beyond words'.[107] Many commentators remarked on the great symbolism of her visit to Croke Park, where in 1921 British soldiers killed 14 civilians.[108] At this place, described as a 'hallowed' place for nationalists, the president of the GAA, Christy Cooney, declared that 'while acknowledging the significance of the past, and honouring all those that died in this place, the GAA has consistently supported and helped the peace process in Northern Ireland'. He referred to the future and spoke of the determination of people and leaders 'to stand together against violence and hatred'.[109] After the event at Islandbridge, one of the northern guests, former leader of the loyalist party, the Progressive Unionist Party, Dawn Purvis, remarked: 'I remembered my own family's involvement in the Great War. I was moved when the tricolour was raised to full mast in memory of those who had fought in that war as Irishmen and Irishwomen. This is another part of the shared history of our island'.[110]

Several weeks later, at the Church of Ireland Cork Diocesan Synod, Bishop Paul Colton spoke of the impact these events had made on him.[111] He talked of how recent acknowledgements of the complexity of Ireland's historical fabric gave 'the lie to the heresy ... that there was only one way in which you could meaningfully be said to be an Irish person – mythical Celtic, oppressed and Roman Catholic'. The dispelling of this myth 'which many of us grew up with', he remarked, made it 'moving ... to see the ceremony at Islandbridge when wreaths were laid by Queen Elizabeth and our President, Mary McAleese'. He explained that recently he had gone to France to visit the grave of his grandmother's soldier first husband, a former Dublin labourer. He saw the ceremony at Islandbridge as 'a public acknowledgement and validation of my ancestors, and, more deep than that, how a family such as mine came to be in Ireland'. He said he believed that this event had been an 'equally potent symbol for many others in our country'.[112]

Final observations

In 2000, on his last official visit to Ireland, the US president Bill Clinton acknowledged that: 'the past is history not destiny'. Of course, this has been true always, not just in 2000. The situation in Ireland cannot be seen as the outcome of some sort of historical regression which has created an inevitable and unavoidable conflict. The problems involved were neither irrevocably rooted in the past nor the outcome of a special history of many hundreds of years of conflict. They are modern day ones, in this case to do with serious divisions over nationalism, and to a lesser extent over religion, although, of course, they have historical roots. At the same time, consciousness in the form of ideas of 'ancient enmities' as part of people's identities has been influential. In other countries as well as Ireland, societies have faced serious religious, ethnic and national divisions, and perceptions of history have come also to play an important part in these places. In the case of the former Yugoslavia, for example, it has been argued that the main cause of the conflict there lay in twentieth-century problems and conditions, rather than 'ancient enmities'.[113] At the same time, historical narratives considerably increased tensions. Pal Kolsto has remarked: 'There is strong evidence that mythicized versions of the past have indeed influenced the thinking of many former Yugoslav citizens and induced them to accept their leaders' call to war'.[114]

Although the core of the difficulty in Ireland lies in this national/religious conflict, it is wrong to underestimate cultural factors in the form of strongly-held historical ideas which have influenced identities. While these views reflect present realities rather than any immutable link with the past, they are still important in their own right and affect the values and actions of the people involved. A sense of history, including actual historical experiences as well as myths, has been a valuable source for the political identity of both individuals and communities. It has helped people to understand and articulate their identity and what it means to be a nationalist or a unionist or British or Irish. At the same time, however, historical narratives have served to sharpen differences between people: also they have strengthened ideas of fatalism and mistrust, as well as justified violence. Such historical views, integral to the contemporary identity of many, have contributed to conflict.

In recent years in Ireland there have been strong efforts to interrogate some of the selective and exclusive views of the past. These developments played an important role in changing the landscape of society and politics in the 1990s, which made possible new political arrangements, first under the Belfast Agreement and subsequently in the effective political accommodation of a decade later. George Mitchell, who chaired the inter-party talks leading to the Belfast Agreement, has described how people came to realise how 'knowledge of their history is a good thing, but being chained to the past is not'.[115] In his memoirs Bertie Ahern recorded how 'the ability to reflect on our history in an open and tolerant way was a central priority of my period as taoiseach'. He continued: 'The 32 counties of Ireland had been a divided society in so many different ways, but we had a shared past. If that history could be commemorated respectfully, I believe that would make an impact on our shared future'.[116] Erosion of the idea of continual conflict back to early history helped to remove some of the distrust and hostility that existed. These developments have encouraged movement within society to allow the emergence of new structures and political arrangements.

The reasons for these changes in historical perceptions require comment. No doubt political events, such as the ceasefires of the mid-1990s or the Belfast Agreement, helped these developments by allowing many to feel more relaxed about new historical views. At the same time, however, changes in understanding and in public discourse about the importance of history have been an important part of the total picture and helped to bring about the new conditions which made political progress easier. This happened at both government and popular level, and is part of a process, which began well before the ceasefires or the 1998 Belfast Agreement. Various factors contributed to these changes: revisionism in Irish history, the exploration of different historical traditions by various groups, and a new approach to commemorations. Such alterations in historical perspectives can be seen as partly élite driven, by some politicians and leading public figures, and by government agencies and intellectuals. At the same time these changes enjoyed support from a wide section of people, from teachers, history enthusiasts and members of the general public, who also saw the need to challenge existing historical narratives. Changes in historical perceptions affected political identities and allowed space for change.

While difficulties remain in the peace process, efforts to achieve political accommodation have won a level of success that would have been unthinkable 40 years ago. Changes in recent years in historical views at the centre of contemporary identities are an influential element of this evolving scene. This historical dimension had helped to deepen conflict and efforts to deal with it have been an essential part of efforts to resolve the situation. The new approach to these historical narratives has won wide although not full public support. An important lesson from the peace process in Ireland is that it is necessary not only to create institutions and systems of government that can win the allegiance of different groups, but also to challenge ideas of 'ancient enmities', which can strongly influence the identities of individuals and communities and so affect the working of such new structures. People have come to gain a better appreciation of their own history and the history of others, which has allowed them to deal with myths. This new understanding has allowed them to escape ideas of inevitability and continual conflict. As President Clinton came to appreciate, eventually, 'the past is history and not destiny'.

A final lesson from these events relates to the importance for contemporary identities of developing a shared sense of history. This has been most evident in the case of the new awareness of all those from Ireland who died in the First World War. A cross-border initiative, organised by a former Fine Gael TD for Donegal North-East, Paddy Harte, and former Derry loyalist leader, Glenn Barr, led to the building of the Island of Ireland Peace Park at Messines in Belgium to remember all the fallen Irish. The 'remarkable ceremony' to dedicate the park in 1998 was recalled later in a speech in Dáil Éireann by one of those who attended, the grandson of a Co. Donegal Orangeman, the British prime minister, Tony Blair. He described how 'representatives of nationalists and unionists travelled together to Flanders to remember shared suffering. Our army bands played together. Our heads of state stood together'. He continued: 'With our other European neighbours, such a ceremony would be commonplace. For us it was a first. It shows how far we have come. But it also shows we still have far to go'.[117]

In Derry city in 2005, at a very different level, the Battle of Messines was recalled with a parade, organised by Glenn Barr. Involving people from Waterford as well as Derry, the event commemorated members of their families who had died at this battle, including a 14-year-old Waterford soldier, believed to be the youngest British army casualty in the entire war. For the first time ever, the tricolour was flown alongside the union flag in the city centre at the cenotaph.[118] In 2007 at Galway Catholic cathedral, a service was held to remember Co. Galway servicemen killed in the First World War. Afterwards a photograph in the press showed two leading politicians, from north and south and from very different backgrounds, standing together on this occasion.[119] One was Sir John Gorman, MC, former British army officer, RUC inspector and Ulster Unionist Party member of the Northern Ireland Assembly. He was also the son of RIC officer, Jack Gorman, a native of Co. Tipperary and last adjutant of the RIC depot in Phoenix Park, Dublin. After the depot was formally vacated by the police in May 1922, he drove north, for 'loyalty to the crown', and joined the RUC. The other was Éamon Ó Cuív, a Fianna Fáil member of Dáil Éireann and an Irish government minister. He was also a grandson of New York born Eamon de Valera, who commanded 'in the name of the Irish republic' the Irish Volunteer garrison at Boland's Mills during the 1916 Dublin Rising, and later became Irish taoiseach and president. Their presence together at this event served to illustrate well how, in the present day, after some 90 years, there has indeed been a significant move, in politics and identities, from partition to peace.

Conclusion

By the end of the period of some 90 years covered here it is clear that there has been both continuity and change in the politics of the two Irelands. Today, political relationships within Northern Ireland and the Republic of Ireland, and between both, are still influenced by matters concerning nationality and, to a lesser extent, religion, which were present in 1921. In a European context, of course, the survival of the importance of such issues is not unusual. The identities that arose from divisions over these matters continue to be expressed in ideas about unionism and nationalism, and in views of Britishness and Irishness. At the same time, the political situation in both states has changed radically. There are now new agreements and structures in place to allow for political differences. More important, however, has been the great change in how people's identities are understood and expressed. We have witnessed a transformation of identities, involving new views of diversity and pluralism and affecting key concepts of sovereignty, nationality and consent. A new political discourse has emerged, north and south, based around the idea of acknowledging and supporting a diversity of identities. It is thanks in large part to such changes that it has been possible to establish and to maintain the political accommodation and relative peace of the present.

We can recognise the considerable success of state building by the two governments after 1921, despite the great difficulties they faced in the early years. The need to establish legitimacy, unity and distinctiveness influenced greatly how identities developed in the decades after 1921. Often people and parties were affected by divisions in their own ranks or by the actions of their opponents. Countries elsewhere in Europe at this time also experienced these difficulties, as well as the question of the relationship between majority and minority national sections. In both cases, in different ways, relations between each state and Britain remained important. Unlike many other European states, both Northern Ireland and the Irish Free State, later Éire and, from 1949, the Republic of Ireland, survived as democratic entities. At the same time, we have seen how these identities developed to become prescriptive, exclusive and confrontational, which created major problems in each state, affecting not just minorities but general stability. This helped to lead eventually to the outbreak of violence in 1968 in Northern Ireland. Although the conflict erupted over the matter of civil rights for the Catholic minority in the north, it became a major confrontation over questions of national allegiance and self-determination, which were seen by many as the 'great unbargainables', and which also involved the south.[1] The continued influence of these restrictive and inflexible identities meant it was impossible to achieve the necessary compromise to bring peace and stability. At a more extreme level, although rejected by the majority of the population, the response by paramilitaries in the form of violence caused many unnecessary deaths and much destruction.

In the end there was a solution. Various factors helped to resolve matters, such as the development of suitable institutions and structures. Essential also was the way in which ideas of identity changed. The growth in an acceptance of ideas of pluralism and diversity affected major concepts of national allegiance and sovereignty, which hitherto had posed such seemingly intractable problems. Ideas of Irishness and Britishness now took on different, broader meanings. Links between religion and political identity were challenged in a significant way. Changes on one side often led to changes on the other. The understanding of the influential idea of national self-determination was qualified by the acceptance of the consent principle, which was accepted by all parties, north and south, as the cornerstone of present and future constitutional relations. Unionism and nationalism were reinterpreted by supporters to allow for new ways of pursuing their objectives. Paramilitaries were persuaded to renounce violence. For many a different approach to history, involving a sense of shared history, became an influential part of changed identities. The modern European context was important, because it helped to create new conditions of co-operation and space. All this meant that problems of government and political relationships could be tackled in a more successful way. Not only were identities transformed but recognition and support of 'diversity of identities' became central to the new political discourse. The Belfast/Good Friday Agreement talks of all the people of Northern Ireland 'in the diversity of their identities and traditions', and recognises their right 'to identify themselves and be accepted as Irish or

British, or both, as they may so choose'.[2] The new article 3 of the Irish constitution speaks of the people of Ireland 'in all the diversity of their identities and traditions'.[3]

What has been achieved in this peace process is very significant. Of course, it involves a successful accommodation, not a removal, of differences. There are still considerable divisions in Ireland, north and south. Unionists remain unionists and nationalists remain nationalists. Religious differences are still relevant. Many people retain their own views of history. In addition, the deaths and injuries of the last 40 years have brought long-term suffering to many families. There are problems over various issues, and there continues to be strong party rivalry within the main groups. In certain quarters there are people who are opposed to these new arrangements. Small groups of dissident republicans have been willing to use violence to promote their aims, leading to the death and injury of a number of police officers and soldiers. In some areas in Northern Ireland loyalist paramilitaries still wield influence and there remain unresolved difficulties over parading.

At the same time it is clear the situation has changed very much for the better. There are now institutions and structures that have wide support. At government and local level there are strong efforts to tackle existing difficulties. We have seen the creation of new narratives about relations within and between the two Irelands. Among individuals, communities and governments identities have altered significantly, which has assisted efforts to bring about and to maintain the new accommodation. What we have today is not just an acknowledgement of differences but the presence of a new sense of generosity and tolerance within existing identities which will assist the creation of a real 'shared society' in Northern Ireland and a fully 'pluralist society' in the Republic of Ireland, as well as better north–south relations. Different identities, arising out of national and religious divisions, have not only been acknowledged but they have also been transformed to become more pluralist and conciliatory. In time, because these divisions have been accommodated, they may well become less pressing for many. Such changes in identity were essential for the emergence and survival of new structures and institutions which have served to deliver relative peace and stability. For the future, it is necessary that such pluralist identities are accepted fully and strengthened.

Notes

Introduction

1. *Irish Times (IT)*, 28 May 2009.
2. Ibid., 24 June 2009.
3. *Northern Ireland House of Commons Debates*, vol.xvi, 24 April 1934, 1095; Dean Godson, *Himself Alone: David Trimble and the Ordeal of Unionism* (London, 2004), p.381.
4. John Bowman, *De Valera and the Ulster Question, 1917–1973* (Oxford, 1982), p.318; *IT*, 3 February 1995.

1 Action and reaction: majority identities, 1921–60

1. *Northern Whig [NW]*, 13 July 1923.
2. *Irish Independent [IND]*, 18 March 1926.
3. Northern Ireland House of Commons Debates, vol.xvi, 24 April 1934, 1095.
4. *IND*, 18 March 1935.
5. Basil Chubb, *The Government and Politics of Ireland* (London, 1982), pp.9–10.
6. Tom Garvin, *1922: The Birth of Irish Democracy* (Dublin, 1996, 2005 edition), pp.147–8.
7. Ibid., pp.189–207; Jonathan Bardon, *A History of Ulster* (Belfast, 2005), p.495.
8. Rogers Brubaker, *Nationalism reframed: Nationhood and the National Question in the New Europe* (Cambridge, 1996), pp.1–10.
9. Karen Stanbridge, Nationalism, International Factors and the 'Irish Question' in the era of the First World War, *Nations and Nationalism*, 2005, vol.11(1), p.23.
10. S.M. Lipset, and Stein Rokkan, 'Cleavage Structures and Voter Alignments: an Introduction' in S.M. Lipset and Stein Rokkan, *Party Systems and Voter Alignments. Cross-national Perspective* (New York, 1967), pp.1–64.
11. B.M. Walker, 'Parliamentary Elections from 1801' in T.W. Moody *et al.* (eds), *A New History of Ireland*, vol.ix. (Oxford, 1984), pp.625–74.
12. For discussion see Peter Mair, 'The Freezing Hypothesis: an Evaluation' in Lauri Karvonen and Stein Kuhnle (eds), *Party Systems and Voter Alignments Revisited* (London, 2001), pp.27–44.
13. John Coakley, 'Religion, Identity and Political Change in Modern Ireland' in *Irish Political Studies*, vol.17, no.1 (2002), pp.15–20; B.M. Walker and Paul Arthur 'Politics and Parties' in R.H. Buchanan and B.M. Walker (eds), *Province, City and People: Belfast and its Region* (Belfast, 1987), pp.305–9.
14. B.M. Walker, *Dancing to History's Tune: History, Myth and Politics in Ireland* (Belfast, 1996), p.115.
15. Thomas Hennessey, *Dividing Ireland: World War 1 and Partition* (London, 1998), pp.1–42.
16. A.C. Hepburn, *The Conflict of Nationality in Modern Ireland* (London, 1980), pp.76 and 95.

17. Garvin, *1922*, p.206.
18. Robert Lynch, *The Northern IRA and the Early Years of Partition* (Dublin, 2006), p.227; Michael Laffan, 'Civil War' in J.S. Donnelly (ed.), *Encyclopedia of Irish History and Culture*, vol.1 (MI, 2004), p.94.
19. Garvin, *1922*, p.190.
20. David Fitzpatrick, *The Two Irelands, 1912–1939* (Oxford, 1998), pp.160–6; Bill Kissane, 'Defending Democracy? The Legislative Response to Political Extremism in the Irish Free State, 1922–39', *Irish Historical Studies*, 2004, xxxiv (134), pp.156–74.
21. Fitzpatrick, *Two Irelands*, p.160.
22. Chris Ryder, *The Royal Ulster Constabulary: A Force under Fire* (London, 1989, 2000 edition), p.60.
23. Ferriter, *Transformation of Ireland*, p.305; Ronan Fanning, *Independent Ireland* (Dublin, 1983), p.66.
24. Ferriter, *Transformation of Ireland*, p.300; Brian Barton, 'Northern Ireland, 1920–25' in J.R. Hill (ed.), *A New History of Ireland. Ireland, 1921–84*. vol.vii. (Oxford, 2003), p.178.
25. Michael Hopkinson, 'The Irish Civil War and Aftermath, 1922–4' in Hill, *New History*, p.34.
26. Fitzpatrick, *Two Irelands*, pp.160–4.
27. *Irish News [IN]*, 10 December 1925.
28. Aodh Quinlivan, *Philip Monahan: a Man apart. The Life and Times of Ireland's First Local Authority Manager* (Dublin, 2006), pp.46–7; Desmond Roche, *Local Government In Ireland* (Dublin, 1982), p.53; Eunan O'Halpin 'Politics and the State, 1922–32' in Hill, *New History*, p.112.
29. Bill Kissane, *The Politics of the Irish Civil War* (Oxford, 2005), pp.163–5.
30. Hopkinson, *Irish Civil War*, pp.54–5; Patrick Buckland, *Ulster Unionism and the Origins of Northern Ireland, 1886 to 1922* (Dublin, 1973), p.178.
31. *IND*, 18 March 1926.
32. J.H. Whyte, *Church and State in Modern Ireland, 1923–1979* (Dublin, 1980), pp.34–5; Patrick Murray, *Oracles of God: The Roman Catholic Church and Irish Politics, 1922–37* (Dublin, 2000), pp.112–16.
33. *IN*, 4 December 1925.
34. Dennis Kennedy, *The Widening Gulf: Northern Attitudes to the Independent Irish State, 1919–49* (Belfast, 1988), p.59.
35. Patrick Buckland, *The Factory of Grievances: Devolved Government in Northern Ireland* (Dublin, 1979), p.21.
36. *IN*, 6 January 1926.
37. Ibid., 18 March 1926.
38. Mary Harris, *The Catholic Church and the Foundation of the Northern Irish State* (Cork, 1993), p.204.
39. Hepburn, *Conflict of Nationality*, p.95.
40. Garvin, *1922*, p.140; Nicholas Mansergh, *Britain and Ireland* (London, 1942), p.65.
41. *Dáil Éireann Debates*, vol.5, 20 September 1923, 49.
42. Ibid., vol.39, 17 July 1931, 2348.
43. David Harkness, *The Restless Dominion* (London, 1969), pp.248–9.
44. Euan Morris, *Our Own Devices: National Symbols and Political Conflict in Twentieth-century Ireland* (Dublin, 2005), pp.38–69, 168–70, and 177.

208   *Notes, pp.12–16*

45. Ronan Fanning, 'Mr de Valera Drafts a Constitution' in Brian Farrell (ed.), *De Valera's Constitution and Ours* (Dublin, 1988), p.35.
46. Mary Daly, *'Irish Nationality and Citizenship since 1922'* in *Irish Historical Studies*, xxxii (127), May 2001, p.385.
47. Maurice Manning, *James Dillon: a biography* (Dublin, 1999), p.130.
48. *Constitution of Ireland*.
49. Chubb, *Politics of Ireland*, pp.43–5.
50. Patrick O'Mahony and Gerard Delanty, *Rethinking Irish History: Nationalism, Identity and Ideology* (London, 1998), pp.155–6.
51. Brian Girvin, *From Union to Union: Nationalism, Democracy and Religion in Ireland-Act of Union to EU* (Dublin, 2002), p.98.
52. *IND*, 27 January 1944.
53. A.J. Ward, *The Irish Constitutional Tradition: Responsible Government and Modern Ireland, 1782–1922* (Washington, 1994), p.251.
54. J.J. Lee, *Ireland: 1912–1985, Politics and Society* (Cambridge, 1989), p.300.
55. Brendan Lynn, 'The Irish Anti-Partition League and the Political Realities of Partition' in *Irish Historical Studies*, vol.xxiv, no.135 (May, 2005), p.330.
56. J.H. Whyte, 'To the Declaration of the Republic and the Ireland Act, 1945–9' in Hill, *New History*, p.56.
57. Buckland, *Ulster Unionism*, p.174.
58. *IN*, 8 December 1925.
59. Michael Kennedy, *Division and Consensus: the Politics of Cross-Border Relations in Ireland, 1925–1969* (Dublin, 2000), p.25.
60. *Dáil Éireann Debates*, vol.22, 22 March 1928, 1645.
61. *IND*, 9 November 1933.
62. John Bowman, *De Valera and the Ulster Question, 1917–1973* (Oxford, 1982), p.115.
63. Kennedy, *Cross-Border*, p.43.
64. Bowman, *De Valera*, pp.137, 146, 171 and 185.
65. Ibid., pp.175–82.
66. Girvin, *Union to Union*, pp.86–7.
67. *IND*, 14 December 1939.
68. Bowman. *De Valera*, p.260.
69. Margaret O'Callaghan, 'Language, Nationality and Cultural Identity in the Irish Free State, 1922–7: the Irish Statesman and the Catholic Bulletin Reappraised', in *Irish Historical Studies*, xxiv (94) November 1984, pp.226–45.
70. Fanning, *Independent Ireland*, p.81.
71. Neil Buttimer and Maire Ni Annrachain, 'Irish Language and Literature, 1921–84' in Hill, *New History*, p.543.
72. R.V. Comerford, *Inventing the Nation: Ireland* (London, 2003), p.81.
73. Fanning, *Independent Ireland*, p.140.
74. Hepburn, *Conflict of Nationality*, p.141.
75. D.H. Akenson, *Education and Enmity. The Control of Schooling in Northern Ireland, 1920–50* (Newton Abbot, 1973), pp.128–30.
76. Garvin, *1922*, p.191.
77. J.H. Whyte, *Church and State in Modern Ireland, 1923–70* (Dublin, 1980), pp.34–9.

78. Ferghal McGarry, *Eoin O'Duffy, A Self-Made Man* (Oxford, 2005), pp.125 and 147.
79. Dermot Keogh, *Ireland and the Vatican: The Politics and Diplomacy of Church–State Relations, 1922–1960* (Cork, 1995), pp.76–81.
80. Lee, *Ireland*, p.161; Keogh, *Ireland and the Vatican*, pp.36–44.
81. Gillian McIntosh, *The Force of Culture: Unionist Identities in Twentieth-Century Ireland* (Cork, 1999), p.91.
82. Comment by Martin Mansergh in *Church of Ireland Gazette*, 2 April 2010.
83. Bowman, *De Valera*, p.107.
84. D.G. Boyce, *Nationalism in Ireland* (London, 1982, second edition, 1991), p.348.
85. *IND*, 9 November 1933.
86. Maurice Curtis, *The Splendid Cause: The Catholic Action Movement in Ireland in the Twentieth Century* (Dublin, 2009). p.174.
87. *IT*, 9 October 1933.
88. Chrystel Hug, *The Politics of Sexual Morality in Ireland* (London, 1999), pp.76–84.
89. *IND*, 18 March 1935.
90. Murray, *Oracles of God*, pp.291–4.
91. Ibid., p.294.
92. Kennedy, *Widening Gulf*, pp.173–4.
93. C.J. Woods, 'Tone's grave at Bodenstown: Memorials and Commemorations, 1798–1913' in Dorothea Siegmund-Schultze (ed.), *Ireland: Gesellschaft und Kultur*-vi (Halle, 1989), pp.141–5.
94. Walker, B.M. (2000) *Past and Present: History, Identity and Politics in Ireland* (Belfast, 2000), pp.58–63.
95. *IT*, 23 June 1924.
96. *IND*, 21 June 1926.
97. Walker, *Past and Present*, p.63.
98. James Loughlin, *Ulster Unionism and British National Identity since 1885* (London, 1995), p.135.
99. D.W. Harkness, *Ireland in the Twentieth Century: Divided Island* (London, 1996), pp.40–1.
100. Loughlin, *Ulster Unionism*, p.95.
101. Nicholas Mansergh, *The Government of Northern Ireland: A Study in Devolution* (London, 1936), p.237.
102. Thomas Hennessey, *A History of Northern Ireland, 1920–1996* (Dublin, 1997), p.77.
103. Mansergh, *Northern Ireland*, pp.235–8.
104. *Belfast News Letter [BNL]*, 17 January 1927.
105. David Kennedy, 'Catholics in Northern Ireland, 1926–1939' in Francis McManus (ed.), *The Years of the Great Test* (Cork, 1967), p.143.
106. *IN*, 4 February 1928.
107. *BNL*, 13 July 1927.
108. *IN*, 11 February and 26 March 1927.
109. Walker, *Parliamentary Elections*, p.651.
110. James Hogan, *Election and Representation* (Cork, 1945), pp.14–15; Chubb, *Politics of Ireland*, pp.144–5.

111. Graham Walker, '"Protestantism before Party!": the Ulster Protestant League in the 1930s', *Historical Journal*, 1985, vol.28 (4), pp.961–7.
112. Paul Bew, Kenneth Darwin and Gordon Gillespie, *Passion and Prejudice: Nationalist–Unionist Conflict in Ulster in the 1930s and the Founding of the Irish Association* (Belfast, 1993), pp.49–50.
113. Walker, *Parliamentary Elections*, p.650.
114. *BNL*, 30 January 1930.
115. *IT*, 30 May 1939.
116. Kennedy, *Widening Gulf*, pp.199–202.
117. *BNL*, 13 July 1927; *IN*, 26 January 1928.
118. Kennedy, *Widening Gulf*, pp.203–20.
119. Northern Ireland House of Commons Debates, vol.xvi, 24 April 1934, 1095.
120. *IN*, 16 November 1937.
121. *IT*, 12 February 1938.
122. Bardon, *History of Ulster*, pp.544–5.
123. Thomas Hennessey, 'Ulster Unionism and Loyalty to the Crown of the United Kingdom, 1912–74' in Richard English and Graham Walker (eds), *Unionism in Modern Ireland* (Dublin, 1996).
124. Morris, *National Symbols*, p.115.
125. Ibid., pp.116–20.
126. Ibid., pp.131 and 201.
127. McIntosh, *Unionist Identities*, p.39.
128. Ibid., p.2.
129. Ibid., pp.45–6.
130. *BNL*, 13 July 1930.
131. *NW*, 13 July 1938.
132. Bardon, *History of Ulster*, p.581
133. Hennessey, *History of Northern Ireland*, p.92.
134. Bardon, *History of Ulster*, p.588.
135. Hennessey, *History of Northern Ireland*, p.98.
136. Lee, *Ireland*, p.300.
137. J.C. Beckett, 'Northern Ireland' in: J.C. Beckett *et al.* (eds), *The Ulster Debate* (London, 1972), p.20.
138. Loughlin, *Ulster Unionism*, p.100; Kennedy, *Widening Gulf*, p.231; McIntosh, *Ulster Identities*, p.133.
139. O'Leary, Cornelius, 'Northern Ireland, 1921–1929: A Failed Consociational Experiment' in Dennis Kavanagh (ed.), *Electoral Politics*. (Oxford, 1992), p.254.
140. *IN*, 18 March 1929.
141. Kennedy, *Widening Gulf*, p.230.
142. *Northern Ireland House of Commons Debates*, vol.x, 5 March 1929, 434.
143. St John Ervine, *Craigavon: Ulsterman* (London, 1949), p.561.
144. B.M. Walker, *Dancing to History's Tune: History, Myth and Politics in Ireland* (Belfast, 1996), pp.121–3.
145. See Jennifer Todd, 'Unionist Political Thought,1920–72', in D.G. Boyce, Robert Eccleshall and Vincent Geoghegan (eds), *Political thought in Ireland since the seventeenth century* (London, 1972). Hugh Shearman, *Anglo-Irish Relations* (London, 1948), pp.241–2.
146. Harkness, *Ireland*, pp.82–3.

147. Mary Harris, *The Catholic Church and the Foundation of the Northern Irish State* (Cork, 1993), p.230.
148. Michael McGrath, *The Catholic Church and Catholic Schools in Northern Ireland: The Price of Faith* (Dublin, 2000), p.103.
149. Ibid., pp.104–5.
150. Fitzpatrick, *Two Irelands*, pp.217–21.
151. Walker, *Past and Present*, pp.81–2.
152. *BNL*, 13 July 1929.
153. Bardon, *History of Ulster*, p.538.
154. *Northern Ireland House of Commons Debates*, vol.16, 24 April 1934, 1091.
155. D.W. Harkness, *Northern Ireland since 1920* (Dublin, 1983), p.80.
156. D.H. Akenson, *et al.*, 'Pre-university Education, 1921–84' in Hill, *New History*, pp.711–20.
157. Fitzpatrick, *Two Irelands*, p.225.
158. *IN*, 22 September 2006.
159. *NW*, 28 May 1945.
160. McIntosh, *Ulster Unionism*, pp.82–3; Walker, *History's Tune*, p.120.
161. Ultach, *Orange Terror: The Partition of Ireland* (1943, new printing, Belfast, 1998), p.69.
162. Brian Lacy, *Siege City: The Story of Derry and Londonderry* (Belfast, 1990), pp.154–8.
163. *Londonderry Sentinel*, 13 August 1946.
164. *NW*, 13 August 1924.
165. *Londonderry Sentinel*, 15 August 1939.
166. *BNL*, 13 August 1947.
167. Garvin, *1922*, p.35.
168. Jane Leonard, 'Facing the "Finger of Scorn": Veterans' Memories of Ireland after the Great War' in M. Evans and K. Lunn (eds), *War and Memory in the Twentieth Century* (Oxford, 1996), p.11.
169. *IN*, 5 May 1995.
170. Yvonne Galligan, 'Women and National Identity in the Republic of Ireland or the Plight of the Poor Dinnerless Husband' in *Scottish Affairs*, no.18, winter 1997, 45–53.
171. Mary Cullen, 'Women, Emancipation and Politics, 1860–1984' in Hill, *New History*, pp.863–80.
172. Ibid., p.864; Frances Gardiner, 'Political Interest and Participation of Irish Women, 1922–1992: The Unfinished Revolution' in Ailbhe Smyth (ed.), *Irish Women's Studies Reader* (Dublin, 1993), p.48.
173. Brian Girvin, *The Emergency: Neutral Ireland, 1939–45* (London, 2006), p.256.
174. *NW*, 13 July 1949.
175. Cabinet documents from 1969 reported in *BNL*, 1 January 1996.
176. Walker, *History's Tune*, p.123.
177. John Sugden and Alan Bairnier, *Sport, Sectarianism and Society in a Divided Ireland* (Leicester, 1993), pp.72–5.
178. Bew, *Irish Association*, p.108.
179. Aaron Edwards, *A History of the Northern Ireland Labour Party: Democratic Socialism and Sectarianism* (Manchester, 2009).

180. Berkley Farr, 'Liberalism in Unionist Northern Ireland' in *Journal of Liberal Democrat History*, 33, Winter 2001-2, pp.29–32.
181. Andrew Gailey (ed.), *Crying in the Wilderness. Jack Sayers: A Liberal Editor in Ulster, 1939–69* (Belfast, 1995), p.80.
182. Harkness, *Northern Ireland*, p.80.
183. Bowman, *De Valera*, p.297.
184. Charles Townsend, 'The Supreme Law: Public Safety and State Security in Northern Ireland' in Dermot Keogh and M.H. Haltzel (eds), *Northern Ireland and the Politics of Reconciliation*, (Washington, 1993), pp.84–116.
185. Garvin, *1922*, p.30.
186. Shearman, *Anglo-Irish Relations*, p.242.
187. Graham Walker, *A History of the Ulster Unionist Party: Protest, Pragmatism and Pessimism* (Manchester, 2004), p.103.
188. Ibid., p.103.
189. Whyte, *Declaration of Republic*, in Hill, *New History*, p.277.
190. Bowman, *De Valera*, pp.269–70.
191. *IT*, 28 Jan. 1949.
192. Bowman, *De Valera*, pp.281–6.
193. Ibid., p.295.
194. Ibid., p.295.
195. M.J. McManus, *Eamon de Valera* (Dublin, 1957 edition), p.385.
196. Bowman, *De Valera*, p.318.
197. Ibid., p.276.
198. Whyte, *Church and State*, pp.232–3.
199. Dermot Keogh, *Ireland and the Vatican; The Politics and Diplomacy of Church–State Relations, 1922–60* (Cork, 1994), pp.29–30.
200. Bowman, *De Valera*, p.281.
201. Kennedy, *Cross-Border*, pp.178–9.
202. *IT*, 22 July 1959.
203. Ibid., 16 Oct. 1959.
204. John Bowman, 'The Wolf in Sheep's Clothing: Richard Hayes's Proposal for a New National Library of Ireland, 1959–60' in R.J. Hill and Michael Marsh (eds), *Modern Irish Democracy: Essays in Honour of Basil Chubb* (Dublin, 1993), pp.44–61.
205. *IT*, 25 January 1949.
206. *BNL*, 3 and 7 February 1949.
207. Bardon, *History of Ulster*, p.600.
208. Ibid., p.600.
209. Ibid., p.207.
210. *BNL*, 12 February 1949.
211. *Northern Ireland House of Commons Debates*, vol.32, 30 November 1948, 3666.
212. *IT*, 17 and 23 February 1950.
213. *Southern Ireland – church or state?* (Belfast, 1951), pp.1–3.
214. *IT*, 26 October 1959.
215. Akenson, *Schooling in Northern Ireland*, p.177.
216. Henry Patterson, *Ireland since 1939: The Persistence of Conflict* (London, 2006), p.123.
217. *IT*, 13 July 1960.

218. *IT*, 28 May 1955.
219. Walker, *Ulster Unionist Party*, pp.115–28; J.H. Whyte, 'Economic Crisis and Political Cold War, 1949–57' in Hill, *New History*, pp.288–93.
220. Bardon, *History of Ulster*, p.609.
221. Whyte, *Political Cold War*, p.289.
222. Hennessey, *History of Northern Ireland*, p.116.
223. Bardon, *History of Ulster*, p.610.
224. Gailey, *Jack Sayers*, p.50.
225. *IT*, 25 August 1958.
226. Enda Staunton, *The Nationalists of Northern Ireland, 1918–1973* (Dublin, 2001), p.222.
227. *IT*, 3 November 1959.
228. *BNL*, 10 November 1959.
229. Bardon, *History of Ulster*, p.610.
230. O'Mahony and Delanty, *Rethinking Irish History*, p.151.
231. Girvin, *Union to Union*, pp.169–200; Tom Garvin, *Preventing the Future. Why was Ireland so poor for so long* (Dublin, 2004).
232. O'Mahony and Delanty, *Rethinking Irish History*, pp.165–9.
233. Garvin, *Preventing the Future*, pp.117 and 149.
234. W.E. Vaughan and A.J. Fitzpatrick (eds), *Irish Historical Statistics: Population 1821–1971* (Dublin, 1978), p.5.
235. Whyte, *Political Cold War*, pp.287–8.
236. Nicholas Mansergh, *The Government of Northern Ireland: A Study in Devolution* (London, 1936), pp.238–41 and 316.

2 Parallel universes: minority identities, 1921–60

1. Rogers Brubaker, *Nationalism Refined: Nationhood and the National Question in the New Europe* (Cambridge, 1996), p.50.
2. Jonathan Bardon, *A History of Ulster* (Belfast, 1992, updated edition, 2005), p.495.
3. *Dictionary of Irish Biography* (*DIB*), vol.9, (Cambridge, 2010), pp.1069–70.
4. Sir John Gorman, *The Times of my Life* (Barnsley, 2002), pp.2–6.
5. *DIB*, vol.1, pp.616–24.
6. Ibid., vol.5, pp.659–60.
7. John Coakley, 'Religion, Ethnic Identity and the Protestant Minority in the Republic' in William Crotty and D.E. Schmitt (eds), *Ireland and the Politics of Change* (London, 1998), p.89.
8. W.E. Vaughan and A.J. Fitzpatrick (eds), *Irish Historical Statistics: Population 1821–1971* (Dublin, 1978), pp.49–37.
9. *Irish Times* (*IT*), 5 July 1921.
10. *IT*, 8 December 1921.
11. Mark Bence-Jones, *Twilight of the Ascendancy* (London, 1987), p.214.
12. *IT*, 17 December 1921.
13. Patrick Buckland, *The Anglo-Irish and the New Ireland 1885–1922* (Dublin, 1972), pp.272–30.
14. *IT*, 12 December 1921.
15. Ibid., 12 December 1921.

16. Ibid., 20 January 1922.
17. Ibid., 10 May 1922.
18. Ibid., 13 May 1922.
19. Buckland, *Anglo-Irish*, pp.259–71.
20. Ibid., pp.263–8; Coakley, 'Protestant Minority', p.233.
21. *IT*, 13 December 1922.
22. J.A. Gaughan, (ed.), *Memoirs of Senator Joseph Connolly: A Founder of Modern Ireland* (Dublin, 1996), pp.386–7.
23. Peter Hart, *The I.R.A. at War, 1916–1923* (Oxford, 2003), pp.223–40.
24. R.B. McDowell, *Crisis & Decline: The Fate of the Southern Unionists* (Dublin, 1997), pp.38–112 and 121–36.
25. Tom Barry, *Guerilla Days in Ireland* (Cork, 1955), pp.114–16.
26. George Seaver, *John Allen Fitzgerald Gregg, Archbishop* (Dublin, 1963), p.121.
27. Ibid.
28. *IT*, 16 May 1923.
29. Ibid., 30 July 1924.
30. Ibid., 28 March 1921.
31. Bardon, *History of Ulster*, p.31.
32. Michael Laffan, *The Partition of Ireland, 1911–1925* (Dundalk, 1983), p.91.
33. Eamon Phoenix, *Northern Nationalism: Nationalist Politics, Partition and the Catholic Minority in Northern Ireland* (Belfast, 1994), pp.154–66.
34. Ibid., pp.167–8; Enda Staunton, *The Nationalists of Northern Ireland, 1918–1973* (Dublin, 2001), pp.167–8.
35. Paul Bew, *Ireland: the Politics of Enmity, 1789–2006* (Oxford, 2007), pp.423–38; Robert Lynch, *The Northern IRA and the Early Years of Partition, 1920–1922* (Dublin, 2006), pp.98 and 119.
36. Phoenix, *Northern Nationalism*, p.181.
37. Bardon, *History of Ulster*, pp.499–500.
38. Ibid., p.500.
39. Thomas Hennessey, *A History of Northern Ireland 1920–1996* (Dublin, 1997), pp.46–51.
40. Mary Harris, *The Catholic Church and the Foundation of the Northern Irish State* (Cork, 1993), pp.145–50.
41. Lynch, *Northern IRA*, pp.177–87.
42. Phoenix, *Northern Nationalism*, pp.247–58.
43. Ibid., p.180.
44. Ibid., p.324.
45. Staunton, *Northern Nationalists*, pp.98–9.
46. Phoenix, *Northern Nationalism*, pp.98–9.
47. Eamon Phoenix, 'Partition, the Catholic church and the Diocese of Clogher' in H.A. Jefferies (ed.), *History of the Diocese of Clogher* (Dublin, 2005), pp.207–22.
48. A.F. Parkinson, *Belfast's Unholy War: the Troubles of the 1920s* (Dublin, 2004), pp.308–16.
49. Phoenix, *Northern Nationalism*, pp.88–9.
50. Ibid., p.183.
51. David Fitzpatrick, *The Two Irelands, 1912–1939* (Oxford, 1998), p.161.
52. Phoenix, *Northern Nationalism*, p.183.
53. *IT*, 6 June 1922.

54. *Irish News (IN)*, 27 April 1922.
55. Bew, *Ireland*, p.436.
56. Hennessey, *History of Northern Ireland*, p.11; Bardon, *History of Ulster*, p.494.
57. Vaughan and Fitzpatrick, *Historical Statistics*, pp.67–70.
58. See Hart, *I.R.A. at War*, pp.223–58.
59. *IT*, 15 February 1929.
60. T.J. Johnston, J.L. Robinson and R.W. Jackson, *A History of the Church of Ireland* (Dublin, 1953), p.269; Wilmot Irwin, *Betrayal in Ireland* (Belfast, n.d.), pp.16–17.
61. Sam Hutchison, *The Light of Other Days. A Selection of Monuments, Mausoleums and Memorials in Church of Ireland Churches and Graveyards and those whom they Commemorate* (Dublin, 2008), p.136.
62. Sir John Ross, *Pilgrim Scrips* (London, 1927), pp.244–51; J.J. Sexton and Richard O'Leary, 'Factors Affecting Population Decline in Minority Religious Communities in the Republic of Ireland' in *Building Trust in Ireland: Studies Commissioned by the Forum for Peace and Reconciliation* (Belfast, 1996), p.263.
63. *IT*, 14 June 1923.
64. Ibid., 6 July 1923.
65. Ibid., 17 February and 8 May 1923.
66. W.A. Phillips, *The Revolution in Ireland, 1906–1923* (London, 1926, second edition), p.v.
67. *IT*, 1 August 1923.
68. W.A. Phillips (ed.), *History of the Church of Ireland*, vol.III. (Oxford, 1933), pp.412–13.
69. Johnston *et al.*, *History of Church of Ireland*, p.269.
70. Harris, *Catholic Church*, p.127; John Hassan (G.B. Kenna), *Facts & Figures: The Belfast Pogroms, 1920–1922* (Dublin, 1922, Belfast, new edition, 1997).
71. A.F. Parkinson, *Belfast's Unholy war: The Troubles of the 1920s* (Dublin, 2004), p.10.
72. *IN*, 27 April 1925.
73. Phoenix, *Diocese of Clogher*, p.220.
74. B.M. Walker, 'Parliamentary elections from 1801' in T.W. Moody *et al.* (eds), *A new history of Ireland*, vol.IX. (Oxford, 1984), pp.642–54.
75. Cornelius O'Leary 'Northern Ireland, 1921–1929: A Failed Consociational Experiment' in Dennis Kavanagh (ed.), *Electoral Politics* (Oxford, 1992), pp.253–5.
76. Phoenix, *Northern Nationalism*, p.353.
77. *IT*, 18 June 1932.
78. *IT*, 20 November 1933.
79. Phoenix, *Northern Nationalism*, p.370.
80. Mary Daly, 'Irish Nationality and Citizenship since 1922' in *Irish Historical Studies*, xxxii, no.127 (May, 2001), p.391. Claire O'Halloran, *Partition and the Limits of Irish Nationalism: An Ideology under Stress* (Dublin, 1987), pp.152–5, 175–60.
81. Eamon de Valera, *Ireland's Stand: Being a Selection of the Speeches of Eamon de Valera during the War (1939–1945)* (Dublin, 1946), p.14; Bardon, *History of Ulster*, p.566.

82. T.J. Campbell, *Fifty Years of Ulster, 1890–1940* (Belfast, 1941), pp.127–32.
83. Brendan Lynn, *Holding the Ground; the Nationalist Party in Northern Ireland, 1945–72* (Aldershot, 1997), p.11.
84. John Bowman, *De Valera and the Ulster Question, 1917–1973* (Oxford, 1982), p.257.
85. Lynn, *Nationalist Party*, pp.327–8.
86. Bardon, *History of Ulster*, p.603.
87. Staunton, *Northern Nationalists*, pp.181–94.
88. *IT*, 28 May 1955.
89. Bardon, *History of Ulster*, pp.606–8; Daithi O Corrain, *Rendering to God and Caesar: the Irish Churches and the Two States in Ireland, 1949–73* (Manchester, 2006), pp.238–41.
90. Ibid., p.240.
91. Walker, *Parliamentary Elections*, p.652.
92. Terence Dooley, *The Plight of Monaghan Protestants, 1912–1926* (Dublin, 2000), p.49.
93. J.L. McCracken, *Representative Government in Ireland: A Study of Dáil Éireann 1919–48* (London, 1958), p.62.
94. Coakley, 'Protestant Minority', p.99.
95. McCracken, *Dáil Éireann*, p.92.
96. Coakley, 'Protestant Minority', p.98.
97. B.M. Walker, (ed.), *Parliamentary Election Results in Ireland, 1918–92* (Dublin, 1992), pp.168–76.
98. *IT*, 4 July 1953.
99. Ibid., 14 October 1961; Walker, *Election Results*, pp.193 and 200; P.M. Sacks, *The Donegal Mafia: an Irish Political Machine* (New Haven,1976), pp.53–4.
100. Walker, *Election Results*, pp.199–205.
101. J.E. and G.W. Dunleavy, *Douglas Hyde: A Maker of Modern Ireland* (Berkeley, 1991), p.356.
102. Coakley, 'Protestant Minority', p.99.
103. W.J. Flynn (ed.), *Irish Parliamentary Handbook – 1939* (Dublin, 1939), p.146.
104. T.P. Coogan, *De Valera: Long fellow, Long shadow* (London, 1993), p.642.
105. Coakley, 'Protestant Minority', p.89.
106. Vaughan and Fitzpatrick, *Historical Statistics*, pp.11–13, 22 and 49.
107. *Census of population*, 1926, vol.iii, pp.8–9.
108. Sexton and O'Leary, *Minority Communities*, pp.10–11, 15 and 30.
109. Kurt Bowen, *Protestants in a Catholic State: Ireland's Privileged Minority* (Dublin, 1983), p.40.
110. Ibid., p.43; Brian Girvin, *From Union to Union: Nationalism, Democracy and Religion in Ireland – Act of Union to EU* (Dublin, 2002), pp.113–14; H.K. Crawford, *Outside the Glow: Protestants and Irishness in Independent Ireland* (Dublin, 2010), p.114.
111. *Irish Times*, 14 February 1951.
112. Tim Fanning, *The Fethard-on-Sea Boycott* (Cork, 2010), pp.173–85 and 198.
113. *Census, 1926*, vol.iii, p.124; *Census of Population, 1961*, vol.vii, pp.75–6.
114. *DIB*, vol.6, pp.482–4; *IT*, 10 October 1942.
115. Anna Bryson, *No Coward Soul: A Biography of Thekla Beere* (Dublin, 2009), p.81: *Census, 1927*, vol.111, p.124.
116. Ibid., p.81.

117. Dennis Kennedy, *The Widening Gulf; Northern Attitudes to the Independent Irish State, 1919–49* (Belfast, 1988), p.156.
118. R.J. Kerr, Comments on 'Protestantism since the Treaty' in *The Bell*, vol.8, no.3 (June, 1944), p.230; Daithi O Corrain, 'Semper fidelis; Eugene O'Callaghan, Bishop of Clogher (1943–1969)' in H.A. Jefferies (ed.), *History of the Diocese of Clogher* (Dublin, 2005), pp.242–3.
119. Pat Walsh, *The Curious Case of the Mayo Librarian* (Cork, 2009).
120. *Catholic Bulletin*, vol.xxi, no.3 (March 1931), pp.209–31.
121. Dermot Keogh, *The Vatican, the Bishops and Irish Politics, 1919–39* (Cambridge, 1986), pp.168–77.
122. *Dáil Éireann*, vol.39, 17 June 1931, 516–20.
123. Walsh, *Mayo Librarian*, pp.202–3.
124. W.B. Stanford, *A Recognised Church. The Church of Ireland in Éire* (Dublin, 1944), p.17.
125. W.B. Stanford, *Faith and Faction in Ireland Now* (Dublin, 1946), p.14.
126. Girvin, *Union to Union*, p.112.
127. Richard Dunphy, *The Making of Fianna Fáil Power in Ireland, 1923–1948* (Oxford, 1995), p.130.
128. Girvin, *Union to Union*, p.112.
129. *Census, 1926*, vol.iii, p.114.
130. *Census, 1961*, vol.vii, p.86.
131. Bowen, *Protestants*, p.86.
132. Quoting information by Terence Dooley, R.V. Comerford, *Inventing the Nation: Ireland* (London, 2003), p.266.
133. Maurice Curtis, *The Splendid Cause: The Catholic Action Movement in Ireland in the Twentieth Century* (Dublin, 2009), pp.72–3.
134. Bowen, *Protestants*, pp.81, 85–6.
135. Ibid., p.181; H.C. Lyster, *An Irish Parish in Changing Days* (London, 1933).
136. James Lydon, The Silent Sister: Trinity College and Catholic Ireland' in C.H. Holland (ed.), *Trinity College Dublin & the Idea of a University* (Dublin, 1991), p.46.
137. *Independent*, 10 March 2004.
138. Vaughan and Fitzpatrick, *Historical Statistics*, pp.68–73.
139. Because of a boycott of the census by some nationalists, it is necessary to estimate these 1971 figures. Paul Compton, 'Population' in R.H. Buchanan and B.M. Walker, *Province, City and People* (Belfast, 1987), p.245.
140. Vaughan and Fitzpatrick, *Historical Statistics*, pp.69–73.
141. Chris Ryder, *The Royal Ulster Constabulary; A force under fire* (London, 1989, 2000 edition), p.60.
142. *Hunt report of the Advisory Committee on Police in Northern Ireland* (Belfast, 1969), p.29. Patrick Buckland, *The Factory of Grievances: Devolved Government in Northern Ireland 1921–39* (Dublin, 1979), pp.20–1.
143. Ibid.
144. Gorman, *Times of my Life*, p.102.
145. Cameron report. *Disturbances in Northern Ireland* (Belfast, 1969), p.91.
146. 'Founding a Legal System-the Early Judiciary of Northern Ireland'. Paper delivered by Lord Justice Carswell to the Irish Legal History Society, to be published shortly by the society.
147. T.J. Campbell, *Fifty Years of Ulster1890–1940* (Belfast, 1941), p.327.

148. Staunton, *Northern Nationalists*, p.239; Lynn, *Nationalist Party*, pp.23–4.
149. *Derry Journal*, 3 December 1945.
150. Buckland, *Factory of Grievances*, p.21.
151. Ibid., p.22.
152. Ibid., p.20.
153. Hennessey, *History of Northern Ireland*, p.132; D.P. Barritt and C.F. Carter, *The Northern Ireland Problem; A Study in Group Relations* (Oxford, 1982), p.97.
154. Ibid., pp.90–1; David Kennedy, 'Catholics in Northern Ireland, 1926–1939' in Francis McManus (ed.), *The Years of the Great Test* (Cork, 1967), p.138.
155. B.M. Walker and Alf McCreary, *Degrees of Excellence: the Story of Queen's, Belfast, 1849–1995* (Belfast, 1995), p.59.
156. Maurice Hayes, *Minority Verdict: Experiences of a Catholic Public Servant* (Belfast, 1995), p.23.
157. Barritt and Carter, *Northern Ireland Problem*, pp.97–8; Cameron report, p.60.
158. David Harkness, *Northern Ireland Since 1920* (Dublin, 1983), p.29.
159. *IN*, 18 March 1960.
160. Barritt and Carter, *Northern Ireland Problem*, p.98.
161. Cameron report, p.60.
162. Bardon, *History of Ulster*, p.538.
163. Alvin Jackson, *Home Rule: An Irish History, 1800–2000* (London, 2003), pp.230–1.
164. *Debates of Northern Ireland House of Commons*, 21 November 1934, vol.xvii, 73.
165. Buckland, *Factory of Grievances*, p.23.
166. Kennedy, *Catholics in Northern Ireland*, p.138.
167. Barritt and Carter, *Northern Ireland Problem*, pp.100–7: J.H. Whyte, 'How much Discrimination was here under the Unionist Regime, 1921–68?' in Tom Gallagher and James O'Donnell (eds), *Contemporary Irish Studies* (Manchester, 1983), pp.14–18.
168. Cameron report, p.15.
169. Barritt and Carter, *Northern Ireland Problem*, p.87; Michael McGrath, *The Catholic Church and Catholic Schools in Northern Ireland* (Dublin, 2000), pp.246–7; Bardon, *History of Ulster*, p.644.
170. *Ulster Herald*, 21 November 1959.
171. Tom Garvin, *Preventing the Future. Why was Ireland so poor for so long* (Dublin, 2004), p.149.
172. Barritt and Carter, *Northern Ireland Problem*, p.60.
173. Hennessey, *History of Northern Ireland*, p.130; Henry Patterson, *Ireland since 1939: The Persistence of Conflict* (London, 2006), p.194.
174. Hennessey, *History of Northern Ireland*, p.130.
175. Cameron report, p.61.
176. Ibid., p.61.
177. Brian Lacy, *Siege City: The Story of Derry and Londonderry* (Belfast, 1990), p.247.
178. Whyte, *Discrimination*, pp.3–4.
179. Ibid., p.4; Christopher Hewitt, 'The Roots of Violence: Catholic Grievances and Irish Nationalism during the Civil Rights Period' in P.J. Roche and Brian Barton (eds), *The Northern Ireland Question: Myth and Reality* (Aldershot, 1991), p.7.

180. Whyte, *Discrimination*, pp.4–5.
181. Ibid., p.7.
182. Buckland, *Factory of Grievances*, p.60.
183. Ibid., p.62.
184. Victor Griffin, *Mark of Protest* (Dublin, 1993), pp.90–1; John Dunlop, *A Precarious Belonging: Presbyterians and the Conflict in Ireland* (Belfast, 1995), p.75; see comments by Ulster Unionist deputy mayor of Derry, Marlene Jefferson to Opshal Commission, *IT*, 26 January 1993.
185. See above, pp.60, 62 and 76–7.
186. *BNL*, 19 November 1959.
187. Marc Mulholland, *Northern Ireland: A Very Short Introduction* (Oxford, 2003), p.45.
188. Vaughan and Fitzpatrick, *Historical Statistics*, p.72.
189. In the northern case see Whyte, *Discrimination*, pp.28–9: in the southern case see debate between Ian Paisley and Garret FitzGerald, *BT*, 13 December 1995 and 9 January 1996.
190. Whyte, *Discrimination*, p.29.
191. Marianne Elliott, *When God Took Sides: Religion and Identity in Ireland – Unfinished History* (Oxford, 2009), p.227.
192. Ibid., p.229; F.S.L. Lyons, 'The Minority Problem in the 26 Counties' in Francis McManus (ed.), *The Years of the Great Test* (Cork, 1967), p.99.
193. *IT*, 21 February 1933.
194. B.M. Walker, *Dancing to History's Tune: History, Myth and Politics in Ireland* (Belfast, 1996), p.119.
195. Michael Viney, *The Five Per Cent. A Survey of Protestants in the Republic* (Dublin, 1961), p.30.
196. *IT*, 10 May 1939.
197. Bew, *Ireland*, pp.482–3.
198. Kennedy, *Widening Gulf*, p.177.
199. D.H. Akenson, *A Mirror to Kathleen's Face: Education in Independent Ireland, 1922–1960* (Montreal, 1975), p.111.
200. *IT*, 14 November, 1 and 6 December 1934. Kennedy, *Widening Gulf*, pp.168–9.
201. See Norma MacMaster, *Over my Shoulder: A Memoir* (Dublin, 2008).
202. *Irish Independent*, 12 March 1957.
203. Victor Griffin, *Mark of Protest – an Autobiography* (Dublin, 1993), pp.25–7.
204. Girvin, *Union to Union*, p.112.
205. *Church of Ireland Gazette*, 2 April 2010; Griffin, *Mark of Protest*, pp.25–7.
206. See Hubert Butler, *Escape from the Anthill* (Mullingar, 1985); *DIB*, vol.2, pp.121–3.
207. *Church of Ireland Gazette*, 13 January 1922.
208. *IT*, 8 February 1933, reprinted in *IT*, 8 February 2010.
209. Hutchison, *Church of Ireland Churches*, p.150.
210. Jack White, *Minority Report: The Protestant Community in the Irish Republic* (Dublin, 1975), p.109.
211. Richard Doherty, *Irish Men and Women in the Second World War* (Dublin, 1999), pp.15–26.
212. *IT*, 11 May 1949.
213. Bowen, *Protestants*, pp.198–9.
214. *DIB*, vol.9, pp.4–5.

215. *IT*, 26 January 1957.
216. Alan Acheson, *A History of the Church of Ireland, 1691–2001*(Dublin, 2002), p.233.
217. Elliott, *Religion and Identity*, p.241.
218. Fionnuala O'Connor, *In Search of a State: Catholics in Northern Ireland* (Belfast, 1993), p.165.
219. Ibid., p.335.
220. Denis Donoghue, *Warrenpoint* (London, 1990), pp.151–2.
221. Sean Farren, *The Politics of Irish Education, 1920–65* (Belfast, 1995), p.104.
222. Elliott, *Religion and Identity*, p.241.
223. Walker, *History's Tune*, p.120.
224. Harkness, *Northern Ireland*, p.76.
225. Hennessey, *History of Northern Ireland*, pp.62–70.
226. Phoenix, *Northern Nationalism*, p.135.
227. Ultach (J.J. Campbell) *Orange terror* (First printed 1943, Belfast, new edition, 1998), pp.13, 24 and 31.
228. Lynn, *Nationalist Party*, pp.23–4; *Derry Journal* 28 November 1945.
229. Michael Kennedy, *Division and Consensus. The Politics of Cross-Border Relations in Ireland, 1925–1969* (Dublin, 2000), p.157.
230. Patterson, *Ireland*, p.132.
231. Kennedy, *Cross-border Relations*, p.218.
232. Staunton, *Northern Nationalists*, p.218.
233. Bardon, *History of Ulster*, p.610; J.H. Whyte, 'Economic Progress and Political Pragmatism, 1957–63' in J.R. Hill (ed.), *A New History of Ireland. Ireland, 1921–84*, vol.vii. (Oxford, 2003), p.306.
234. *IT*, 5 August 1958.
235. Staunton, *Northern Nationalists*, p.221.
236. *IN*, 18 March 1960; Staunton, *Northern Nationalists*, p.230.
237. John Bowman, 'The wolf in sheep's clothing': Richard Hayes's proposal for a new National Library of Ireland, 1959–60' in *Modern Irish Democracy: Essays in honour of Basil Chubb* (Dublin, 1993), p.45.
238. William Watts, *Provost Trinity College Dublin: A Memoir* (Dublin, 2008), p.208.
239. *Hansard*, vol. 656, 30 March 1962, 1747.
240. Lynn, *Nationalist Party*, p.143.

3   Remembering and forgetting: commemorations and identity, 1921–60

1. Pauline Mooney, 'A Symbol for the Nation: the National Holiday Campaign, 1901–3' MA thesis, Maynooth University College, 1992), p.76.
2. Ibid.
3. *Irish Independent* [*IND*], 18 March 1926.
4. Ibid., 16 March 1930.
5. Ibid., 18 March 1931.
6. Ibid., 18 March 1932, 19 March 1934.
7. See speech by Eamon de Valera in Maurice Moynihan (ed.), *Speeches and Statements by Eamon de Valera* (Dublin, 1980), pp.217–9.
8. *IND*, 18 March 1935.

9. *Northern Whig* [*NW*], 18 March 1939.
10. *IND*, 18 March 1939.
11. Moynihan, *De Valera's Speeches*, p.466.
12. *IND*, 18 March 1950.
13. Ibid., 18 March 1953.
14. Ibid., 18 March 1955.
15. *Capuchin Annual*, (1962), p.218.
16. *NW*, 18 March 1930.
17. Rex Cathcart, *The Most Contrary Region: The BBC in Northern Ireland, 1924–84* (Belfast, 1984), p.32.
18. *Irish News*, [*IN*]18 March 1932; *Belfast News Letter* [*BNL*], 17 March 1932.
19. *NW*, 18 March 1930.
20. *BNL*, 18 March 1946, 18 March 1950, 17 March 1952.
21. Document is quoted in *BNL*, 1 January 1996.
22. *IND*, 18 March 1954; for complaints about schools not closing see *BNL*, 16 March 1961.
23. Ibid., 17 March 1961.
24. *Belfast Telegraph* [*BT*], 17 March 1956.
25. *BNL*, 17 March 1961.
26. *IND*, 19 March 1956; *BT*, 10 March 1964.
27. David Fitzpatrick, *The Two Irelands, 1921–1939* (Oxford, 1998), p.54.
28. Brian Girvin, *The Emergency: Neutral Ireland, 1939–45* (London, 2006), pp.276–7; Richard Doherty, *Irish Men and Women in the Second World War* (Dublin, 1999), pp.20–6.
29. Girvin, *The Emergency*, p.257.
30. Jane Leonard, *The Culture of Commemoration: The Culture of War Commemoration* (Dublin, 1996), p.20.
31. *IN*, 12 November 1924.
32. Keith Jeffery, 'The Great War in Modern Irish Memory' in T.G. Fraser and Keith Jeffery (eds), *Men, Women and War: Historical Studies*, xviii (Dublin, 1993), p.151.
33. Leonard, *Culture of Commemoration*, p.20.
34. Keith Jeffery, *Ireland and the Great War* (Cambridge, 2000), p.133.
35. Jeffery, *The Great War in Memory*, p.150.
36. Ibid., pp.150–1.
37. *BT*, 11 November 1930.
38. *BNL*, 11 November 1937; *Londonderry Sentinel* [*LS*], 13 November 1934.
39. *BNL*, 11 November 1946, 13 November 1950.
40. Ibid., 7 November 1955; 12 November 1956; *NW*, 7 November 1955, 12 November 1956; *IN*, 7 November 1955, 12 November 1956.
41. Jane Leonard, 'The Twinge of Memory: Armistice Day and Remembrance Sunday in Dublin since 1919' in Richard English and Graham Walker (eds), *Unionism in Modern Ireland* (Dublin, 1996), p.101.
42. Ibid.
43. Judith Hill, *Irish Public Sculpture* (Dublin, 1998), pp.189–90.
44. See Jeffery, *Ireland and the Great War*, pp.107–23.
45. *IN*, 12 November 1924.
46. Leonard, *Armistice Day in Dublin*, p.105.

47. Brian Hanley, 'Poppy Day in Dublin in the '20s and '30s' in *History Ireland*, vol.7, no.1. (Spring 1999), pp.5–6.
48. Leonard, *Armistice Day in Dublin*, p.106.
49. David Fitzpatrick, 'Commemorating in the Irish Free State: a Chronicle of Embarrassment' in Ian McBride (ed.), *History and Memory in Modern Ireland* (Cambridge, 2001), p.194.
50. Ibid.
51. Brian Girvin and Geoffrey Roberts, 'The Forgotten Volunteers of World War II' in *History Ireland*, vol.6, no.1 (Spring 1998), pp.46–51.
52. *BNL*, 13 November 1950.
53. Jane Leonard, 'Facing the "finger of scorn": Veterans' Memories of Ireland after the Great War' in Martin Evans and Kenneth Lunn (eds), *War and Memory in the Twentieth Century* (Oxford, 1997), pp.59–72.
54. See Rosemary Ryan *et al.*, 'Commemorating 1916' in *Retrospect* (1984), pp.59–62.
55. Fitzpatrick, *Commemorating in the Irish Free State*, p.196.
56. *IND*, 2 April 1934.
57. Fitzpatrick, *Commemorating in the Irish Free State*, p.197.
58. *IND*, 5 April 1935.
59. Hill, *Irish Sculpture*, pp.188–9.
60. *IND*, 14 April 1941.
61. Ibid., 19 April 1954.
62. Ryan, *Commemorating 1916*, p.61.
63. *Northern Ireland House of Commons Debates*, vol.ix, 15 May 1928.
64. Ibid., vol.xiv, 22 March 1932.
65. See Neil Jarman and Dominic Bryan, 'Green Parades in an Orange State' in Tom Fraser (ed.), *The Irish Parading Tradition: Following the Drum* (London, 2000), pp.95–110.
66. *IN*, 22 April 1935.
67. Ibid., 17 April 1933.
68. Ibid., 6 April 1942.
69. Ibid., 10 April 1950.
70. Jarman and Bryan, *Green Parades*, pp.103–5.
71. *Northern Ireland House of Commons Debates*, vol.II, 15 July 1922; vol.VI, 19 May 1925.
72. Brian Walker, *Past and Present: History, Identity and Politics in Ireland* (Belfast, 2000), pp.80 and 136.
73. *NW*, 13 July, 1922.
74. Ibid., 13 July 1923.
75. Ibid., 14 July 1925.
76. Ibid., 13 July 1926.
77. Ibid., 13 July 1927.
78. A.D. McDonnell, *The Life of Sir Denis Henry, Catholic Unionist* (Belfast, 2000).
79. Jonathan Bardon, *A History of Ulster* (Belfast, 1992), p.511.
80. See Chapter 1, p.17.
81. Keith Jeffery, 'Parades, Police and Government in Northern Ireland, 1922–69' in Fraser, *Irish Parading Tradition*, pp.84–6.
82. *NW*, 13 July 1933.
83. Ibid., 13 July 1932.

84. Ibid., 13 July 1939.
85. *Portadown News*, 13 July 1940, 12 July 1941, 18 July 1942, 17 July 1943.
86. *NW*, 13 July 1955, 14 July 1958.
87. Ibid., 12 July 1960.
88. Ibid., 13 July 1960 and 13 July 1961.
89. Ibid., 13 July 1960.
90. Ibid., 13 July 1923.
91. Ibid., 14 July 1925.
92. Ibid., 14 July 1930.
93. *LS*, 15 July 1930.
94. *NW*, 14 July 1931.
95. Ibid.; *IND*, 13 August 1931.
96. Aiken McClelland, 'Orangeism in Co. Monaghan' in *Clogher Record* (1978), pp.401–2.
97. Walker, *Past and Present*, pp.98 and 138.
98. Ibid.
99. *BNL*, 11 July 1936.
100. Jeffery, *Ireland and the Great War*, p.107. This comment about 11 November was made by General Sir William Hickie.
101. See Craig's comments in 1934 and 1938. Dennis Kennedy, *The Widening Gulf: Northern Attitudes to the Independent Irish State, 1919–49* (Belfast, 1988), pp.166 and 173–4.
102. Paul Arthur, *Political Realities, Government and Politics of Northern Ireland* (London, 1980), p.92.

4 Conflict and conciliation: identities and change, 1960–2011

1. D.H. Akenson, *Conor: A Biography of Conor Cruise O'Brien* (Montreal and Kingston, 1994), p.335.
2. S.M. Lipset and Stein Rokkan, 'Cleavage and Voter Alignments: an Introduction' in S.M. Lipset and Stein Rokkan (eds), *Party Systems and Voter Alignments. Cross-national Perspectives* (New York, 1967), pp.1–64; Peter Mair, 'The Freezing Hypothesis; an Evaluation' in Lauri Karvonen and Stein Kuhnle (eds), *Party Systems and Voter Alignments Revisited* (London, 2001), pp.27–44.
3. Richard Rose and Derek Urwin, 'Social Cohesion, Political Parties and Strains in Regimes' in Mattei Dogan and Richard Rose (eds), *European Politics; a Reader* (London, 1971), p.220; Gordon Smith, *Politics in Western Europe* (London, 4th edition 1983), pp.18–26.
4. Smith, *Politics*, p.19; Basil Chubb, *The Government and Politics of Ireland* (Stanford, 1970), pp.53–5.
5. Smith, *Politics*, p.15.
6. Hugh Thomas in *Listener*, 15 April 1976.
7. See Rogers Brubaker, *Nationalism Reframed: Nationhood and the National Question in the New Europe* (Cambridge, 1996).
8. R.F. Foster, 'Forward to Methusalah: The Progress of Nationalism' in Terence Dooley (ed.), *Ireland's Polemical Past: Views of Irish History in Honour of R.V. Comerford* (Dublin, 2010), p.147.

9. Thomas Hennessey, *Northern Ireland; the Origins of the Troubles* (Dublin, 2005), p.377.
10. John Cole, *As it Seemed to Me: Political Memoirs* (London, 1995), p.131.
11. Richard Rose, *Governing without Consensus: An Irish Perspective* (London, 1971), pp.208–17.
12. Jonathan Bardon, *A History of Ulster* (Belfast, 2005), p.622; Marc Mulholland, *Northern Ireland at the Crossroads: Ulster Unionism in the O'Neill Years* (Basingstoke, 2000), p.61.
13. Michael Kennedy, *Division and Consensus: The Politics of Cross-border Relations in Ireland, 1925–1969* (Dublin, 2000), pp.175–317.
14. Andrew Gailey, *Crying in the Wilderness: Jack Sayers, a Liberal Editor in Ulster, 1939–69* (Belfast, 1995), p.102.
15. Fergal Cochrane, 'Meddling at the Crossroads: The Decline and Fall of Terence O'Neill within the Unionist Community' in Richard English and Richard Walker (eds), *Unionism in Modern Ireland* (London, 1996), p.157.
16. Gailey, *Sayers*, p.84.
17. Ibid., p.99.
18. Ibid., p.117.
19. Kennedy, *Cross-border*, p.171.
20. Brendan Lynn, *Holding the Ground: The Nationalist Party in Northern Ireland, 1945–72* (Aldershot, 1997), p.182.
21. M.E. Daly and Margaret O'Callaghan, 'Introduction' in Daly and O'Callaghan (eds), *1916 in 1966: Commemorating the Easter Rising* (Dublin, 2007), p.4.
22. Enda Staunton, *The Nationalists of Northern Ireland, 1918–1973* (Dublin, 2001), p.248.
23. Denis Barritt and Charles Carter, *The Northern Ireland Problem: A Study in Group Relations* (Oxford, 1962).
24. Henry Patterson, *Ireland Since 1939: The Persistence of Conflict* (London, 2006), p.195.
25. Hennessey, *Northern Ireland Troubles*, p.25.
26. Pauline McClenaghan (ed.), *Spirit of '68: Beyond the Barricades* (Derry, 2009).
27. Desmond O'Malley, 'Redefining Ireland' in John Coakley (ed.), *Changing Shades of Orange and Green: Refining the Union and the Nation in Contemporary Ireland* (Dublin, 2002), p.64.
28. Patrick Keatinge and Brigid Laffan, 'Ireland; a Small Open Polity' in John Coakley (ed.), *Politics in the Republic of Ireland* (London, 3rd edition, 1999), p.325.
29. Chubb, *Politics of Ireland*, pp.53–4.
30. Katy Hayward, *Irish Nationalism and European Integration; The official redefinition of the Island of Ireland* (Manchester, 2009), p.108.
31. Kennedy, *Cross-border*, p.222.
32. Mary Daly, 'Less a Commemoration of the Actual Achievements and More a Commemoration of the Hopes of the Men of 1916' in Daly and O'Callaghan (eds), *Commemorating 1916*, pp.27–9.
33. John Bowman, *De Valera and the Ulster Question, 1917–1973* (Oxford, 1982), p.318; Clare O'Halloran, *Partition and the Limits of Irish Nationalism* (Dublin, 1987), p.187.
34. Report of the Committee on the Constitution (Dublin, 1967), p.5.
35. Kennedy, *Cross-border*, p.285.

36. Bowman, *De Valera*, p.285.
37. O'Halloran, *Partition*, p.188.
38. David Fitzpatrick, 'The Orange Order and the border' in *Irish Historical Studies*, vol.xxxiii, no.129 (May 2002), pp.63–4; Dominic Bryan, 'Rituals of Irish Protestantism and Orangeism: The Transnational Grand Lodge of Ireland' in *European Studies*, 19 (2003), pp.105–23.
39. Daly, 'Commemoration' in Daly and O'Callaghan (eds), *Commemorating 1916*, pp.46–50.
40. Kennedy, *Cross-border*, p.198.
41. Henry Patterson, *Ireland Since 1939: The Persistence of Conflict* (London, 2006), p.193.
42. Ibid., pp.153–9.
43. Hayward, *European Integration*, p.108.
44. Patterson, *Ireland Since 1939*, p.191.
45. See Mair, 'Freezing Hypothesis' in Karvonen and Kuhnle (eds), *Party Systems*.
46. See later accounts by witnesses, *Belfast Telegraph* (*BT*), 10 and 11 August 2009.
47. J.H. Whyte, 'How much Discrimination was there under the Unionist Regime, 1921–68?' in Tom Gallagher and James O'Donnell (eds), *Contemporary Irish Studies* (Manchester, 1983), p.4.
48. Letter from former RUC Sergeant Ian Duncan, *BT*, 8 October 2004.
49. Hennessey, *Northern Ireland Troubles*, p.138.
50. Ibid., p.162.
51. Gailey, *Sayers*, pp.136–7.
52. Lord Scarman, *Violence and Civil Disturbances in Northern Ireland in 1969: Report of Tribunal of Inquiry* (Belfast, 1973), p.11.
53. David Bleakley, *Faulkner: Conflict and Consent in Irish Politics* (London, 1974), p.94.
54. Richard English, *Armed Struggle: A History of the I.R.A.* (London, 2003), p.106.
55. Ibid., pp.123–30.
56. David McKittrick *et al.* (eds), *Lost Lives: The Stories of the Men, Women and Children who Died as a Result of the Northern Troubles* (London, 2007 edition), p.1552.
57. Bleakley, *Faulkner*, p.82.
58. *Irish Times* [*IT*], 22 August 1970.
59. Ibid., 22 April 1970.
60. Ibid., 2 October 1971.
61. Dermot Keogh, *Jack Lynch: A Biography* (Dublin, 2008), pp.171–2.
62. *IT*, 21 August 1969.
63. Keogh, *Lynch*, p.197.
64. Scarman, *Tribunal*, vol.2, p.37.
65. John Walsh, *Patrick Hillery: The Official Biography* (Dublin, 2008), p.174.
66. Ibid., pp.175–6.
67. Paul Bew, *Ireland: the Politics of Enmity 1789–2006* (Oxford, 2007), pp.499–502.
68. Keogh, *Lynch*, p.302.

69. Richard Deutsch and V. Magowen, *Northern Ireland:Chronology of Events*, vol.i, (Belfast, 1973), p.95.
70. Ibid., p.366.
71. Basil Chubb, *The Constitution and Constitutional Change in Ireland* (Dublin, 1978), p.97.
72. *IT*, 22 February 1974.
73. *Belfast News Letter [BNL]*, 14 March 1974.
74. Walsh, *Hillery*, p.172.
75. *IT*, 2 February 1972.
76. Cole, *Political Memoirs*, p.135.
77. Bleakley, *Faulkner*, p.131.
78. *IT*, 1 January 1974.
79. Thomas Hennessey, *A History of Northern Ireland, 1920–1996* (Dublin, 1997), p.228.
80. Richard Deutsch and V. Magowen (eds), *Northern Ireland; Chronology of Events*, vol.iii (Belfast, 1975), p.59.
81. Paddy Devlin, *Straight Left: An Autobiography* (Belfast, 1993), p.231.
82. English, *Armed Struggle*, p.166.
83. Deutsch and Magowen, *Northern Chronology*, vol.iii, p.1.
84. Paul Bew and Gordon Gillespie, *Northern Ireland: A Chronology of the Troubles, 1968–1999* (Dublin, 1999), p.69.
85. Deutsch and Magowen, *Chronology*, p.81.
86. Alvin Jackson, *Home Rule: An Irish History, 1800–2000* (London, 2003), p.2003.
87. Akenson, *O'Brien*, p.407; Devlin, *Autobiography*, p.205.
88. Akenson, *O'Brien*, p.407; Garret FitzGerald, *All in a Life: An Autobiography* (Dublin, 1993), p.198. Gill and Macmillan).
89. *IT*, 22 February 1974; Bew, *Politics of Enmity*, p.513.
90. Brian Faulkner, *Memoirs of a Statesman* (London, 1978), pp.247–8.
91. Hennessey, *Northern Ireland History*, pp.231–3.
92. *Listener*, 16 November 1978.
93. J.D.Cash, *Identity, Ideology and Conflict: The Structuration of Politics in Northern Ireland* (Cambridge, 1996), p.199.
94. *BNL*, 9 September 1975.
95. Cash, *Identity*, p.202.
96. *IT*, 6 November 1978.
97. Chris Ryder, *Fighting Fitt* (Belfast, 2006), p.327; Devlin, *Autobiography*, p.277. Brehon Press.
98. Keogh, *Lynch*, pp.422–4; C. O'Donnell, *Fianna Fail, Irish Republicanism and the Northern Ireland Troubles, 1968–2005* (Dublin, 2007), pp.44–5.
99. T.R. Dwyer, *Charlie: The Political Biography of Charles J. Haughey* (Dublin, 1987), pp.133 and 136–7.
100. FitzGerald, *Autobiography*, p.378.
101. Dermot Keogh, 'Ireland, 1972–84' in J.R. Hill (ed.), *A New History of Ireland. Ireland, 1921–84*, vol.vii (Oxford, 2003), p.391.
102. New Ireland Forum Report, 2 May 1984 (Dublin), pp.25–30.
103. FitzGerald, *Autobiography*, p.491.
104. Ibid., p.482.
105. Hennesey, *Northern Ireland History*, p.273.

106. Recorded in an article by Stephen Collins, *IT*, 15 November 2010.
107. Gordon Gillespie, *Historical Dictionary of the Northern Ireland Conflict* (Lanham, Maryland, 2008), p.24.
108. *IT*, 21 November 1985.
109. Debates of Irish Senate, vol.110, 27 November 1985, pp.225–37.
110. *IT*, 19 November 1985.
111. *Dáil Éireann Debates*, vol.361, 19 November 1985, 2580–600.
112. McKittrick, *Lost Lives*, pp.1551–62.
113. Brendan O'Duffy and Brendan O'Leary 'Violence in Northern Ireland, 1969–June 1989' in John McGarry and Brendan O'Leary (eds), *The Future of Northern Ireland* (Oxford, 1990), p.324.
114. Ibid., p.328.
115. John Hume, *A New Ireland: Politics, Peace and Reconciliation* (Dublin, 1994), p.72; McKittrick, *Lost Lives*, p.1558.
116. Adrian Guelke, 'Political violence and the paramilitaries' in Rick Wilford and Paul Mitchell (eds), *Politics in Northern Ireland* (Oxford, 1999), p.47.
117. Marc Mulholland, *Northern Ireland: A Very Short Introduction* (Oxford, 2002), p.90.
118. English, *Armed Struggle*, p.384.
119. Bew, *Politics of Enmity*, p.237.
120. Katy Hayward, 'National Territory in European Space: Reconfiguring the Island of Ireland' in *European Journal of Political Research* 45(2006), pp.907–14.
121. Bew, *Politics of Enmity*, p.534.
122. Neil Buttimer and Máire Ní Annracháin, 'Irish Language and Literature, 1921–84' in J.R. Hill (ed.), *A New History of Ireland, 1921–84*, vol.vii. (Oxford, 2003), p.569.
123. J.J. Sexton and Richard O'Leary, 'Factors Affecting Population Decline in Minority Religious Communities in the Republic of Ireland' in *Building Trust in Ireland: Studies Commissioned by the Forum for Peace and Reconciliation* (Belfast, 1996), p.292.
124. Article by Peter Murtagh, *IT*, 16 June 2010.
125. B.M. Walker, *Parliamentary Election Results in Ireland, 1918–92* (Dublin, 1992), pp.228–76.
126. FitzGerald, *Autobiography*, pp.184–5.
127. Richard O'Leary, 'Change in the Rate and Pattern of Religious Intermarriage in the Republic of Ireland' in *The Economic and Social Review*, vol.30, no.2, April, 1999, p.131.
128. Daithi O Corrain, *Rendering to God and Caesar: The Irish Churches and the two States in Ireland, 1949–73* (Manchester, 2006), p.191.
129. *IT*, 6 September 1974.
130. See H.K. Crawford, *Outside the Glow: Protestants and Irishness in Independent Ireland* (Dublin, 2010), pp.106–36.
131. Census of Ireland, 2002, vol.12, p.9.
132. John Dunlop, *A Precarious Belonging: Presbyterians and the Conflict in Ireland* (Belfast, 1995), p.34.
133. Cathal McCall, *Identity in Northern Ireland: Communities, Politics and Change* (London, 1999).
134. Quoted by Louis McRedmond, *Guardian*, 1 January 2010.

135. Jonathan Bardon, *History of Ulster* (Belfast, 1992), pp.802–3.
136. Karen Trew, 'The Northern Irish Identity' in A. Kershen (ed.), *A Question of Identity* (Aldershot, 1998), p.66. See chapter one, p.110.
137. Ibid., p.73.
138. Marianne Elliott (ed.), *The Long Road to Peace in Northern Ireland* (Liverpool, 2002), pp.207–11.
139. Ibid., pp.212–22.
140. McKittrick, *Lost Lives*, p.1552.
141. Bew, *Politics of Enmity*, p.537.
142. Sean Byrne *et al.*, 'The International Fund for Ireland: Economic Assistance and the Northern Ireland Peace Process' in *Peace and Conflict Studies*, 14 (2), pp.49–73.
143. Cathal McCall, 'The Production of Space and Realignment of Identity' in *Regional and Federal Studies*, vol.11, no.2, Summer 2001, pp.1–24.
144. Maria Power, *From Ecumenism to Community Relations: Inter-church Relationships in Northern Ireland, 1980–2005* (Dublin, 2007).
145. Norman Richardson and Tony Gallagher (eds), *Education for Diversity and Mutual Understanding: The Experience of Northern Ireland* (Oxford, 2010).
146. *IT*, 4 December 1990.
147. Ibid., 12 November 1997.
148. Thomas Bartlett, *Ireland: A History* (Cambridge, 2010), pp.533–7.
149. *Building Trust in Ireland* (Belfast, 1996), p.v.
150. *IT*, 3 February 1995.
151. Ibid., 7 May 1997.
152. *BT*, 13 December 1995.
153. *Irish Census, 2002*, vol.12, p.9.
154. *IT*, 8 August 2005.
155. *Church of Ireland Gazette*, 28 May 2010. See Crawford, *Outside the Glow*.
156. G.T. Dempsey, 'The American Role in the Northern Ireland Peace Process' in *Irish Political Studies*, 14, 1999, pp.104–17.
157. Michael Kerr, *Imposing Power-sharing: Conflict and Co-Existence in Northern Ireland and Lebanon* (Dublin, 2006); Robert Taylor (ed.), *Consociational Theory: McGarry and O'Leary and the Northern Ireland Conflict* (London; 2009).
158. Christopher Farrington, *Ulster Unionism and the Peace Process in Northern Ireland* (Basingstoke, 2006), p.48.
159. Bew, *Politics of Enmity*, p.539.
160. *IT*, 23 October 1995.
161. Dean Godson, *Himself Alone: David Trimble and the Ordeal of Unionism* (London, 2004), p.296.
162. Ibid., p.381.
163. *IT*, 28 November 1988.
164. Gerald Murray, *John Hume and the SDLP: Impact and Survival in Northern Ireland* (Dublin, 1998), p.154.
165. Peter McLaughlin, *John Hume and the Revision of Irish Nationalism* (Manchester, 2010), pp.184–5, 228–9.
166. *IT*, 11 December 1998.
167. Ibid., 19 April 1996.
168. Kate Fearon and Rachel Rebouche 'What happened to the Women? Promises, reality and the Northern Ireland Women's Coalition' in Michael

Cox *et al.*, *A Farewell to Arms? Beyond the Good Friday Agreement* (Manchester, second edition, 2006), pp.280–2.
169. Albert Reynolds, *My Autobiography* (London, 2009), p.207.
170. Ibid., p.209.
171. Godson, *Trimble*, p.303.
172. Bertie Ahern, *The Autobiography* (London, 2009), pp.210–30.
173. *IT*, 11 April 1998.
174. *Hansard*, vol.188, 26 March 1991, 765.
175. *IT*, 10 November 1990.
176. *IT*, 17 December 1992.
177. Godson, *Trimble*, pp.252–9.
178. Ibid., p.266.
179. *IT*, 15 May 1998.
180. Rogelio Alonso, *The IRA and Armed Struggle* (London, 2003, 2007 edition), p.189.
181. Quote from Kevin Bean in Henry Patterson, *The Politics of Illusion; A Political History of the I.R.A.* (London, 1997), p.260.
182. Jonathan Tonge, *Northern Ireland* (Cambridge, 2006), p.121.
183. Roy Garland, *Gusty Spence* (Belfast, 2001), p.279.
184. Gillespie, *Historical Dictionary*, p.590.
185. David McKittrick, *The Nervous Peace* (Belfast, 1996), pp.39–40.
186. David Ervine, 'Redefining Loyalism' in Coakley (ed.), *Orange and Green*, pp.59–60.
187. Christopher Farrington, 'Loyalists and Unionists: Explaining the Internal Dynamics of an Ethnic Group' in Aaron Edwards and Stephen Bloomer, *Transforming the Peace Process in Northern Ireland: From Terrorism to Democratic Politics* (Dublin, 2008), p.36.
188. From Belfast Agreement, reprinted in Elliott, *Road to Peace*, pp.223–39.
189. Irish Constitution, 6.
190. McKittrick, *Lost Lives*, p.1552.
191. *IT*, 9 May 2007.
192. Ibid., 12 May 2007.
193. Ibid., 11 March 2009.
194. Ibid., 28 May 2009.
195. *IND*, 19 March 1962.
196. www.president.ie; *IT*, 4 June 2011.
197. Ed Moloney and Andy Pollak, *Paisley* (Dublin, 1986), pp.97–8.
198. *BT*, 23 June 2011.
199. Quoted by Conor O'Clery in *Irish Times*, 6 April 1998.
200. Ibid., 12 April 2008.
201. *IND*, 16 May 2007.
202. *IT*, 11 April 2008.
203. Ibid., 10 April 2010.
204. Ibid., 21 April 2010.
205. Ibid., 27 November 2008.
206. Ibid., 15 November 2004.
207. *BNL*, 5 April 2007.
208. *Agenda NI*, issue 16, April 2008.
209. *IT*, 29 May 2009.

210. *IT*, 31 October 2001.
211. *BT*, 8 November 2010.
212. *IT*, 26 May 2003.
213. *BT*, 29 April 2010.
214. *IT*, 13 June; www.britishirish.org. See 42nd plenary address Enda Kenny.
215. *BT*, 14 April 2011.
216. Ibid., 10 June 2011.

5   Remembering and reclaiming: commemorations and identity, 1960–2011

1. *Irish Times [IT]*, 3 February 1995; *The Times*, 26 December 1995.
2. Edna Longley, *The Living Stream: Literature and Revisionism in Ireland* (Newcastle upon Tyne, 1994), p.69.
3. G.B. Graff-McRae, 'Forget Politics! Theorising the Political Dynamics of Commemoration and Conflict' in M.E. Daly and Margaret O'Callaghan (eds), *1916 in 1966: Commemorating the Easter Rising* (Dublin, 2007), p.235.
4. Longley, *Living Stream*, p.69.
5. Kenneth Bloomfield, *Stormont in Crisis: A Memoir* (Belfast, 1994), p.92.
6. Jane Leonard, 'The Twinge of Memory: Armistice Day and Remembrance Sunday in Dublin since 1919' in Richard English and Graham Walker (eds), *Unionism in Modern Ireland* (Dublin, 1996), pp.102–3.
7. *Irish Independent, [IND]*, 13 November 1967.
8. *Belfast News Letter [BNL]*, 13 November 1961.
9. *BNL*, 15 November 1965 and 13 November 1967.
10. *IT*, 7–9 November 1978.
11. *Belfast Telegraph [BT]*, 15 November 1982.
12. *BNL*, 12 November 1984.
13. Leonard, 'Twinge of Memory', pp.107–10.
14. *IT*, 11 November 1998.
15. Leonard, 'Twinge of Memory', p.103.
16. Kevin Myers, *IT*, 11 November 1998.
17. John Walsh, *Patrick Hillery: The Official Biography* (Dublin, 2008), pp.466–71.
18. Leonard, 'Twinge of Memory', pp.107–9.
19. Jane Leonard, 'Facing the "finger of scorn"; Veterans memories of Ireland in the Twentieth Century' in Martin Evans and Kenneth Lunn (eds), *War and Memory in the Twentieth Century* (Oxford, 1997), p.9.
20. *BNL*, 13 November 1989, 14 November 1994.
21. Leonard, 'Twinge of Memory', p.111.
22. *IND*, 15 November 1993.
23. Leonard, 'Twinge of Memory', p.111.
24. *IT*, 29 April 1995.
25. *BNL*, 14 November 1994.
26. Ibid., 9 November 1992.
27. Ibid.,13 November 1995.
28. *BT*, 10 November 1997; *Irish News[IN]*, 10 November 1997.
29. Report of television programme on Magennis, *Sunday Times*, 3 October 2004.

30. *IT*, 12 November 1998.
31. *BNL*, 12 November 1998.
32. *IN*, 14 February 2002.
33. *IT*, 21 May 2008.
34. Ibid., 21 February 2008.
35. *IT*, 1 July 2002.
36. *IT*, 1 March 2004 and 1 July 2008.
37. *BT*, 1 May 2003.
38. *BNL*, 7 November 2005; *IT*, 7 November 2005.
39. *BT*, 11 September 2007.
40. Ibid., 11 and 15 November 2010; *IN*, 12 November 2010.
41. *IN*, 17 March 1960.
42. *IND*, 19 March 1962.
43. Ibid., 17 March 1966.
44. Ibid., 18 March 1964 and 16 March 1965.
45. *BNL*, 18 March 1960.
46. *IN*, 17 March 1960.
47. *IND*, 17 and 18 March 1964.
48. *BNL*, 17 March 1961.
49. *BT*, 17 March 1967.
50. *IND*, 18 March 1971, 18 March 1983, 18 March 1987.
51. *IT*, 17 March 1972.
52. Ibid., 19 January 1996.
53. *IND*, 18 March 1985; *BT*, 18 March 1990.
54. *BNL*, 17 March 2008.
55. Diarmuid Ferriter, 'Commemorating the Rising, 1922–65: A Figurative Scramble for the "Bones of the Patriot Dead"' in Daly and O'Callaghan, *Commemorating 1916*, p.213.
56. *Irish Press* [*IP*] 18 April 1960.
57. *IN*, 18 April 1960.
58. M.E. Daly and Margaret O'Callaghan, 'Introduction-Irish Modernity and the "Patriot Dead of 1916" in Daly and O'Callaghan, *Commemorating 1916*, p.8.
59. *IP*, 11 April 1966.
60. Ibid.
61. *IT*, 3 April 1972.
62. *IN*, 1 April 1991.
63. Ibid., 11 April 1977.
64. Ibid., 27 March 1978.
65. *IN*, 31 March 1997.
66. Ibid., 6 May 2004.
67. Ibid., 17 April 2006.
68. Ibid.
69. *IND*, 15 April 2006.
70. *IN*, 17 April 2006.
71. *IT*, 10 April 2009.
72. BNL, 13 July 1960.
73. Ibid., 13 July 1965.
74. Ibid., 13 July 1960; *Londonderry Sentinel* [*LS*], 20 July 1960.

75. *BNL*, 13 July 1960.
76. Ibid.
77. Ibid., 13 July 1965.
78. *IT*, 13 July 1966.
79. Ibid., 13 July 1966.
80. *BT*, 13 July 1986.
81. *BNL*, 13 July 1990.
82. *LS*, 16 July 1970: *IT*, 7 July 1970.
83. *Dáil Éireann Debates*, vol. 248, 9 July 1970, 889.
84. *LS*, 13 July 1975 and 19 July 1978.
85. *IT*, 12 July 1993 and 13 July 1987.
86. *BNL*, 14 July 2003.
87. *IT*, 14 July 2008.
88. Ibid., 27 November 2008.
89. *Sunday Times*, 11 July 2010.
90. *IT*, 13 July 2006 and 14 July 2008.
91. www.qub.dup
92. *IT*, 6 June 2006.
93. www.Catholicnews.com
94. Ian McBride 'Memory and National Identity in Modern Ireland' in Ian McBride (ed.), *History and Memory in Modern Ireland* (Cambridge, 2001), p.2.

6   The past and the present: history, identity and the peace process

1. Report of the Independent Review of Parades and Marches, 1997 (Belfast, 1997), p.29.
2. Dermot Bolger, 'Shift your shadow or I'll burst you' in *Sunday Independent*, 16 August 1992.
3. For example, *The Times*, 5 September 1998.
4. *Belfast News Letter* [*BNL*], 10 February 1995.
5. Conor O'Clery, *Ireland in Quotes. A History of the Twentieth Century* (Dublin, 1999), p.130.
6. *Irish Times* [*IT*], 17 February 1996.
7. *Belfast Telegraph* [*BT*], 13 October 2009.
8. Nicholas Mansergh, *Britain and Ireland* (London, 1942), p.95.
9. A.D. Smith, *National Identity* (Nevada, published 1991, reprinted 1993), p.14.
10. Eric Hobsbawm, 'Introduction: Inventing Traditions' in Eric Hobsbawm and T. Ranger (eds), *The Invention of Tradition* (Cambridge, published 1983, reprinted 1995), pp.13–14; John Coakley, 'Mobilising the Past: Nationalist Images of History' in *Nationalism and Ethnic Politics*, vol.10, no.4 (2004), pp.531–60; B.M. Walker, '1641, 1689, 1690 and all that: The Unionist Sense of History' in *Irish Review*, no.12 (Summer, 1992), pp.56–64.
11. John McGarry and Brendan O'Leary, *The Northern Ireland Conflict: Consociational Engagements* (Oxford, 2004), p.186.
12. Walker Connor, 'A Few Cautionary Notes on the History and Future of Ethnonational Conflicts' in Andreas Wimmer *et al.* (eds), *Facing Ethnic Conflicts: Towards a New Realism* (Lanham, MD, 2004), p.30.

13. See Ronald McNeill, *Ulster's Stand for Union* (London, 1922), p.9; Lord Robert Armstrong, 'Ethnicity, the English and Northern Ireland' in Dermot Keogh and M.H. Haltzel (eds), *Northern Ireland and the Politics of Reconciliation* (Cambridge, 1993), p.203.
14. A.T.Q. Stewart, *The Narrow Ground: Aspects of Ulster, 1609–1969* (London, 1977), p.16.
15. *Hansard*, lxxxvii, (1985–6), 779, 783, 904 and 907.
16. Martin Mansergh (ed.), *The Spirit of the Nation: The Speeches and Statements of Charles J. Haughey* (Cork, 1986), p.738.
17. Richard Davis, *Mirror Hate: The Convergant Ideology of Northern Ireland Paramilitaries, 1966–92* (Aldershot, 1994), p.3.
18. Shane O'Doherty, *The Volunteer: A Former IRA Man's True Story* (London, 1993), pp.27–30.
19. Geoffrey Beattie, *Protestant Boy* (London, 2004), p.126.
20. *IT*, 25 February 1998.
21. Ibid., 3 March 1994.
22. Ibid., 13 April 1994.
23. *Sunday Tribune Magazine*, 31 March 1996.
24. Report of the International Body on Decommissioning, 22 January 1996 (Belfast and Dublin, 1996), p.5.
25. Arthur Aughey, 'Learning from the Leopard' in Rick Wilford (ed.), *Aspects of the Belfast Agreement* (Oxford, 2000), pp.184–201.
26. George Mitchell, 'Towards Peace in Northern Ireland' in Marianne Elliott (ed.), *The Long Road to Peace in Northern Ireland; Peace Lectures from the Institute of Irish Studies at Liverpool University* (Liverpool, 2002), p.88.
27. J. Bowyer Bell, *The Irish Troubles: A Generation of Violence, 1967–92* (Dublin, 1993), p.829.
28. Andy Pollak (ed.), *A Citizen's Inquiry: The Opsahl Report on Northern Ireland* (Dublin, 1993), p.122.
29. M.E. Smith, *Reckoning with the Past* (Maryland, 2005), pp.143–79.
30. Jonathan Bardon, *A History of Ulster* (Belfast, 1992).
31. Máiréad Nic Craith, *Plural Identities – Singular Narratives: The Case of Northern Ireland* (Oxford, 2002), p.30.
32. R.D. Edwards, *Patrick Pearse: The Triumph of Failure* (London, 1977): C.C. O'Brien *States of Ireland* (London, 1972).
33. Ian McBride (ed.), *History and Memory in Modern Ireland* (Cambridge, 2001), p.38; Ciaran Brady (ed.), *Interpreting Irish History: The Debate on Historical Revisionism* (Dublin, 1994), pp.13–14; D.George Boyce and Alan O'Day (eds), *The Making of Irish History: Revisionism and the Revisionist Controversy* (London, 1996), pp.1–14.
34. R.F. Foster, *Modern Ireland* (London, 1988); Marianne Elliott, *Wolfe Tone: Prophet of Irish Independence* (London, 1989); Tim Pat Coogan, *De Valera: Long Fellow, Long Shadow* (London 1993); C.C. O'Brien, *Ancestral Voices: Religion and Nationalism in Ireland* (Dublin, 1994).
35. Jane Leonard, *The Culture of Commemoration: The Culture of War Commemoration* (Dublin, 1996), p.21.
36. *IT*, 12 November 1998.
37. D. George Boyce, '"No Lack of Ghosts"; Memory, Commemoration and the State in Ireland' in Ian McBride (ed.), *History and Memory in Ireland* (Cambridge, 2001), p.270.

38. Mary Daly, 'History a la Carte? Historical Commemoration and Modern Ireland' in Eberhard Bort (ed.), *Commemorating Ireland: History, Politics, Culture* (Dublin, 2004), pp.34–55; Boyce and O'Day, *Making of Irish History*, p.4.
39. Peter Collins, *Who Fears to Speak of '98? Commemoration and the Continuing Impact of the United Irishmen* (Belfast, 2004), pp.168–9.
40. *BT*, 2 July 1992.
41. *IT*, 25 February 1995.
42. Ibid., 17 December 1992.
43. *IND*, 14 November 1992.
44. Ibid., 19 April 1993.
45. *IT*, 8 November 1993.
46. *Sunday Times*, 7 March 1993.
47. *BT*, 28 October 1993.
48. *IT*, 23 March and 19 April 1993.
49. Ibid., 8 April 1993.
50. Ibid., 13 April, 1994.
51. Marianne Elliott (ed.), *The Long Road to Peace in Northern Ireland* (Liverpool, 2002), pp.207–11.
52. *Frameworks for the Future* (Belfast, 1995), pp.iii and 23.
53. *IT*, 2 October 1993.
54. *Irish News [IN]*, 6 January 1994.
55. *IT* 26 May 1994.
56. Ibid., 4 March 1996.
57. *BT*, 19 September 1996: *IND*, 30 July 1996.
58. *IT*, 11 June 1996.
59. *Sunday Independent*, 15 September 1996.
60. *BT*, 7 August 1996.
61. Jonathan Powell, *Great Hatred, Little Room: Making Peace in Northern Ireland* (London, 2008), p.94.
62. *Sunday Times*, 5 March 1995; *BT*, 9 June 1995.
63. *IT*, 1 August 1996.
64. Ibid., 25 December 1995.
65. *IN*, 4 February 1998.
66. *Sunday Times*, 21 March 1999.
67. Report of the International Body on Decommissioning, 22 January 1996 (Dublin and Belfast), pp.5–6.
68. Report of the Independent Review of Parades and Marches, January, 1997 (Belfast), p.5.
69. B.M. Walker, *Past and Present: History, Identity and Politics in Ireland* (Belfast, 2000), p.83.
70. *Sunday Times*, 9 July, 2000.
71. *IT*, 27 February 1995: 25 March 1996.
72. *BNL*, 10 February 1995.
73. Ibid., 14 June 1996.
74. The Belfast Agreement, 1998 (Belfast, 1998).
75. Tom Hennessey, *The Northern Ireland Peace Process. Ending the Troubles* (Dublin, 2000), pp.217–20.
76. *Independent*, 8 April 1998.
77. *Times*, 5 September 1998.

78. Ibid., 13 December 2000 and *BT*, 13 December 2000.
79. Ibid., 26 November 1998.
80. From copy of speech in possession of author who attended the lecture.
81. *IN*, 6 August 2005.
82. *IT*, 11 December 1998.
83. *BNL*, 21 November 1998: David Trimble, *To Raise up a New Northern Ireland: Articles and Speeches* (Belfast, 2001), pp.47–8.
84. *IT*, 2 March 2002.
85. *BNL*, 5 November 2007.
86. *IT*, 9 May 2003.
87. *IT*, 23 February 2007.
88. Bertie Ahern, *Bertie Ahern: The Autobiography* (London, 2009), p.293.
89. Sir Kenneth Bloomfield, 'The Report of the Northern Ireland Victims Commission' in Elliott, *Peace in Northern Ireland*, pp.235–9.
90. Arthur Aughey, *The Politics of Northern Ireland* (London, 2004), p.97.
91. Norman Porter, *The Elusive Quest: Reconciliation in Northern Ireland* (Belfast, 2003), p.145.
92. Dominic Bryan and Gillian McIntosh, 'Sites of Creation and Contest in Northern Ireland', *SAIS Review of International Affairs*, vol.25, no.2, Summer/Fall (2005), pp.127–37.
93. *BT*, 16 July 2001.
94. *Daily Telegraph*, 12 July 2001.
95. Richard English, *Armed Struggle: A History of the IRA* (London, 2003), p.316.
96. *IT*, 25 November 2002.
97. Powell, *Peace in Northern Ireland*, pp.312–3.
98. *IT*, 5 April 2007.
99. Ibid., 11 May 2007.
100. *IN*, 11 September 2007.
101. *BT*, 3 April 2008.
102. Ahern, *Autobiography*, p.296.
103. *IT*, 1 May 2008.
104. Ibid., pp.314–15.
105. *Times*, 17 May 2011.
106. *IT*, 19 May 2011.
107. Ibid., 18 May 2011.
108. *IND*, 19 May 2011.
109. *IT*, 19 May 2011.
110. Ibid., 19 May 2011.
111. Ibid., 14 June 2011.
112. *Sunday Independent*, 19 June 2011.
113. See Fintan O'Toole on Kosovo, *Irish Times*, 30 April 1999; Noel Malcolm, *Bosnia: A Short History* (London, 1994, reprinted 1996), pp.xix–xxiv.
114. Pal Kolsto (ed.), *Myths and Boundaries in South-Eastern Europe* (London, 2005), p.1.
115. George Mitchell, *Making Peace* (London, 1999), p.186.
116. Ahern, *Autobiography*, pp.292–3.
117. *IT*, 27 November 1998.
118. *BNL*, 7 November 2005.
119. *IT*, 5 November 2007.

Conclusion

1. See reference to comments by Richard Rose in Maurice Hayes, 'Neither Orange March nor Irish Gig: Finding Compromise in Northern Ireland' in Marianne Elliott (ed.), *The Long Road to Peace in Northern Ireland* (Liverpool, 2002), p.97.
2. Reprinted in Elliott, *Peace in Northern Ireland*, p.266.
3. Constitution of Ireland (Dublin, 2005), pp.4–6.

Select Bibliography

Newspapers

An Phoblacht, Belfast News Letter, Belfast Telegraph, Church of Ireland Gazette, Daily Telegraph, Guardian, Independent, Irish Independent, Irish News, Irish Press, Irish Times, Listener, Londonderry Sentinel, Northern Whig, Portadown News, Sunday Independent, Sunday Times, Sunday Tribune, Ulster Herald.

Books, chapters and articles

Acheson, Alan, *A History of the Church of Ireland 1669–1997* (Dublin, 1997).

Akenson, D.H., *Education and Enmity: The Control of Schooling in Northern Ireland, 1920–50* (Newton Abbot, 1973).

Akenson, D.H., *A Mirror to Kathleen's Face: Education in Independent Ireland, 1922–1960* (Montreal and Kingston, 1975).

Akenson, D.H., *Conor: A Biography of Conor Cruise O'Brien* (Montreal and Kingston, 1994).

Aughey, Arthur, *The Politics of Northern Ireland* (London, 2004).

Bardon, Jonathan, *A History of Ulster* (Belfast, 1992, updated edition, 2005).

Barritt, D.P. and Carter, C.F., *The Northern Ireland Problem: A Study in Group Relations* (Oxford, 1982).

Bew, Paul, Darwin, Kenneth and Gillespie, Gordon, *Passion and Prejudice: Nationalist–Unionist Conflict in Ulster in the 1930s and the Founding of the Irish Association* (Belfast, 1993).

Bew, Paul and Gillespie, Gordon, *Northern Ireland: A Chronology of the Troubles, 1968–1999* (Dublin, 1999).

Bew, Paul, *Ireland: The Politics of Enmity, 1789–2006* (Oxford, 2007).

Bowen, Kurt, *Protestants in a Catholic State: Ireland's Privileged Minority* (Dublin, 1983).

Bowman, John, *De Valera and the Ulster Question, 1917–1973* (Oxford, 1982).

Boyce, D.G., *Nationalism in Ireland* (London, 1980, second edition, 1991).

Boyce, D.G., and O'Day, Alan (eds), *The Making of Irish History: Revisionism and the Revisionist Controversy* (London, 1996).

Brady, Ciaran (ed.), *Interpreting Irish History: The Debate on Historical Revisionism.* (Dublin, 1994).

Brown, Terence, *Ireland: A Social and Cultural History, 1922–2002* (London, 2004).

Brubaker, Rogers, *Nationalism Reframed: Nationhood and the National Question in the New Europe* (Cambridge, 1996).

Buckland, Patrick, *The Factory of Grievances: Devolved Government in Northern Ireland 1921–39* (Dublin, 1979).

Cameron, Lord, *Disturbances in Northern Ireland* (Belfast, 1969).

Campbell, T.J., *Fifty years of Ulster, 1890–1940* (Belfast, 1941).

Chubb, Basil, *The Government and Politics of Ireland* (Stanford, first edition, 1970), (London: second revised edition, 1982).

Coakley, John, 'Religion, Identity and Political Change in Modern Ireland' in *Irish Political Studies*, vol.17, no.1 (2002), pp.4–28.

Coakley, John (ed.), *Changing Shades of Orange and Green: Redefining the Union and the Nation in Contemporary Ireland* (Dublin, 2006).

Comerford, Vincent, *Inventing the Nation: Ireland* (London, 2003).

Cox, Michael *et al.*, *A Farewell to Arms? Beyond the Good Friday Agreement* (Manchester, second edition, 2006).

Crawford, H.K., *Outside the Glow: Protestants and Irishness in Independent Ireland* (Dublin, 2010).

Curtis, Maurice *The Splendid Cause: The Catholic Action Movement in Ireland in the Twentieth Century* (Dublin, 2009).

Dáil Éireann and Senate Debates.

Daly, M.E. and O'Callaghan, Margaret (eds), *1916 in 1966: Commemorating the Easter Rising* (Dublin, 2007).

Deutsch, Richard and Magowen, V., *Northern Ireland: Chronology of Events*, vols 1–3 (Belfast, 1973–75).

Dictionary of Irish Biography (Cambridge, 2010).

Edwards, Aaron and Bloomer, Stephen (eds), *Transforming the Peace Process in Northern Ireland: From Terrorism to Democratic Politics* (Dublin, 2008).

Edwards, R.D., *Patrick Pearse: The Triumph of Failure* (London, 1977).

Elliott, Marianne, *The Catholics of Ulster: A History* (London, 2000).

Elliott, Marianne, *When God took Sides: Religion and Identity in Ireland – Unfinished History* (Oxford, 2009).

Elliott, Marianne (ed.), *The Long Road to Peace in Northern Ireland* (Liverpool, 2002 and 2007).

English, Richard and Walker, Graham (eds), *Unionism in Modern Ireland* (Dublin, 1996).

English, Richard, *Armed Struggle: A History of the I.R.A.* (London, 2003).

Fanning, Tim, *The Fethard-on-Sea Boycott* (Cork, 2010).

Farrington, Christopher, *Ulster Unionism and the Peace Process in Northern Ireland* (Basingstoke, 2006).

Faulkner, Brian, *Memoirs of a Statesman* (London, 1978).

Ferriter, Diarmaid, *The Transformation of Ireland, 1900–2000* (London, 2005).

FitzGerald, Garret, *All in a Life: An Autobiography* (Dublin, 1993).

Fitzpatrick, David, *The Two Irelands, 1912–1939* (Oxford: 1998).

Foster, R.F., *Modern Ireland, 1600–1972* (London, 1988).

Foster, R.F., *Luck and the Irish: A Brief History of Change, c. 1970–2000* (London, 2007).

Gailey, Andrew, *Crying in the Wilderness. Jack Sayers: A Liberal Editor in Ulster, 1939–69* (Belfast, 1995).

Garvin, Tom, *1922: The Birth of Irish Democracy* (Dublin, 1996 new edition, 2005).

Garvin, Tom, *Preventing the Future: Why was Ireland so poor for so long?* (Dublin, 2004).

Gillespie, Gordon, *Historical Dictionary of the Northern Ireland Conflict* (Lanham, Maryland, 2008).

Girvin, Brian, *From Union to Union: Nationalism, Democracy and Religion in Ireland – Act of Union to EU* (Dublin, 2002).
Godson, Dean, *Himself Alone: David Trimble and the Ordeal of Unionism* (London, 2004).
Harkness, David, *Northern Ireland since 1920* (Dublin, 1983).
Harkness, David, *Ireland in the Twentieth Century: Divided Island* (London, 1996).
Hart, Peter, *The IRA at War, 1916–1923* (Oxford, 2003).
Hayward, Katy 'National Territory in European Space: Reconfiguring the Island of Ireland' in *European Journal of Political Research*, 45 (2006), 897–920.
Hayward, Katy, *Irish Nationalism and European Integration: The Official Redefinition of the Island of Ireland* (Manchester, 2009).
Hennessey, Thomas, *A History of Northern Ireland, 1920–1996* (Dublin, 1997).
Hennessey, Thomas, *The Northern Ireland Peace Process: Ending the Troubles* (Dublin, 2000).
Hennessey, Thomas, *Northern Ireland: The Origins of the Troubles* (Dublin, 2005).
Hill, J.R. (ed.), *A New History of Ireland. Ireland, 1921–84.* vol.vii (Oxford, 2003).
Hobsbawm, Eric and Ranger, T. (eds), *The Invention of Tradition* (Cambridge, published 1983, reprinted 1995).
Jackson, Alvin, *Home Rule: An Irish History, 1800–2000* (London, 2003).
Jeffrey, Keith, *Ireland and the Great War* (Cambridge, 2000).
Kennedy, Dennis, *The Widening Gulf: Northern Attitudes to the Independent Irish State, 1919–49* (Belfast, 1988).
Kennedy, Michael, *Division and Consensus: The Politics of Cross-Border Relations in Ireland, 1925–1969* (Dublin, 2000).
Keogh, Dermot, *Ireland and the Vatican: The Politics and Diplomacy of Church–State Relations, 1922–1960* (Cork, 1995).
Keogh, Dermot, *Jack Lynch: A Biography* (Dublin, 2008).
Kerr, Michael, *Imposing Power-sharing: Conflict and Co-Existence in Northern Ireland and Lebanon* (Dublin: Irish Academic Press, 2006).
Lee, J.J., *Ireland: 1912–1985, Politics and Society* (Cambridge, 1989).
Leonard, Jane, *The Culture of Commemoration: The Culture of War* (Dublin, 1996).
Lipset, S.M. and Rokkan, Stein, 'Cleavage Structures and Voter Alignments: An Introduction' in S.M. Lipset and Stein Rokkan, *Party Systems and Voter Alignments. Cross-National Perspectives* (New York, 1967), pp.1–61.
Lynn, Brendan, *Holding the Ground: The Nationalist Party in Northern Ireland, 1945–72* (Aldershot, 1997).
Mansergh, Nicholas, *The Government of Northern Ireland: A Study in Devolution* (London, 1936).
Mansergh, Nicholas, *Britain and Ireland* (London, 1942).
McBride, Ian (ed.), *History and Memory in Modern Ireland* (Cambridge, 2001).
McCall, Cathal, *Identity in Northern Ireland; Communities, Politics and Change* (London, 1999).
McCall, Cathal, 'The Production of Space and Realignment of Identity' in *Regional and Federal Studies*, vol.11, no.2, Summer 2001, pp.1–24.
McGarry, John, and O'Leary, Brendan (eds), *The Future of Northern Ireland* (Oxford, 1990).
McGarry, John, and O'Leary, Brendan, *The Northern Ireland Conflict: Consociational Engagements* (Oxford, 2004).

McIntosh, Gillian, *The Force of Culture: Unionist Identities in Twentieth-Century Ireland* (Cork, 1999).

McKittrick, David *et al.*, *Lost Lives: The stories of the men, women and children who died as a result of the Northern Troubles* (London, 1999, 2007 edition).

Mc Laughlin, P.J., *John Hume and the Revision of Irish Nationalism* (Manchester, 2010).

Milne, Kenneth, 'The Protestant Churches in Independent Ireland' in Mackay, J.P., and Mcdonagh, Enda (eds), *Religion and Politics in Ireland at the Turn of the Millennium* (Dublin, 2003), pp.64–83.

Mitchell, George, *Making Peace* (London, 1999).

Morris, Euan, *Our Own Devices: National Symbols and Political Conflict in Twentieth-century Ireland* (Dublin, 2005).

Murray, Patrick, *Oracles of God: The Roman Catholic Church and Irish Politics, 1922–37* (Dublin, 2000).

Mulholland, Marc, *Northern Ireland at the Crossroads: Ulster Unionism in the O'Neill Years* (Basingstoke, 2000).

Mulholland, Marc, *Northern Ireland: A very short Introduction* (Oxford, 2003).

New Ireland Forum Report (Dublin, 1985).

Nic Craith, Máiréad, *Plural Identities–Singular Narratives: The Case of Northern Ireland* (Oxford, 2002).

Northern Ireland Parliamentary and Assembly Debates.

O'Brien, C.C., *States of Ireland* (London, 1972).

O'Brien, C.C., *Ancestral Voices: Religion and Nationalism in Ireland* (London, 1994).

O'Callaghan, Margaret, 'Language, Nationality and Cultural Identity in the Irish Free State, 1922–7: The Irish Statesman and the *Catholic Bulletin* Reappraised', *Irish Historical Studies*, xxiv (94), pp.226–45.

Ò Corráin, Daithì, *Rendering to God and Caesar: The Irish Churches and the two States in Ireland, 1949–73* (Manchester, 2006).

O'Halloran, Clare, *Partition and the Limits of Irish Nationalism* (Dublin, 1987).

O'Mahony, P.J. and Delanty, Gerard, *Rethinking Irish History: Nationalism, Identity and Ideology* (London, 1998).

Parkinson, A.F., *Belfast's Unholy War: The Troubles of the 1920s* (Dublin, 2004).

Patterson, Henry, *Ireland since 1939: The Persistence of Conflict* (London, 2006).

Phoenix, Eamon, *Northern Nationalism: Nationalist Politics, Partition and the Catholic Minority in Northern Ireland* (Belfast, 1994).

Porter, Norman, *The Elusive Quest: Reconciliation in Northern Ireland* (Belfast, 2003).

Roche, P.J., and Barton, Brian (eds), *The Northern Ireland Question: Myth or Reality* (Aldershot, 1991).

Rose, Richard, *Governing without Consensus: An Irish Perspective* (London, 1971).

Shearman, Hugh, *Anglo-Irish Relations* (London, 1948).

Smith, A.D., *National Identity* (Nevada, published 1991, reprinted 1993).

Smith, Gordon, *Politics in Western Europe* (London: Heinemann, 1972, 4th edition 1983).

Smith, M.E., *Reckoning with the Past* (Maryland, 2005).

Staunton, Enda, *The Nationalists of Northern Ireland, 1918–1973* (Dublin, 2001).

Stewart, A.T.Q., *The Narrow Ground: Aspects of Ulster, 1609–1969* (London, 1977).

Todd, Jennifer, 'Two Traditions in Unionist Political Culture' in *Irish Political Studies*, vol.2, 1987), pp.1–26.

Todd, Jennifer and Ruane, Joseph, *The Dynamics of Conflict in Northern Ireland: Power, Conflict and Emancipation* (Cambridge, 1996).

Tonge, Jonathan, *The New Northern Ireland Politics?* (Basingstoke, 2004).

Vaughan, W.E. and Fitzpatrick, A.J., *Irish Historical Statistics: Population 1821–1971* (Dublin, 1978).

Violence and Civil Disturbances in Northern Ireland in 1969: Report of Tribunal of Inquiry (Lord Scarman) (Belfast, 1973).

Walker, B.M., 'Parliamentary Elections from 1801' in T.W. Moody *et al.*, *A New History of Ireland*, vol. ix (Oxford, 1984), pp.625–74.

Walker, B.M. (ed.), *Parliamentary Election Results in Ireland, 1918–92* (Dublin, 1992).

Walker, B.M., *Dancing to History's Tune: History, Myth and Politics in Ireland* (Belfast, 1996).

Walker, B.M., *Past and Present: History, Identity and Politics in Ireland* (Belfast, 2000).

Walker, Graham, *A History of the Ulster Unionist Party: Protest, Pragmatism and Pessimism* (Manchester, 2004).

Walsh, John, *Patrick Hillery: The Official Biography* (Dublin, 2008).

Walsh, Pat, *The Curious Case of the Mayo Librarian* (Cork, 2009).

Whyte, J.H., *Church and State in Modern Ireland, 1923–79* (Dublin, 1980).

Whyte, J.H., 'How much Discrimination was there under the Unionist regime, 1921–68?' in Tom Gallagher and James O'Donnell (eds), *Contemporary Irish Studies* (Manchester, 1983), pp.1–33.

Wilford, Rick (ed.), *Aspects of the Belfast Agreement* (Oxford, 2000).

Woods, C.J., 'Tone's Grave at Bodenstown: Memorials and Commemorations, 1798–1913' in Dorothea Siegmund-Schultze (ed.), *Ireland: Gesellschaft und Kultur*-vi (Halle), pp.141–5.

Index

abortion 133
Acheson, Alan 79
Adams, Gerry 130, 133, 141, 153, 187, 188, 190, 195
Adamson, Dr Ian 161
Ahern, Bertie xi, 6, 95, 143, 149, 151, 170, 189–90, 194, 196–7, 200
Akenson, Don 108
Alderdice, John 142, 167
Aldershot bomb 120
Alliance Party 117, 121, 124, 142, 153
Ancient Order of Hibernians (AOH) 80, 89, 90, 164
Anderson, Rev J.C.M. 77
Andrews, J.M. 10, 25, 26, 27, 61, 68
Andrews, Judge James 68
Anglo-Irish Agreement (1985) 127, 130–1, 147, 181, 188
Anglo-Irish Intergovernmental Council 129
Anglo-Irish Treaty (1921) 3, 6, 9, 10, 20, 47, 50
Anglo-Irish, term rejected 75
Anti-Partition League 38, 40, 58, 59, 81, 82
Apprentice Boys of Derry 29–30, 166, 193
Armistice Day *see* Remembrance Sunday
Atkins, Humphrey 126
Atwood, Alex 150
Aughey, Arthur 183

'B' specials 8, 68, 117
Babington, Sir Anthony 23
Ballynahinch, Battle of (1798), bicentenary of 186
Bardon, Jonathan
A History of Ulster 184
Barr, Glenn 127, 161, 162–3, 201
Barritt, Denis and Carter, Charles
The Northern Ireland Problem 71, 113

Barry, Tom 49
Bates, Sir Dawson 20, 99
Batterbee, Sir Harry 34
Beatty, Geoffrey 181
Beckett, J.C. 25
Beere, Thekla 63–4
Belfast Agreement (1998) xi, 107, 136, 144, 145, 146–7, 153, 191–2, 195, 200, 204
Belfast News Letter 87, 90–1, 101, 157
Belfast Telegraph 28
Bell, J. Bowyer
The Irish Troubles 183–4
Berry, Bishop Sterling 55
Black, Justice William 63
Blair, Tony 144, 151, 186, 189–90, 192, 193, 201
Blaney, Neil 60, 122, 164
Bloody Friday 120
Bloody Sunday 120, 134
Bloomfield, Sir Kenneth 156
Blythe, Ernest 7, 9, 14, 46, 59
Bodenstown, ceremony at grave of Wolfe Tone 18–19
Bogside, Battle of the (1969) 117
Boland, Kevin 115, 122
Bolger, Dermot 178
Booth, Lionel 60
boundary commission 9, 20, 50–1, 52
Bowen, Kurt 66
Bowman, John 58, 185
Boyce, George 186
Boyd, R.N. 33
Boyne, Battle of the (1690) xii, 182, 187
Twelfth of July commemoration 86–7, 98–103, 104, 115, 156, 171–5, 176, 194
Bradley, Denis 195
Briscoe, Robert 37

Britain
 relations with Irish Free State/
  Republic of Ireland 11–12,
  24, 51, 124, 127, 129, 130, 153
 relations with Northern
  Ireland 20, 23–5, 34–5, 123–4
British Legion 94, 157, 158, 160
Brooke, Field Marshal Alan 25
Brooke, Peter 143
Brookeborough, Lord (Sir Basil
  Brooke) 25, 28, 38, 39, 40, 41,
  70, 80, 90, 101, 150, 171
Browne, Noel 39, 66
Brubaker, Roger 4–5
Bruton, John 32, 143, 160, 189
BSR (later Monarch Electric) 73
Butler, Hubert 77–8, 79

Caird, Archbishop Donald 76
Cameron Commission (1969) 70,
  71, 72
Cameron, David 153
Campaign for Democracy in
  Ulster 113
Campaign for Social Justice
  (CSJ) 113
Campbell, J.J. 81, 116
Campbell, T.J. 58, 68, 81
Carswell, Lady 162
Carter, Charles 71
Cassidy, Michael 178
Catholic Emancipation Centenary
  Celebrations (1929) 16
Catholic Social Study Conference
  (1958) 82–3
Catholic Truth Society of Ireland
  conference (1934) 80
Catholics (in Northern Ireland) 41,
  84–5, 135
 in (1960s) 113, 116
 civil rights movement and
  violence 116–18
 community interests 79–83
 early days 45–56
 and education 71–2, 137
 and employment 67–71, 80, 137
 and housing 72–3, 84, 118
 importance of religion to 80
 and Irish language 80

 and judiciary 68
 marginalisation of and
  discrimination against 44, 80,
  113, 116
 political representation 56–7, 58
 population and areas concentrated
  in 44, 46–7, 67, 84, 137
 reforms removing injustices and
  discrimination 117, 137
 rise in Northern Irish identity 135
 setting up of Campaign for Social
  Justice 113
 social and economic profile of
  67–74
 violence against and death
  toll 53–4, 55, 132
Central Community Relations
  Unit 135
Charlemont, Lord 10, 22, 26
Childers, Erskine 60, 65, 77, 133, 134
Chubb, Basil 114
Church of Ireland 19, 46, 55, 79, 91,
  139, 164
Church of Ireland Gazette 54, 59, 78
Churchill, Winston 25
Civil Authorities (Special Powers)
  Act 51
civil rights movement
 rise of in Northern Ireland 116–17
civil service
 and northern Catholics 69
 and southern Protestants 63
Clann na Poblachta 13
Clark, Sir George 41, 171
Clarke, Henry 84
Clarke, James Chichester 120
Clarke, P.C. 58
Clinton, Bill 178–9, 189, 192, 193,
  198–9, 201
Clinton, Hillary 179
Co-operation Ireland 137
Coholan, Bishop Daniel 55
Cole, John 110, 124
Colgan, Michael 165
Colley, George 164
Collins, Michael 48, 50–1, 101
Colton, Bishop Paul 198
Combined Loyalist Military
  Command (CLMC) 145, 146

Comerford, Vincent 15
Comiskey, Bishop Brendan 63
commemorations 29, 193, 201
  1798 rebellion bicentenary 186
  (1921–60) 86–104
  (1960–2011) 155–77
  Easter Rising (1916) 86, 95–8, 104,
    167–71, 176, 194
  Great Irish Famine 186
  Remembrance Sunday 87, 91–5,
    103–4, 156, 157–63, 175, 185–6,
    193
  St Patrick's Day 86, 87–91, 103–4,
    156, 163–7, 175–6
  Siege of Derry 29–30
  Twelfth of July anniversary of the
    Battle of the Boyne (1690)
    86–7, 98–103, 104, 115, 156,
    171–5, 176, 194
  used to recall important events in
    history 185–6
community interests 75–83
  and northern Catholics 79–83
  and southern Protestants
    75–9
Community Relations Council 135
Condon, John 162
Connolly, Joseph 48–9
Connor, Walker 180
consent principle 14, 141–2, 144,
    145, 204
Constabulary Act (Northern Ireland)
    (1922) 67
constitution, Irish (1937) *see under*
    Irish Free State/Irish Republic
Cooney, Christy 198
Cooper, Ivan 113
Cooper, Major Bryan 10, 59
Cootehill 102
Cosgrave, James 123, 124
Cosgrave, Liam 169
Cosgrave, W.T. 3–4, 9, 11, 14, 18–19,
    48, 64, 88
Costello, Declan 123, 126
Costello, J.A. 13, 35–6, 38, 89, 97
council employment
  and northern Catholics 69–70
  and southern Protestants 63–4
Cowen, Brian 151–2

Craig, Sir James (later Craigavon)
    xiii, 3, 4, 10, 18, 23, 24, 26, 27,
    28, 34, 50, 61, 70, 92, 99,
    100, 194
Craig, William 118, 125, 127
Crawford, Seymour 139
Criminal Law Amendment Act
    (1935) 17
Croke Park 198
Cultural Traditions Group 135, 184
Cumann Gaelach na hEaglaise (Irish
    Guild of the Church) 76
Cumann na nBan 31
Cumann na nGaedheal
  government 7, 10, 11, 12, 15,
    16, 96
Currie, Austin 121
Currin, Brian 191
Curtis, Edmund 75
Czechoslovakia 4, 45, 109

Daly, Cardinal Cahal 79, 119, 135
D'Arcy, Archbishop Charles 49
Davis, Richard 181
Davison, Sir John 27
Day, Bishop Fitzmaurice 49
de Valera, Eamon xiv, 4, 12, 13, 14–16,
    64, 97, 114, 150, 163–4, 167
  and northern nationalists 57
  opposition to Armistice Day 94,
    103
  opposition to partition 14–16, 23,
    35–6, 57, 88
  religious views 17
  St Patrick Day broadcasts 57, 88,
    89, 150
Deane, Declan 134
decommissioning 140, 147, 148,
    183, 191, 195
Delanty, Gerard 42
Democratic Unionist Party *see* DUP
Dempsey, G.T. 139
Dempsey, Noel 162
Derrig, Thomas 16
Derry 72–3, 74, 97, 113
  civil rights marches 117, 118
  employment in 73
  housing policies 72
  population 74

Derry, Siege of (1688–89)   182, 187
  commemoration of   29–30
Devlin, Joseph   10, 22, 25–6, 50, 52,
    55–6, 97
Devlin, Paddy   121, 126, 128
Diamond, Harry   68, 98
divorce   133, 138
Dockrell, Henry   60, 134
Dockrell, Maurice   60
Donoghue, Denis   80, 126–7
Donegal protestants   60, 62, 74,
    76–7, 101–3, 115
Downing Street Declaration
    (1993)   136, 142–3, 144, 188,
    189
Dowse, Bishop C.B.   54
Drumm, James   169
Dublin
  Easter Rising (1916)
    commemorations   96–7
  Remembrance Sunday
    commemorations   93–4
  St Patrick's Day parade   165
Dublin Forum for Peace and
    Reconciliation   142
Dublin Rising *see* Easter Rising (1916)
Dufferin, Lord   34
Duffy, John   186
Dunlop, Dr John   134, 187
Dunmanway murders (1922)   48, 49
DUP (Democratic Unionist
    Party)   117, 121, 125, 140–1,
    148, 195
Durkan, Brendan   68
Durkan, Mark   68, 147, 152

Eames, Archbishop Robin   142
East Donegal Protestants   76–7
Easter Rising (1916)   6, 10, 12,
    181, 189
  commemorations of   86, 95–8,
    104, 167–71, 176, 194
education
  and northern Catholics   71–2, 137
  and Irish Free State/Republic of
    Ireland   42, 138
Education Act (1947)   71, 72
Education for Mutual
    Understanding   137

Edwards, Ruth Dudley   185
electoral practices (Northern
    Ireland)   73–4
electoral practices (Irish Free State/
    Republic of Ireland)   60
Elizabeth II, Queen   155
  visit to Republic of Ireland   xi, 153,
    197–8
Elliott, Marianne   75, 79
emigration, Irish   42, 62, 77
employment
  and northern Catholics   67–71,
    80, 137
  and southern Protestants   63–4
Enniskillen bomb (1987)   159, 160
Ervine, David   146, 190
EU (European Union)   133, 137
Eucharistic Congress (1932)   80
External Relations Act (1936)
    12–13, 35

Fagan, Niall   168
Falklands War   129
Fallon, John   157
Farnham, Lord   47
Farren, Dr Neil   72
Farrington, Christopher   139–40
Faulkner, Brian   32, 39, 40, 41, 120,
    124, 125, 126
Fethard-on-Sea boycott case   77
Fianna Fáil   6, 11, 12, 13, 22, 57
Field, Dorita   160
Fine Gael   6, 13, 60, 123, 168
First World War   91
Fitt, Gerry   31, 113, 121, 124, 128
FitzGerald, Garret   123, 126, 127,
    129, 130, 131, 133, 134, 138–9
Fitzgibbon, Justice Gerald   63
Fitzpatrick, David   27
Flags and Emblems (Display) Act
    (1954)   40
Fogarty, Bishop Michael   55
football   32
Football Association of Ireland   32
Forde, David   149, 153, 194
Forum of Peace and
    Reconciliation   138
Fox, Billy   134
Fox, Johnny   139

'Frameworks for the Future' document (1995)   136, 188
Free Presbyterian church   111
Frontier Sentinel   52

Gaelic Athletic Association (GAA)   79, 198
Gaelic League   76, 88
'Gaelicisation'   11, 15, 75–6
Gallagher, Frank   70
Garda Siochana   8, 63
Garden of Remembrance,   168, 197–8
Garron Tower social study conference (1958)   41, 82, 84–5
Garvin, Tom   7, 8, 31, 72
general elections
    (1918)   47, 49, 81, 141, 181
    (1921)   86
    (1925)   56
    (1929)   21, 56, 57
    (1938)   22, 23, 82
    (1949)   38
    (1957)   60
    (1961)   60
    (1962)   59
    (1973)   123
    (1977)   134
    (1992)   139
Germany   108, 179
Gibney, Jim   144–5
Gilmartin, Archbishop Thomas   64
Girvin, Brian   65
Glenavy, Lord   48
Glentoran, Lord   39
Good Friday Agreement *see* Belfast Agreement
Gore-Booth, Sub-Lieutenant Brian   78
Gore-Booth, Sub-Lieutenant Hugh   78
Gorman, Major Jack   46, 201
Gorman, Sir John   68, 201
Government of Ireland Act (1920)   3, 6, 19, 20, 49–50, 147
Graff-McRae, Rebecca   155
Graham, Sir Clarence   41, 150
Grand Lodge of Ireland   98
Gransden, Sir Robert   115
Gray, David   15

Great Irish Famine, commemorations of   186
Greece   179
Gregg, Archbishop John   47, 49, 75–6, 78
Griffin, Victor   74, 77, 159
Griffith, Arthur   7, 47
Gwynn, Stephen   75

Hall-Thompson, Lt. Col. Samuel   39–40
Hanna, George   40
Harkness, David   69
Harris, Eoghan   185
Harrison, Letitia Dunbar   64
Harte, Paddy   161, 162, 201
Hartley, Tom   160, 162, 163, 189
Hassan, Father John   55
Haughey, C.J.   83, 122, 129, 131, 133, 142, 159, 169, 181
Hayes, Maurice   69
Healy, Cahir   57, 72, 81, 83
Heath, Edward   124, 151
Henderson, Thomas   24
Hennessey, Thomas   24–5, 109–10, 140
Henry, Sir Denis   7, 68, 100
Hickey, Dr Eileen   59
Hillery, Patrick   121, 123, 124, 151, 159
historical perceptions   180–4
history (and identity)   178–202, 204
    attitude to by politicians and parties   189–90
    changes in public discourse from early 1990s to Agreement   184–92
    changes in public discourse since the Agreement   192–8
    and Belfast Agreement   191–2
    importance of to the present   178–84
    north–south relations and shared   196–7
    and peace process   179, 187, 190, 191
    references to in key governmental papers   188
    references to in Queen's Irish visit   197–8

teaching of in schools 184
use of commemorations to recall
important events in 185–6
Holland 108
housing
and northern Catholics 72–3, 84,
118
Howard, Lady Alice 47
Hume, John 72, 113, 121, 126, 128,
132, 135, 141–2, 181, 182, 187,
188, 190, 194
hunger strikes 126, 130, 133
Hurley, Father Michael 165
Hyde, Douglas 61, 76, 89

Independent Group (Irish Senate) 61
Inglis, Brian 75
International Fund for Ireland 137
internment, introduction of 120, 121
IRA (Irish Republican Army) 22–3,
36, 112, 119–20, 181
bombing campaigns in Britain 23
campaign against Northern
Ireland 40, 51, 58
ceasefire (1994) 136, 189
declared illegal (1936) 18
and decommissioning 148
formal declaration of end of
campaign (2005) 148
government action taken
against 8, 14, 36
growth in numbers 23
and historical tradition 181
intensification of violence 125
and peace process 141, 143–4
split of into provisional and official
(1970) 117, 119–20, 132
violence committed by 131–2
Ireland Act (1949) 25
Ireland, Denis 33
Irish Association 33, 113
Irish Citizenship Act (1935) 57
Irish Football Association 32
Irish Free State/Republic of Ireland
(1929–41) 10–19
(1949–50) 35–8
(1960s) 113–15
(1968–74) 121–3
(1974–1990) 127–8, 128–9

(1990–98) 136, 137–9
accession to EEC/EU (1973) 133,
135
and Anglo-Irish Agreement
(1985) 127, 130
and Belfast Agreement 147
and Catholicism/Catholic
Church 16–18, 36–7, 39
civil war 7, 8, 11, 15, 17, 48, 49
constitution (1922) 15, 17
constitution (1937) 13, 14,
17–18, 23, 31–2, 130–1, 142–3,
147, 191
constitutional review 114–15
de Valera's anti-partition
campaign 14–16, 23, 35–6,
57, 88
declaration of a republic (1949) 3,
25, 26, 34, 35–6, 78
early security measures 8
Easter Rising commemoration
95–7, 104, 114, 115, 156, 167–9,
170–1, 176, 194
economic nationalism 42
education 138
election of Lemass as taoiseach and
changes brought in by 114
establishment of Irish Free State
(1921) xi, 3, 6, 10–11
establishment of New Ireland
Forum 127, 129
fall of Fianna Fáil government
(1973) 123
and historical public
discourse 182–3, 185
ideas of nationalism and Irishness
remain important 151–2
intra-nationalist conflict 7
and Irish language 15–16, 75–6,
133
and mother and child scheme
37, 39
neutrality during Second World
War 13, 78, 91
and peace process 142–3
promotion of pluralism 138,
150, 154
prosperity and economic
growth 138

Irish Free State/Republic of
    Ireland – *continued*
    Protestants in *see* Protestants (in
        Irish Free State/Republic of
        Ireland)
    Queen's visit   xi, 153, 197–8
    relations and dealings with
        Britain   11–12, 24, 51, 124, 127,
        129, 130
    relations with the north and unity
        issue   3–4, 14–15, 21, 23, 33, 37,
        39, 42, 43, 51, 82, 107, 111–12,
        114, 121–3, 137, 149, 151–2
    and religion   8, 16–17
    Remembrance Sunday   93–4,
        157–9, 158, 161–2, 175, 185–6
    response to violent events in the
        north (1969)   121–2
    St Patrick's Day
        commemoration   87–9, 163–4,
        165–6, 176
    steps taken to develop dimensions
        of Irish identity and to reduce
        elements of British identity
        12–13
    tricolour and national anthem   12
    Twelfth of July
        commemoration   171–2, 173–4,
        194
    unionists in *see* southern unionists
    view of history   194
    violence and loss of lives (1922–23)
        7
    war of independence (1918–21)
        11, 47, 49, 94, 187
    women's movement and position
        in   31–2, 137–8
Irish Historical Society   33
Irish Historical Studies   33
Irish Independent   18
Irish language   76, 88
    and Republic of Ireland/Irish Free
        State   15–16, 75–6
    and Northern Ireland   26–7, 80
Irish National War Memorial
    (Islandbridge, Dublin)   94, 95,
    157, 158, 160, 198
Irish Nationality and Citizenship Act
    (1935)   13

Irish News   27, 73, 79, 80, 83, 92,
    157, 161
Irish Press   17
Irish Statesman   21
Irish Times   19, 38, 76, 78, 115
Irish Turf Club   66
Irish Unionist Party   6
Irish Volunteers (later IRA)   5, 31
Italy   108

Jackson, Alvin   126
Jeffery, Keith   92
John Paul XXIII, Pope   111
Johnson, Thomas   36, 59
Jones, W.E.   74
judiciary
    and northern Catholics   68
    and southern Protestants   63

Kane, Pamela   170
Keatinge, Patrick   113–14
Kelly, John   130
Kennedy, David   71
Kenny, Enda   153
Keogh, Dermot   129
Kerr, John   161
Kerr, Ronan   151
Kidd, Sir Robert   67
Kingsmill, Justice Theodore   63
Kolsto, Pal   199

Laffan, Brigid   113–14
Laffan, Michael   50
Lavery, Danny   163
Leech commission   51, 69
Lemass, Sean   37, 38, 41, 42, 61, 83,
    107, 111, 114, 116, 163, 164, 167
Lenihan, Brian   162
Lenihan, Conor   182–3
Lennon, James   168
Leonard, Jane   31, 94, 159, 185
Lipset, S.M.   6
Little, Dr James   30
local government elections
    and northern nationalists   73–4
local government employment
    and northern Catholics   69–70
    and southern Protestants   63
Logue, Hugh   126

Londonderry, Lord 71, 100
Longley, Edna 155–6
Loughlin, James 20
Lowe, Dr W.J. 53
loyalist paramilitaries 132, 181
  ceasefire (1994) 89, 136
  death toll 131
  growth of organizations 117
  and peace process 145–6
  violence committed by 131–2
Lucy, Bishop Cornelius 89
Lynch, Jack 114, 115, 121, 122,
  124, 164
Lynn, Dr Kathleen 46

McAleese, President Mary x, 138,
  150, 152, 153, 156, 160, 163, 170,
  174, 176, 186, 193, 194, 197
McAliskey, Bernadette 182
McAllister, T.S. 52, 56
McAteer, Eddie 82, 83, 112
McBride, Ian 175
MacBride, Sean 13, 39
McCabe, Eugene 186
McCall, Cathal 137
McCann, Eamon 113
McCann, Hugh 115
McCarroll, J.J. 80
McCaughey, Terence 76
McClenaghan, Dermot 113
McCloskey, Conn 113
McCloskey, Patricia 113
McCrea, John 172–3
MacDermot, Frank 15
MacDonald, Malcolm 34
McElroy, Albert 33
MacEntee, Sean 15, 89
McGilligan, Patrick 12
McGimpsey, Michael and
  Christopher 130–1
McGlinchey, Bernard 173
McGonigal, Ambrose 68
McGowan, Paddy 160
McGuigan, Brian 116
McGuinness, Martin 148, 149, 196
McGurk's Bar bomb (Belfast) 120
McGurran, Malachy 169
McIntosh, Gillian 24
McLoughlin, John 48

MacMahon murders (1922) 53
MacManaway, Rev. J.G. 30
McMichael, Gary 190
McMichael, John 132
McNeill, Ronald 7
McQuaid, Archbishop John
  Charles 38, 66
MacRory, Archbishop Joseph 53
McSorley, Dr Frederick 59
Madden, J.A. 19
Magee College, Derry 67
Mageean, Archbishop Daniel 81
Magennis, Brian 112, 150
Magennis, James 161, 193
Maginnis, Ken 140, 187
Maginess, W.B. 41
Maguire, Rev. C.W. 28
Major, John 188, 189
Malan, Rian 188
Mallon, Seamus 147, 169, 188
Mansergh, Martin 77, 143
Mansergh, Nicholas 179
  *The Government of Northern
    Ireland* 43
Mansion House Committee 36, 38
Markevicz, Countess Constance 78
marriage
  southern Protestants and mixed
    marriages 62–3, 133, 134, 138
Martin, Archbishop Diarmuid 170
Martin, Leo 167
Maskey, Alex 162
May, W.M. 101
Mayhew, Sir Patrick 37–8, 144, 160,
  187, 189
Meehan, Martin 162
Meredith, Justice James 63
Messines, Battle of 201
Messines, Ireland Peace Park at 161,
  162, 186, 201
Midgley, Harry 40
Mitchell commission (1996) 183
Mitchell, Gary 182
Mitchell, Senator George 139, 183,
  189, 190, 199
Mitchell, T.J. 58
Moore, Bishop W.R. 54–5
Moore, Sir William 68
Morris, Ewan 12, 24

mother and child scheme
  controversy   37, 39
Mulcahy, General Richard   13, 16
Murnaghan, Sheelagh   33
Murphy, Father Hugh   158
Murray, Patrick   17–18
Myers, Kevin   158, 185

National Graves Association   98, 167
National University of Ireland   66
Nationalist Party   6, 49
nationalists, in Northern Ireland *see*
  northern nationalists
Ne Temere decree (1908)   62, 138
Neill, Archbishop John   139
Netherlands   179, 183
New History of Ireland   185
New Ireland Forum   127, 129, 134
Newe, G.B.   41, 82–3, 120
Nic Craith, Máiréad   184
Nixon, District Inspector J.W.   53
Nixon, Dr R.S.   74, 101
North, Peter   190
Northern Ireland   19–20
  (1921–49)   19–35
  (1949–60)   38–41
  (1960s)   109–13
  (1968–74)   116–26
  (1974–1990)   126–35
  (1990–98)   136–7, 140–2
  abolition of proportional
    representation   21–2, 51, 56,
    57, 73
  anti-partition campaign   38, 39,
    40, 81
  Catholics in *see* Catholics (in
    Northern Ireland)
  cooperation between unionists and
    nationalists in 1990s   140
  Craig's proposed voluntary unionist/
    SDLP coalition idea   127–8
  early security measures   8
  Easter Rising commemoration
    97–8, 167, 168, 169–70, 176
  establishment of (1920)   xi, 3, 6,
    19, 50
  formation of power-sharing
    executive in 1974 and collapse
    of   118, 124–6, 128

  formation of power-sharing
    executive (1998)   147
  formation of power-sharing
    executive (2007)   xi, 148–9, 196
  Good Friday Agreement and
    aftermath   146–9
  guaranteeing right to stay in UK
    (1949)   3, 34
  and historical public discourse
    184–5
  influence of Protestant
    churches   28
  internal rivalry within unionist
    government   21, 22, 40
  introduction of internment   120,
    121
  IRA campaign against   40, 51, 58
  and Irish language   26–7, 80
  links between Orange Order and
    unionist government   27–8, 40,
    43, 99, 100, 101, 110, 140
  local government controls   8–9, 51
  local government elections   73
  national anthem and union
    flag   23–4
  and peace process   136, 140–2,
    143–4
  population   42
  and Protestantism   27–30, 39–40
  public housing   72–3, 84, 118
  reforms (1990–98)   137
  relations with Britain   20, 23–5,
    34–5, 123–4
  relations with the south and unity
    issue   3–4, 14–15, 21, 23, 33, 39,
    42, 43, 51, 82, 107, 111–12, 114,
    121–3, 137, 149, 151–2
  religion as dividing factor in
    politics   7–8
  Remembrance Sunday   92–3,
    157–8, 160–1, 162–3, 175, 185
  rise of civil rights movement and
    violence   116–19, 204
  St Patrick's Day commemoration
    89–91, 156, 164–5, 166–7, 176
  and Second World War   25,
    58, 91
  sense of Irishness retained by some
    unionists   26, 32

suspension of parliament and direct rule introduced from London (1972) 118, 124
Twelfth of July commemoration of the Battle of the Boyne 99–101, 171–3
and Ulster identity 25–6, 110
union flag 40
unionism and Britishness still remains important 152–3
view of history 193–4
violence and conflict (1968–74) 116–21
violence and deaths (1920–22) 7
violence and deaths (1989–2006) 136, 148
violence and deaths (1998–2006) 148
women's position in 31–2
Northern Ireland Civil Rights Association 113
Northern Ireland Housing Trust 72
Northern Ireland Labour Party (NILP) 33, 38, 56, 59, 113, 124
Northern Ireland Women's Coalition (NIWC) 142
northern nationalists 6, 49–50, 80–1, 110, 112, 120, 152
abstention of MPs from parliament 22, 50, 52, 58
anti-partition 81–2
and boundary commission 50–1, 52
concern over electoral practices 73
and de Valera 57
discrimination against 110
and historical narratives 182
and local government elections 73–4
and political representation 56–9, 110
violence against 53
Northern Whig 26, 30
Nugent, Sir Roland 29

Ó Brádaigh, Ruari 179
O'Brien, Conor Cruise 123, 126, 185
O'Callaghan, Bishop Eugene 59
O'Callaghan, Margaret 15

O'Connor, Roderick 82
O'Doherty, Hugh 52
O'Doherty, Shane Paul 181
O'Donnell, Cardinal Patrick 56, 92
O'Donnell, Nellie 161–2
O'Hanlon, Paddy 128
O'Hare, Canon Frank 52
O'Higgins, Kevin 12, 48
O'Kelly, Sean T. 17, 97
Old Comrades Association 157
Omagh bombing 148
O'Mahony, Patrick 42
O'Malley, Desmond 113, 173
O'Neill, Captain Terence 107, 110, 111, 112, 116, 117, 164, 171, 172
Opsahl Commission 184
Orange Order 27–9, 39, 41, 70–1, 98–9, 115, 140, 186
links with unionist government 27–8, 40, 43, 99, 100, 101, 110, 140
parades 101–3, 191
and Twelfth of July commemorations 171–5, 176
Orangefest 174–5, 176
'Over the Bridge' (play) 111
Oxford Union debate (1959) 37

Paisley, Ian x, xi, 91, 111, 121, 125, 148, 149, 150, 152, 163, 179, 181, 187, 190, 195, 196
parades/marches
Orange 101–3, 191
report on (1997) 190–1
see also loyalists paramilitaries *and* IRA (Irish Republican Army)
paramilitary groups 132
rise of (1969–74) 119
violence caused by 131–2
see also loyalist paramilitaries and IRA
peace process 136–46, 200–1, 204–5
and Alliance Party 142
and Belfast Agreement (1998) x, 107, 136, 144, 145, 146–7, 153, 191–2, 195, 200, 204
and British government 137, 143–4
and DUP 140–1

peace process – *continued*
  factors bringing about   136–9
  and history   179, 187, 190, 191
  and Hume   141–2
  influence of United States   137,
    139
  and IRA/Sinn Féin   141, 143–4
  and Irish Republic   142–3
  and loyalist paramilitaries   145–6
  and NIWC   142
  and republicans   144–5
  and UUP   140
Pearse, Patrick   189
Philbin, Bishop William   111
Phillips, W. Alison   55
Pius XII, Pope   88
Poland   4, 45, 109
political representation   56–61
  and northern nationalists/
    Catholics   56–7, 58
  and southern Protestants   45,
    59–61, 133, 134, 139
Porter, Norman   195
Powell, Jonathan   195
power-sharing executive,
    establishment of *see* Northern
    Ireland
Prior, James   126
prisoners, early release of   145, 147,
    148
Progressive Unionist Party (PUP)
    132, 146, 190
Progressive Unionist Party (1938)   22
property franchise   73
proportional representation
  abolishment of in Northern
    Ireland   21–2, 51, 56, 57, 73
Protestants (in Irish Free State/
    Republic of Ireland)   44–85, 47–9,
    83–4, 109, 115, 133–4, 138–9
  advantages enjoyed   65–6
  and Anglo-Irish treaty (1921)   47
  bearing of new pluralism policy
    on   138–9
  changes in   1960s   115, 116
  community interests   75–9
  decline in numbers and
    reasons   42, 45, 46, 54–5, 62, 66,
    67, 75, 84, 134

discrimination against   64–5
early days   45–56
emigration of   42, 62, 77
and employment   63–4
as farmers   65
feelings of isolation from
  mainstream society   77, 84
increase in numbers (2002)   139
and Irish language   75–6
and judiciary   63
marginalisation continues   134
mixed marriages and religious
  upbringing of children   62–3,
  133, 134, 138
political representation   45, 59–61,
  133, 134, 139
prominence amongst professions
  and business   65–6
response to declaration of
  a republic   78–9, 84
social and economic profile   62–7,
  74–5
violence and intimidation
  against   48, 49, 54–5
Provisional IRA   120, 132–3 *see also*
  IRA
Purvis, Dawn   198

Queen's University of Belfast   69

Rebellion (1798), commemoration
  of   186
Reid, John   194
Remembrance Sunday   87, 91–5,
  103–4, 156, 157–63, 175, 185–6,
  193
Republic of Ireland Bill (1948)   13
Reynolds, Albert   142, 143, 187
Ritchie, Margaret   152–3, 163
Robb, J.H.   27
Roberts, Colonel E.   54
Robinson, David Lubbock   61
Robinson, Nicholas   159
Robinson, Peter   148, 150–1, 152,
  174–5
Robinson, President Mary   xiv, 131,
  137–8, 140, 143, 155, 159–60,
  169
Rockwell lectures   184

Rokkan, Stein 6
Rose, Richard 32, 108, 110
Royal Black Institution 64, 102
Royal Irish Academy 32–3
Royal Irish Constabulary (RIC) 46
Royal Ulster Constabulary (RUC) 8, 67–8
RUC Special Constabulary *see* 'B' specials
Rugby, Lord 35

Sabatarianism 28
St Andrews Agreement (2006) 148, 196
St Patrick's Day 86, 87–91, 103–4, 156, 163–7, 175–6
Sargent, Trevor 139
Sayers, Jack 33, 41, 111–12, 118
Scarman Tribunal report (1972) 119
SDLP (Social Democratic and Labour Party) 117, 120–1, 124, 126, 128, 135, 141, 144, 152–3, 160, 190
Second World War 13, 24–5, 25, 58, 78, 91
Shea, Patrick 69
Shearman, Hugh 35
Sheil, Charles Leo 68
Sheldon, William 60, 61
Simms, Archbishop George Otto 63, 79, 115
Sinn Féin 6, 40, 47, 50, 58, 132, 153
   adoption of broader political platform 133
   attitude towards history 188–9
   and Easter Rising commemoration 169–70
   and Good Friday Agreement 148
   and peace process 141, 143, 144
Skeffington, Owen Sheehy 61
Smith, Anthony D.
   National Identity 180
Smith, Gordon 109
Smyth, Samuel 125
Social Democratic and Labour Party *see* SDLP
social and economic conditions
   and northern Catholics 67–74
   and southern Protestants 62–7

Somme Association 161
Somme, Battle of the (1916) 156, 161, 181, 182
Somme Heritage Centre 161, 163
southern Protestants *see* Protestants (in Irish Free State/Republic of Ireland)
southern unionists 47–8, 49, 55, 59, 78
Spence, Gusty 132, 145
Stanbridge, Karen 5
Stanford, W.B. 65, 79
Statute of Westminster (1931) 12
Stephenson, Sean 168
Stewart, A.T.Q. 181
Stewart, Charles 59
Stewart, Joseph 82, 83
Stewart, Michael 123
Stewart, W.J. 22
Sunningdale Agreement (1973) 118, 123, 124, 125, 188
Switzerland 183

Taylor, John 171
temperance movement 21, 28
Tennant, Emerson 152
Thatcher, Margaret 127, 129, 130
Thomas, Hugh 109
Thompson, Sam 111
Tilson case 63
Tone, Theobald Wolfe 18–19, 65
Trew, Karen 135
Trimble, David xiii, 127, 140, 142, 143, 144, 147, 152, 191, 194
Trinity College Dublin 38, 47, 55, 66–7
Tripartite Agreement (1925) 14, 23
Trousdell, General Philip 162
Tumelty, Father William 84
Twelfth of July *see* Boyne, Battle of the
Tyrie, Andy 132

Ulster Defence Association (UDA) 117, 120, 132
Ulster Defence Regiment 117
Ulster Democratic Party (UDP) 132
Ulster Liberal Party 113
Ulster Museum 184

Ulster Protestant League   22
Ulster Sabbath Day   29
Ulster Society for Irish Historical
    Studies   33
Ulster Unionist Council   20, 21, 22,
    23, 39, 41, 110, 125
Ulster Unionist Party *see* UUP
Ulster Vanguard Party   125
Ulster Volunteer Force *see* UVF
Ulster Women's Unionist Council   31
Ulster Workers' Council Strike   124
United States
role in peace process   137, 139
United Ulster Unionist Council
    (UUUC)   125, 127
Urwin, Derek   108
UUP (Ulster Unionist Party)   6, 21,
    110, 111, 120, 124, 126, 140, 174
UVF (Ulster Volunteer Force)   111,
    120, 132, 173, 181
UVF (Ulster Volunteer Force)
    (1912)   5, 8

Vanguard Party   127

Walker, Cecil   190
Walshe, Joseph   13
Warnock, Edmund   65
Watts, William   84
Webb, Michael   139
White, Bishop H.V.   76
White, James   134
Whyte, John   74
Wilton, Claude   33, 113
women, position of   31–2, 137–8,
    142
Workers' Party   132, 142
Wyse, A.G. Bonaparte   46, 69

Yates, Ivan   139
Young Unionist Council   41, 91,
    165, 171
Yugoslavia, former   4, 45, 199